EXCELLENCE IN PRACTICE Series
Katharine G. Butler, Editor

SUCCESSFUL INTERACTIVE SKILLS FOR SPEECH-LANGUAGE PATHOLOGISTS AND AUDIOLOGISTS

Dorothy Molyneaux, Ph.D.
Vera W. Lane, Ph.D.
Department of Special Education
Communicative Disorders Program
San Francisco State University
San Francisco, California

AN ASPEN PUBLICATION®
Aspen Publishers, Inc.
Rockville, Maryland
1990

Library of Congress Cataloging-in-Publication Data

Molyneaux, Dorothy.
Successful interactive skills for speech-language pathologists
and audiologists/Dorothy Molyneaux, Vera W. Lane.
p. cm.
"An Aspen publication."
Includes bibliographical references.
ISBN: 0-8342-0106-2
1. Speech therapist and patient. 2. Audiologist and patient.
I. Lane, Vera W.
RC428.8.M65   1989   616.85'50232--dc20   89-37240
CIP

Editorial Services: Marsha Davies

Library of Congress Catalog Card Number: 89-37240
ISBN: 0-8342-0106-2

Printed in the United States of America

1 2 3 4 5

To our students, clients, and colleagues—
and to our families

Table of Contents

Foreword

Successful Interactive Skills for Speech-Language Pathologists and Audiologists is designed to assist these professionals and others in health and education settings to use *communication* to serve those with *communication disorders* and their families. The authors, Drs. Molyneaux and Lane, bring to this difficult task an rich understanding of the complexities inherent in using language of text to explicate that which is essentially a verbal process in inordinate subtlety. How is it that professionals gain the necessary interpersonal, verbal, and nonverbal skills to assist clients or patients solve myriad communication difficulties?

From 1930–1960, educators of communication disorders specialists paid considerable attention to both the technical aspects of interviewing and the exploration of feelings by speech, language, and hearing professionals. In the first half of the twentieth century, the literature in the field reflected the close ties of the emerging profession with psychology and psychiatry, as a review of the early publications in speech correction journals and texts indicate. Indeed, many of the pioneers were psychologists and psychiatrists. As the profession developed its own speech and hearing scientists, the quest for rigorous scientific bases in communication sciences and disorders addressed those issues which became more highly technical and data-based. Research in the latter half of the century has begun to unravel some of the earlier mysteries and to provide substantive changes in the knowledge base of the profession. In the same vein, curricula in institutions of higher education reflect this trend. Increased knowledge has required increased attention to a multiplicity of basic and applied scientific discoveries. However, an unfortunate result of the ongoing increase in the scientific and technical aspects of the profession has been diminution of attention to critical clinical precepts until recently.

The heart of the clinical enterprise includes the ability to function effectively at the interpersonal level in a variety of roles and work settings (Molyneaux & Lane, Chapter 1, pp. 1–2), and the authors' longitudinal research enhances the exemplars provided throughout the text by drawing from the transcripts of more than 500 interviews conducted over time with a variety of individuals with varying communication disorders. In addition, their collective wisdom regarding the initiation of, progress in, and conclusion of therapeutic interactions provides an adaptable framework for readers at many levels of sophistication. The questions they ask and answer also take into account far more than traditional discussions of methodological issues or interviewing techniques. For example, facilitation of the assessment process is highlighted, a process which is frequently thought to be rather limited in scope, particularly when utilizing normative tests and assessment instruments. New and not-so-new clinicians will find information related to client motivation to change, a matter sometimes given little attention within various paradigms that stress objectives, goals, and data-based accountability. Far too frequently it is assumed that the clinician-established goals and objectives will be submissively assumed by the therapy recipient. Not necessarily so, of course.

The era ushered in by the passage of Public Law 99-457, commonly identified as the infants and toddlers legislation for service delivery to children 0–3, will require enhanced knowledge and skills in a number of domains. Not the least of these will be working with the families of these children as integral members of the intervention team, and increased interactions in multidisciplinary, transdisciplinary, or intradisciplinary settings. The authors' discussion of contemporary family patterns and the interactive sequences involved in the delivery of services on a one-to-one or team basis is useful across the wide age span of individuals and families seen within a variety of settings.

Finally, the recent interest in collaborative consultation models and the provision of services indirectly rather than directly in school-based settings require extensive familiarity with how professional effectiveness may be attained in such work settings. As with so many modifications in delivery system components, the seemingly simple is extraordinarily complex. It is to the authors' credit that this book reflects a careful analysis of the role of the communication disorders specialist across settings and models of services. Moreover, this book further exemplifies how the clinical enterprise may best be approached in this less than perfect world.

Katharine G. Butler, Ph.D.
Syracuse University
Syracuse, New York

Preface

This book is intended for speech-language pathologists, audiologists, and others interested in improving their professional interpersonal skills. As a communication specialist, you are likely to be called upon to function in a wide variety of roles using both traditional and innovative service delivery models. Regardless of your work setting, you must be able to interact effectively with individuals and groups of communicatively impaired clients and their families, with colleagues, and with professionals in other disciplines.

Experienced professionals and recent graduates in our own and related fields—as well as clients and families receiving services—repeatedly mention the importance of a professional's knowledge and skill in certain areas that often are not emphasized in academic programs. These areas include interpersonal communication, counseling, group work, problem solving, time utilization, and stress management. This book addresses these and related topics. We hope it will assist you in achieving increased success and satisfaction in your professional and personal life.

Acknowledgments

Special thanks go to the following colleagues who, through lengthy interviews, provided us with many valuable suggestions from their varying professional perspectives: Carol Fleming, Carol Freidenberg, Minnie Graham, Stanford Lamb, Hilda Man, Nancy McConnell, Jean Nisbet, and Penelope Wayte.

The excerpts from clinician/client and clinician/family interviews have been selected from over 500 verbatim transcribed interviews that have been collected over a period of years. Our appreciation goes to the clients and family members who participated in the interviews, and to the graduate students at San Francisco State University who conducted and transcribed many of them.

We also express our appreciation to the authors and publishers who granted permission for the use of quoted material.

1

Introduction

This book is for speech-language pathologists, audiologists, and other communication specialists who are interested in improving their professional interpersonal skills. It is designed for professionals who are knowledgeable in the basic speech and hearing sciences and in techniques and procedures vital to assessing and/or remediating a variety of communication disorders and difficulties. As a practicing professional, or a well-trained soon-to-be professional, you are not entering this reading project with an empty kit. You probably already have served your apprenticeship and have certificates and licenses that attest to your clinical competence. In other words, you already are well supplied with the tools of your trade. Our task is to help you augment your tool kit with some useful tools that are not always supplied with the basic package. These are the tools involving interpersonal and counseling skills.

Today's communication specialists must be prepared to improve and expand their activities not only in traditional areas of interest and service, but also in new and vital areas. If you are to be on the cutting edge of an expanding profession, you must use tools adapted and honed to new levels of competence and excellence.

ROLES OF THE COMMUNICATION DISORDERS SPECIALIST

Today, speech-language pathologists and audiologists play a number of roles. Some professionals are serving in school settings. Their clients may range in age from a few months to many years, since school districts now comprise facilities serving clients of all ages. A recent development in service delivery in educational settings is that of serving as a collaborative consultant (Marvin, 1987) to classroom teachers, other primary caregivers, and special education personnel. Some communication specialists serve in that capacity. They often work with clients in the classroom or in a child care facility rather than limiting service to a therapy

1

room. Colleges and universities are other educational settings serving a special population, and a number of speech and hearing professionals work full time or part time in those areas.

Other specialists are serving in community agencies, often working with people of many nationalities. Sometimes these specialists work not only with men, women, and children with speech and hearing difficulties, but also with people whose lack of proficiency in English is preventing them from satisfying some basic needs. Some specialists are supplying knowledge and stimulation to children deprived of even low levels of attention and care. Others are working with the severely disabled population, often helping members of that population live more stimulating and satisfying lives than would have been possible a few years ago.

Still other communication specialists (or some of the same ones, if they hold more than one job) are employed in hospital settings, in rehabilitation centers, or extended care facilities. Personnel in hospitals or centers may serve clients of all ages or those of a specific age range. Some may limit their services, specializing in clients with particular disorders, while others treat a wider range of clients with varied medical conditions.

An increasing number of communication disorders specialists are developing private practices. These specialists may devote their energies to individual therapy with many types of clients or may limit their practice to populations with specific needs. For example, a private practitioner may work with singers or actors to improve vocal quality and/or diction. Another may have a contract to provide speech and/or hearing services in a long-term care facility. Others may serve as consultants to business or industry.

In addition to other duties, many speech-language pathologists and audiologists serve administrative functions. Many serve in supervisory capacities such as supervising aides, student teachers, beginning professionals, or a large staff. Others conduct research; write grant proposals, books, and journal articles; serve as expert witnesses; conduct workshops and in-service training sessions; plan fundraising activities; participate in professional organizations and conferences; and engage in legislative and civic activities.

No college or university program can prepare a student to assume all of these roles and perform all of these functions. As a result, many learn on the job. Success depends not only on professionals' mental capabilities or on their academic preparation. It depends greatly on their interpersonal skills, their ability to assess personal strengths and limitations, and their capability to profit from experience.

REQUISITE INTERPERSONAL SKILLS

To be able to function effectively in this variety of roles and work settings, speech-language pathologists and audiologists need certain interpersonal skills.

Twila Griffith (1987, p. 119), director of speech, language, and hearing services in a community hospital, described the characteristics most necessary for success in a hospital setting. The characteristics she lists are desirable for clinicians in all work settings. Some of those are quoted below.

> Experience suggests that certain traits make it easier to work comfortably and effectively. Included in these are: (a) flexibility to deal with the constant daily changes which affect most aspects of care; (b) the ability to work independently; (c) willingness to continue to learn; (d) ability to communicate well with families and other professionals who are involved; and (e) readiness to provide coverage and to accept the assignment of a patient not previously seen. . . .
>
> There is no room in the hospital setting for a staff member who needs to be told when to begin work. Speech-language pathologists and audiologists must be ready to initiate programs and be confident and assertive enough to request support services and resources.
>
> Professional credibility is important to the success of the treatment program as well as the overall success of the hospital. All staff members are expected to present a professional appearance in dress and demeanor and to conduct themselves in a professional manner. . . .
>
> Good writing skills are required because of the number of professional persons providing written documentation on a given patient. Each professional must be able to convey the maximum amount of information in the fewest number of words.

Patricia Cole (1986, p. 8) described some personal prerequisites for success in private practice. These too would be advantageous in many work settings.

> As clinicians, businesspersons, and public relations specialists, private practitioners deal with many persons and situations. They must move forward in the face of uncertainty, make decisions in a timely and determined manner, be creative yet systematic, and be flexible enough to adjust to changing opportunities and demands.

We concur with the above statements. In our years of experience working and talking with students and professionals in our own and related fields, and particularly with clients and families receiving professional services, the vital importance of knowledge and skill in the areas of interpersonal communication, counseling, group work, problem solving, time utilization, and stress management has been repeatedly emphasized.

OVERVIEW OF CHAPTER CONTENT

This book is concerned with interpersonal skills that will assist you in achieving success and satisfaction in your profession, regardless of the areas or settings in which you serve. The chapters cover a variety of topics that are previewed here. To permit adequate discussion of these topics, it has been necessary to exclude some important aspects of evaluation, differential diagnosis, case management, therapy for communication disorders, and clinical supervision. Many volumes already have been published concerning them. The topics that we have included in this book are not as frequently addressed and should prove interesting and beneficial.

Chapter 2 discusses the elements involved in meeting a new client. A clinician must be concerned with preparing for the meeting—keeping in mind the purposes of the meeting and the unique characteristics that each participant brings to the interaction. Preparing for a first meeting involves consideration of the physical setting, of the special needs of individual clients, and of data recording procedures. First meetings serve many purposes, including information getting, information giving, expression and exploration of feelings, problem solving, and planning for future action. The chapter includes a discussion of basic human needs, organismic variables, and the dynamics of personal interaction. We consider the understanding of these topics to be vital in effective interpersonal relationships.

Chapter 3 addresses factors involved in assessing clients. Some important goals of the assessment process are discussed: determining the nature and extent of the communication problem; determining contributing causal factors; determining therapeutic direction and procedures; strengthening the client/clinician relationship; and encouraging client involvement. Techniques to facilitate the assessment process included in the chapter are as follows: conforming to the requirements of the work setting; adapting to the client's age; helping the client feel at ease; previewing the evaluation procedures; making the most of available time; supporting the client's self-esteem; minimizing unproductive behavior; sharing evaluation results and recommendations; and understanding the grief process.

Motivating clients for effective therapy is the topic of Chapter 4. Techniques for initiating and maintaining effective therapy are included, as well as suggestions for establishing therapy goals. Strategies to promote behavioral change are described. The section on dealing with counterproductive factors includes discussion of physiological factors, resistance, defense mechanisms, stress, and depression.

Working with family members is the special focus of Chapter 5. Contemporary family patterns are explored. Examples are given of types of interactions with family members. Ways to enlist family participation in therapy are discussed, as well as ways to encourage environmental change supportive to therapy.

Chapter 6 is designed to aid clinicians in developing skills for working with groups. Basic principles of group process and participation are discussed, with particular consideration regarding types of groups, stages of group development, and characteristics of group members. A section of the chapter is devoted to characteristics of an effective group leader. Examples of therapy groups for clients with specific communication disorders are given. The structuring of effective groups for families of clients is also considered.

The focus of Chapter 7 is on helping clients and families become effective problem solvers. Some of the topics include professional applications of problem solving, steps in problem solving, strategies for client and family participation in problem solving, and problem solving in group settings. Discussion of various problem-solving styles concludes the chapter.

Chapter 8 is concerned with the conclusion of therapy. Factors involved in the final stages of therapy are addressed, including preparing a client for leaving therapy and referral to other agencies. Record keeping, documentation, and follow-up procedures receive special attention. The difficulties of facing a client's death are also discussed.

In Chapter 9, we round out our discussion of factors contributing to professional interpersonal effectiveness with suggestions on working with colleagues and on transdisciplinary teams. Sections of the chapter are devoted to skills involved in making professional presentations and in evaluating professional effectiveness. Interpersonal relationships can be time-consuming and stressful. Attention is therefore given to time management and to the recognition and avoidance of burnout.

As mentioned earlier, topics included in this book are those that have been repeatedly mentioned as important by clients, parents and other family members, students preparing for the profession, and professionals working in the field. The book addresses skills that may only be covered briefly in academic preparation programs. Yet these skills often spell the difference between mediocrity and excellence in clinical practice. It is our hope that the topics explored here will add to your clinical competence and professional satisfaction.

REFERENCES

Cole, P.R. (1986). Private practice: Personal prerequisites and potential. In K.G. Butler (Ed.), *Prospering in private practice: A handbook for speech-language pathology and audiology* (pp. 3–11). Rockville, MD: Aspen Publishers, Inc.

Griffith, T.S. (1987). Administration of community hospital speech-language-hearing programs. In H.J. Oyer (Ed.), *Administration of programs in speech-language pathology and audiology* (pp. 100–128). Englewood Cliffs, NJ: Prentice-Hall.

Marvin, C.A. (1987). Consultation services: Changing roles for SLPs. *Journal of Childhood Communication Disorders, 11*(1), 1–15.

2

Meeting a New Client

What is involved in a significant new experience? There are elements of anticipation and challenge, and at the same time, elements of fear and uncertainty. Basically everyone in a new situation has these positive and negative emotions, in varying combinations or proportions. These feelings therefore exist when meeting a new client or when meeting a potential client for the first time.

You are pleased that someone has chosen to come to you as a professional and that your expertise is being sought. You have an opportunity to use your professional knowledge and hone your professional techniques. You also have the chance to play detective in facing a challenging new case. You have the opportunity to meet an interesting new person, perhaps from a culture or milieu different from those with which you are familiar. At the same time, there is the possibility that the client will be disappointed. The client may not be happy with the diagnosis, or the proposed treatment, or the fee, or your background or experience. Or the client may not want to return because of some unexplained reason. You may see a great need for your services, but, because of tight scheduling, you may have difficulty arranging for the appropriate sessions. In a sense, some of these positive and negative feelings occur with each subsequent meeting, but there is no doubt that it is the first meeting when the basic nature of the relationship will be established.

The client has mixed feelings also. He or she is coming in with the hope that you will be instrumental in solving a problem or bettering a condition that is interfering with effective communication. You and your agency represent an ally in helping to face the problem. The client knows that you are the expert, and that is an important assurance. Often, however, a client has more feelings of uncertainty and anxiety than positive feelings. There may be fear that the problem is insoluble. There may be feelings of guilt and shame that such a problem exists. There also may be the fear that the treatment process will be long and expensive with no guarantee that the gain will be great. Clients will be concerned about your opinion of them as people—whether they are worthy, whether they have contributed to the problem by past actions or errors, whether they will be able to follow the proposed treatment and achieve their desired objective.

What are the goals for a first meeting or interview with a client? In the first meeting, you will find out what the client is like and what he or she hopes to gain from your services. You hope that the client will recognize your professional ability to handle the particular problem, your willingness to work with the client, and your acceptance of the client as a worthy and respected person. To convey to a client that this relationship will be a positive one, you must exhibit confidence regarding your professional skill and competence.

The participants and what they bring to the first meeting, including their goals and expectations, are critically important to the outcome of this initial contact. Before we explore further the purposes of the meeting and the characteristics of the participants, it is important to consider what preparations should be made prior to the actual meeting. Thus, this chapter will first include a discussion of preparing for the first meeting and then consider the purposes that such meetings can serve. The final portion of the chapter will discuss characteristics of the meeting's participants and some basic dynamics of human motivation and interaction.

PREPARATIONS FOR THE MEETING

In making preparations for the meeting, one factor to consider is how the client came to you. If it is a self-referral, how did the client happen to select you? Was it through advertising, word-of-mouth referral by a friend, or the "yellow pages"? Did an agency or another professional recommend you? If so, was the referral made by a pediatrician, an otolaryngologist, a preschool director, a classroom teacher, an employer, another speech-language pathologist or audiologist, a senior center, a refugee center, or other professionals at your agency who may also be seeing the client? Not only do you need to know this in order to submit appropriate reports and recommendations, but from a long-range standpoint, if you are in a private practice or agency, you will find the information useful in developing clientele by broadening and strengthening your referral base. In most situations, strictly ''drop-in'' clients are unlikely. Usually, a written or telephone contact precedes the first meeting.

In preparing for meeting with a client, it is important to consider what first impressions you or your organization make upon a new client. A client's preliminary telephone contact, whether with you or with some employee or staff member, can often significantly affect a future relationship. If the person representing you or your agency is friendly, helpful, polite, intelligible, and intelligent, and provides pertinent and requested information (such as the fee schedule or available appointment times), then the overall impression will be positive. If, however, clients are made to feel insignificant or troublesome, if their questions are not answered satisfactorily, or if the staff person is not patient and perceptive in dealing with a communicatively handicapped person, the overall impression will be negative. Be certain that the person making preliminary contacts for you understands desired procedures and the questions that need to be addressed. The importance of the telephone contact or receptionist cannot be overemphasized. Clients can be lost before they are ever seen by the professional. Check out the nature of these preliminary contacts in your office or agency and make suggestions for improvement if needed.

If you rely on an answering machine to receive telephone messages, it is important that your recorded message is clear and professional. Here are some examples.

- "Thank you for calling the Speech and Hearing Center. Please leave your name and telephone number. Your call will be returned as soon as possible."
- "This is 555-1234. If you would like to leave your name and phone number, one of us will return your call as soon as possible. You may leave a detailed message if you wish. Wait for the beep."

A telephone conversation is often followed by a written contact. Careful attention should be directed toward any materials to be mailed to the client: a brochure describing the available services, a card confirming a scheduled appointment, a fee schedule, a note from a school speech-language specialist outlining the services a child will be receiving, a map describing the location of the office or facility, parking information and a parking permit if necessary, or any questionnaires or forms that need to be completed.

The Physical Setting

First meetings with clients can take place in a variety of settings. Sometimes professionals have complete control over the settings in which they meet their clients, and sometimes they have no choice whatsoever. Offices and/or therapy rooms run the gamut from broom closets to elegant suites. Whatever can be done to enhance even the simplest of settings can be productive. Appropriate artwork, an attractive bulletin board, a small plant, neatly organized files and therapy materials, and useful visual aids can make a significant difference. Physical settings, including decor, furniture, even the colors chosen to decorate offices, convey information to the client. Rooms are described as homey, lived-in, comfortable, masculine, feminine, formal, cold, sterile, and so forth. Whatever the setting, it should be one that is comfortable and workable for both you and your clients.

The setting in which you conduct professional business can be considered a form of nonverbal communication to the client. It should therefore be congruent with any messages you wish to convey. For instance, you want clients to feel they have your undivided attention. Thus, privacy is an important consideration. Anyone who has ever conducted an important session with someone while people came in and out of the room or phones rang and buzzers sounded recognizes the need for privacy. If provisions are not made to meet this need, the session will suffer.

The same is true regarding the physical comfort of the setting. The clients should feel as comfortable as possible. Therefore, attention must be paid to seating and working arrangements and to the room's temperature and ventilation. You also want clients to know that you are efficient and well-organized. File folders, therapy materials, correspondence, and other personal effects scattered about the room in a haphazard manner give quite the opposite impression. Signs or slogans that reveal your position on controversial issues certainly convey messages that may affect a client's response to you.

People vary in their sensitivity to physical settings. Some find themselves distracted or actually upset if the room is either excessively cluttered or inordinately barren. Others do not seem to be affected, provided there is a place to sit, the air is relatively pleasant and fresh, and it is possible to hear without acute discomfort or strain. An unusual or humble setting does not necessarily make for an inferior session, providing both participants can still devote the necessary time and attention to the interaction. Nevertheless, if your current office and work setting can be easily improved, it is wise to make the effort.

Today, the issue of smoking versus nonsmoking is a consideration. A smoker can be very uncomfortable in a setting where smoking is not permitted. On the other hand, if one person smokes and the other is a nonsmoker, this can also cause discomfort. You will have to handle this issue in your own way. However, a sign requesting "no smoking, please" in a speech pathologist's office is appropriate.

In summary, minimum requisites for the setting of a first meeting include a pleasant, quiet room; chairs of relatively equal dimensions to foster equality of participation; an uncluttered desk or table for needed materials; and desired recording and diagnostic equipment. Basically, most professionals are concerned with the setting only insofar as it facilitates work with clients and is consistent with the professional's personality and work style.

Personal Furnishings

We have talked about office furnishings. Now let us consider personal "furnishings." Beyond the essentials of body cleanliness lies personal grooming and "dressing for success." Magazine articles as well as entire books provide guidance in this area (for example, Molloy, 1977; Cho & Lueders, 1982; Wallach, 1986).

Certain styles of grooming and dress may lead to being stereotyped by a client. The clinician may thus arouse some of the client's attitudes and feelings customarily directed to that stereotype. For instance, an audiologist may think that wearing a white laboratory coat enhances his professional image, whereas the client may have negative reactions to such a potent reminder of medical crises.

The degree of formality in dress is dependent upon the work setting. Many clinicians select a wardrobe that is comparable to that worn by other professionals at the site. Activities that will be required during the day must also be considered. For example, clinicians working with young children in a preschool setting may find informal dress more desirable. In general, conservative dress is preferred.

Special Considerations

Another important aspect of the setting is the consideration of any special needs that clients may present. For instance, it may be necessary to provide a wheelchair or other assistance to an aged or physically handicapped person. The office itself must be accessible to clients who have impaired mobility.

Not only must you consider physical needs; you must also consider possible communicative barriers. If, for example, you know that the person with whom you are to meet communicates minimally or not at all in your language, you must arrange for an interpreter, either accompanying the person or provided by you. This applies as well to clients who communicate via manual communication such as American Sign Language. As a professional, you cannot overlook the fact that there can be a language barrier even when both participants in a conversation ostensibly speak the same language. We are referring to the use of vocabulary and sentence structure that is inappropriate for the communication level of the client (either too complex or too simple) and to the inordinate use of professional jargon.

In addition to possible language barriers, you must consider possible barriers related to cultural differences. This is where knowledge of other cultures can serve you well. For example, a client's maintaining eye contact is considered desirable in many cultures and yet can be insulting in others. Researchers in the fields of kinesics (the study of facial expressions and body movements) and proxemics (the study of space usage and territoriality) have explained how an individual from one culture can unwittingly offend someone from another culture. For example, you may find yourself backing off from another person who continues to move closer as both of you try to establish what is perceived to be a socially appropriate and comfortable conversational position. Preparation for professional interactions, then, may involve special efforts to become better acquainted with the cultures from which clients come.

Another consideration in planning for the first session is deciding whether to include or exclude potential participants. For example, when you are meeting an adolescent and her parents for the first time, you may wish to provide an opportunity to meet individually with the adolescent. Otherwise you may find the presence of a parent inhibiting frank communication with the client. Often the presence of a spouse may inhibit the establishment of communication with a client, particularly if the spouse tends to monopolize or misdirect the conversation.

One of the considerations in meeting a client for the first time concerns data regarding the client that you may wish to know before the meeting. Professionals vary in their philosophy regarding this. Some feel that prior knowledge will trigger selective perception causing them to focus on certain information at the first meeting and ignore or overlook other equally important data. In selective perception, preconceived notions regarding somebody actually affect the way that person is viewed initially. Other professionals argue that the more information available before the meeting, the better able they are to plan effective initial procedures. The clinician may want to have a preliminary questionnaire or checklist completed before the meeting. If the client has been referred by another professional or agency, information may have been included in the referral packet or obtained through telephone contact with the source of referral. Two questions need to be addressed: (1) How much information do I want to obtain prior to the first meeting? and (2) How carefully will I study the available information prior to the first meeting? You must decide what you feel is desirable and appropriate for each new case.

Depending on the age of the client (child or adult) and on the general nature of the presenting problem, the selection and assortment of materials to be used at the first meeting will also have to be considered. A few interesting toys strategically placed in the meeting room can make or break an initial meeting with a four-year-old child. On the other hand, toys scattered about the room used for a meeting with a 60-year-old laryngectomized client can be disconcerting. If you plan on using diagnostic or evaluative materials at a first session, all the necessary supplies should be conveniently located in the meeting room. Disrupting a first session by rushing off to borrow a test booklet from a colleague or rummaging through desk drawers to find the tokens for a token test wastes valuable time and conveys a message of disorganization to the client. If an audiologist first meets with a client in an office and then escorts the client to a test suite, all audiometric equipment and supplies should be ready and functional so that testing can be readily begun.

Recording Data

At the first meeting, the clinician will no doubt obtain important information. Personal note taking is often the method of choice for recording such information.

Note taking is so much a part of business and professional life that it is readily accepted by the vast majority of clients. The procedure ordinarily does not affect the progress of the meeting unless the clinician becomes so involved in the process that it interferes with attending to and communicating with the client.

You have to face the fact that, even with a personal shorthand system of note taking, you can record only the barest essentials of what transpires in a meeting. If you wish to analyze in detail the content and dynamics of a session, it is preferable to rely on a more objective, extensive method of recording such as an audiotape or videotape recorder. The most important consideration in the first meeting with a client is the establishment of rapport. For that reason, personal note taking may be the method of choice for recording information from that session. A client may feel very self-conscious, apprehensive, or uncomfortable in the first session (particularly if it is a preliminary informational session rather than a diagnostic evaluation) if more than occasional note taking is used. You should be sensitive to these feelings. If more detailed recording is necessary at the first meeting, you may wish to explain the purpose for it.

Most clients tend to pay less attention to a tape recorder as they become more engrossed in actual conversation and interaction. It has been our experience that the clinician plays an important role in bringing this about. Your attitude toward the recording procedure influences your client's attitude and consequently the degree to which these procedures intrude upon the meeting. The more unobtrusive a recording procedure, the easier it is to ignore. However, ethical considerations dictate that the client's (or parent's) permission be obtained before initiating the recording.

Comments to the client regarding the recording system should be straightforward and brief. One approach might be, "If it's all right with you, I'm going to tape record this session so I can go over it later and make notes regarding it. You and I may go over parts of it together also. Of course, the tape is for our use only." If the intention is to share the record of the session with anyone else, this should be made clear to the client. Many communicative disorders specialists routinely record all sessions with clients. The tapes are used for analysis and discussion purposes with the clients and form the basis of a permanent record of each client's progress. Many clinicians encourage the client to tape each session also, so that the client in home practice sessions can replay assigned practice exercises or materials as well as the comments and instructions of the therapist.

So far in this chapter, we have discussed necessary preparations for meeting with clients. Another important consideration is the purpose or purposes that the meeting can serve.

PURPOSES OF THE MEETING

In our textbook on effective interviewing (Molyneaux & Lane, 1982), we described interviews (defined as "directed conversations with a purpose") as fulfilling one or more of the following goals: information getting; information giving; expression and exploration of feelings; problem solving; and planning for future action. Implicit in the successful accomplishment of most, if not all, of these interviewing purposes is that learning and/or observable behavioral change will take place in one or both participants as a result of the interaction. Since first meetings are interviews and thus serve one or more of the functions mentioned above, we will now examine these purposes in greater detail.

Information Getting

In *information-getting* interactions, the goal of the professional is to acquire certain factual information. For example, an information-getting session may involve obtaining a case history from the client. The information obtained on aspects of the client's background, communicative experiences, daily habits, and/ or personality characteristics, as well as on the client's perception of his or her communication problem, will have a bearing on your professional actions or recommendations.

There are several ways you can gather information about a person. You can observe him or her in a variety of situations or circumstances, observing both verbal and nonverbal behavior. You can also examine a variety of documents relating to that person: existing documents (including diaries, medical records, school records, etc.) and elicited documents prepared or completed at your request (questionnaires or rating scales). These documents may be prepared or completed by your client or by others. In addition to observation and examination of documents, interviewing (of the client and of others who have had contact with him or her) is an important source of information.

Information Giving

In *information-giving* interactions, the major purpose is to give the person with whom you are meeting information that will prove helpful and worthwhile. As a speech-language pathologist or audiologist, you will often be in interpersonal situations where the other person is expecting you to provide information. The requests for information may be framed in a variety of ways; for instance, as direct, straightforward questions or as hypothetical situations to which you are encouraged to respond. The person is basically asking for authoritative information from you. Perhaps an anxious mother is asking you what can be discovered by testing Johnny for two hours on a variety of language tests. Perhaps an elderly hearing-impaired client wants you to tell him about the different types of hearing aids and what they can do to improve his ability to get along with his family and friends. Perhaps you have been asked to meet with a new member of your agency's staff to explain the agency's general philosophy as well as the paperwork and procedures required of all employees. In each of these instances, your effectiveness in the session will certainly depend upon your professional acumen and judgment and the depth of your understanding of the subject matter. But equally important to your effectiveness in the session is your ability to relate well to the other person and to convey the required information in an appropriate and understandable manner.

Expression and Exploration of Feelings

Another frequent outcome of professional interactions is the *expression and exploration of feelings*—the opportunity for one or both participants to make known their feelings about something or someone. Many psychotherapists attempt to stimulate and encourage the expression of feelings, not only positive feelings but negative and ambivalent feelings as well. Professionals in the communicative disorders field often find it advisable to do the same. The feelings that are revealed during the course of a session may be familiar ones to the person expressing them. Often, however, the feelings that emerge may be feelings that have been hitherto ignored, suppressed, or disavowed.

The goal of the counselor or therapist during a session, then, may be to increase the client's awareness and acceptance of feelings. The general rationale behind this expression and exploration of feelings is the conviction that until a person is fully aware and accepting of the underlying feelings that are motivating his or her behavior or triggering his or her defense mechanisms, that person will be unable to devote attention and psychic energy to changing behavior patterns and altering communicative style. Many professionals are convinced of the importance of providing an atmosphere in which clients and their families can express their innermost feelings with a minimum of defensive reactions. They feel that in such an atmosphere, coping responses will be heightened and facilitated so as to allow for more effective ways of behaving in the environment.

Problem Solving

Another purpose that professional sessions can serve is that of *problem solving*. Often, clients will come to you with a specific problem that has already been identified and acknowledged. The bulk of time in that type of session may then be spent examining different ways of dealing with the situation causing the difficulties. The participants might then select what appears to be a workable behavioral alternative, or plan of action, given the current circumstances. At other times, the client and/or the client's family may be aware of ineffective or unsatisfying communicative functioning but may be unable to pinpoint any precise problem or whether or not circumstances can be changed. Your role as a communicative disorders specialist is then to identify the problem (perhaps through more extensive diagnostic evaluation) before helping to explore possible solutions. At any time in an ongoing therapeutic relationship, problems may arise that require problem-solving techniques. We consider problem-solving skills so important that Chapter 7 will be devoted to further discussion on helping clients and families become effective problem solvers.

Planning for Future Action

Another purpose that first meetings often serve is *planning for future action*. On some occasions, a general plan of action or a future goal may have already been decided upon prior to the first actual meeting. In that case, the session may be devoted to planning and scheduling specific activities (perhaps enrollment in your speech-language therapy program or in an aural rehabilitation workshop) designed to implement the chosen plan or achieve the chosen goal. In order to decide on an appropriate direction for behavioral change, a person must first be aware of where the trouble lies and what possibilities there are for change in the troublesome circumstances. Many other factors come into play in determining what direction change will take. These factors include the person's physical and mental capacities, general level of understanding and experience, degree of insight into communicative weaknesses and strengths, tolerance for risk taking, and general flexibility and adaptability, as well as available services, agencies, support groups, and funds, to name a few.

The first interview or meeting with a client is seldom limited strictly to a single one of the five purposes listed above. Often, a session that is especially effective or satisfying to one or both participants turns out to have accomplished more than one of these goals. This is true of the first meeting with a client whether that meeting is an informal introductory meeting or a complete diagnostic evaluation. It can also hold true for any therapy session.

PARTICIPANTS IN THE MEETING

We come now to examining more directly what happens when two people come together in the communicative interaction of a first meeting. People and communicative situations come in infinite variety, and the progress and outcome of any particular situation will be influenced by a number of factors. The nature of the communicative setting, the circumstances under which the interaction takes place, and the reasons for it certainly affect the interaction. The personality and characteristics of each individual and his or her effects upon the other participant are also crucial determinants of the quality of the interaction and its outcome.

S-O-R Variables

One way of describing the coming together of individuals in a communicative interaction is to consider what are often termed the "S-O-R variables" involved. The S, O, and R variables refer to the variations that can occur in the "stimulus," within the "organism," or in the "response."

Let us first consider the *stimulus, or S, variables*. In their efforts to survive, humans are constantly taking in information from the environment, processing it, and responding to that information in some way. The actual objects and events (the stimuli) in the environment at any one moment, as well as the richness or paucity of stimuli, will differ. We have already discussed some aspects of the external environment that can serve as stimuli to affect the behavior of participants in a conference or therapy session. Various internal happenings, including unmet basic needs, can also serve as stimuli to which the individual will attend. These internal happenings could be a sudden increase in heartbeat or perspiration; a severe abdominal, chest, or head pain; "grumblings" of the stomach if mealtime is past due; or fantasies or daydreams that are more appealing than external realities. These and many other internal stimuli can capture a person's attention as well as noises, sights, smells, or other sensations coming from the outside. The variety of these messages that can be picked up by sense receptors and transmitted to the central nervous system for processing are termed stimulus (or S) variables.

What is *available* to be responded to will be different from situation to situation. In any one situation, what *will* be responded to differs from individual to individual. Thus, a distinction can be made between *potential* and *actual* stimuli. Potential stimuli are all the happenings or disturbances in the individual's environment to which his or her sense receptors are capable of responding, even though he or she may not do so. Actual stimuli are those taken into and processed by the nervous system.

At any particular time, many stimuli available in the external environment, as well as within a person's body, may evoke responses. These responses may take many different forms. These, then, can be termed the *response, or R, variables* in the situation. At any one time, there are likely to be many stimuli impinging on the sense receptors. People respond to some and disregard others; those to which they do respond are processed at a variety of levels within the nervous system. Some responses occur at a level of the nervous system below that which triggers conscious awareness of the information. For instance, minor variations in respiration rate, body temperature, or postural adjustments go unnoticed even though they take place in our bodies to maintain physiological balance (homeostasis).

Sometimes people are aware of reflexive responses as they occur because messages are sent to the cerebral cortex at the same time the response occurs involuntarily at another part of the body. You realize, for example, that you have blinked your eye to avoid an insect that has flown near your eyelid, but the defensive maneuver took place without your conscious direction. Emotional responses are often of this nature. Sometimes, for example, you may be first aware that you are fearful of something when you feel your heart beating faster and your mouth getting dry.

Still other responses are voluntarily accomplished after processing, interpreting, and integrating various stimuli at a completely conscious level. You may decide deliberately to move closer to your client in a session, for example, when you sense that the distance between your chairs seems too stiff and formal for the confidential material being discussed. Or you may decide to rephrase and repeat a question you have asked when you hear how vague and confused it sounds the first time.

In any human interaction, the response, or R, variables can be remarkably numerous. Responses to stimuli can be one-cell simple or extraordinarily complex. They can be completely reflexive or involuntary or intricately calculated and voluntary, and they can be all stages in between. From a wide variety of potential stimuli, you selectively perceive only a small portion of those that will then determine your responses. This selectivity of perception is vital in enabling you to concentrate your attention. However, this selective perception is also often the cause of stereotyped responses, in which a limited set of visual, auditory, tactile, or even olfactory stimuli automatically evokes a particular behavior or emotional response. The sight of food particles on a man's beard may automatically evoke a frown, for example; a command received over an intercom from a voice of authority may evoke an automatic "Yes, sir"; and the smell of freshly brewed coffee may lure you from your desk no matter how high the work is stacked or how near the deadline.

In each of the above examples, a person is exhibiting a habitual, ready-made response to a limited set of perceived stimuli. As we mentioned earlier, people often form judgments of others in just such a stereotyped manner. They note a limited set of stimuli, those indicating male or female, young or old, white or black, and the like. They quickly classify the observed person into a general category on the basis of that limited set. They then react with a habitual, automatic response to that general category. As can be expected, such a limited response repertoire on the part of a clinician can interfere markedly with relating to a client on the basis of his or her individual attributes and needs. A limited response repertoire on the part of a client may account for the fact that the client has just dismissed his eighth speech-language therapist because "all of them were just too bossy."

The variety of voluntary responses available to humans is a result of the extensive development of the cerebral cortex. This potential for varied response is a vital factor in humans' supremacy in the animal hierarchy. We must note, however, that having the potential for a variety of appropriate responses does little good if a person's actual response repertoire is limited to a few habitual, stereotyped behaviors.

In addition to voluntary, involuntary, and stereotyped responses, another set of terms used to describe responses is the overt/covert classification. If a response to a stimulus or combination of stimuli can be observed by another person, it is termed an *overt* response. If it is unobservable by another, it is called a *covert* response. Both types of responses are taking place in both participants throughout a conference or therapy session.

Sometimes, there can be "leakage" of clues (often nonverbal) that provide an attentive observer with some information regarding basically covert responses in the session participants. However, there are still many reactions going on inside the head of each participant. These are unknown to the other participant unless there is a later voluntary sharing of previously undisclosed information. An astute professional is alert to nonverbal clues to a client's responses and reactions and emotional state. Many clients are equally alert to subtle clues revealing the therapist's covert responses.

In the realms of psychology and learning theory, the stimulus/response paradigm has been described, researched, and manipulated for centuries. Within the past century, speech-language pathologists, audiologists, and members of many other professions have become more and more adept at precise manipulation of human behavior through the selective reinforcement of certain behavioral responses. They have also become more alert to the role past conditioning may play in current behavior. Ivan Pavlov (1927) and B.F. Skinner (1938, 1953) are two of the best known pioneer investigators in the behaviorist tradition.

Pavlov demonstrated the existence of what is now known as classical or Pavlovian conditioning. When the sight, sound, smell, or feel of something in the environment automatically brings forth an emotional response (which may or may not be similar to the response of other people in the same situation), a person may well be demonstrating the results of classical conditioning that occurred at an earlier point in life. For example, a child, when asked to open his or her mouth for an oral mechanism examination, may draw away fearfully because of prior painful experiences with a dentist.

In contrast to Pavlovian conditioning, which involves the substitution of one stimulus for another in calling up a particular response, the early work of B.F. Skinner concentrated primarily on what is often termed operant conditioning. This involves the strengthening or increased recurrence of a particular response out of a variety of possible ones, and is accomplished through positive reinforcement of the desired response. Today, the principles of behavior modification based on selective reinforcement of various behaviors are widely known and employed.

In any situation, the selection of a particular behavioral response (out of the variety of possible behaviors) is due in large part to the fact that, in the past, that particular behavior has proved beneficial in some way. The payoff may have been relief of tension, satisfaction of a basic need, or approval by someone respected or admired. Or perhaps the behavior merited a mark on a progress chart, ten of which earned a gold star or other tangible treat. Previous conditioning may be playing an important role in the communication problems of some of the clients in your caseload. A nonverbal child may have been rewarded for silence and punished for speaking in the past. A grown woman may still be rewarded for speaking in a "little girl" voice by her doting and paternalistic husband.

One other point to be made regarding behavior modification as it applies directly to behavior in the professional situation: either participant in an interaction may be engaged in modifying the other's behavior during the session itself. This is done by selectively rewarding (positively reinforcing) certain types of verbal responses or other behavior. It is also done by ignoring other responses or actually punishing them by disapproval or other unpleasantness. The clinician who voices immediate disapproval when a parent states that she does not read to her child because of her long working hours may find the parent increasingly unwilling to discuss her relationship with her child.

Thus far, we have been concerned with S (stimulus) and R (response) variables. The particular nature of S and R variables can be noted and described in any behavioral situation or human interaction. In contrast to the traditional behaviorists' emphases upon these S and R variables, other investigators (known as perceptual theorists, cognitive theorists, Gestaltists, field theorists, personality theorists, phenomenologists, and humanists, to name a few) focus major attention on what have been termed the *organismic, or O, variables* in human behavior. The O variables are present in the individual and determine the perception, processing, and integration of stimulus information and the selection, formulation, and execution of a behavioral response.

Each participant in a communicative interaction will come to the interaction as a unique personality with a set of personal characteristics that will greatly affect perception and processing of available information and the responses made to it. Listed below are some of these organismic variables that clinician, client, and other session participants will bring to a session. Perhaps there are others that you can add to this list.

- age, sex, skin color, physical build, and other physical characteristics
- capacity and functioning of the sense receptors, other bodily systems, and the central nervous system
- perceptual experience and the concepts acquired to organize and make sense of perceptions
- personality characteristics—habitual ways of reacting to stimuli and of maintaining homeostasis
- previously learned responses and memories of past events
- basic need structure, including the degree to which those needs were met in the past and the extent to which any one of the needs is currently frustrated or satisfied
- pattern of motivation and goal selection—habitual ways of striving to satisfy basic needs
- beliefs and attitudes—the emotional component of the individual's conceptual structure
- injunctions and constraints imposed by the individual's culture
- value system under which the individual operates
- self-concept and the individual's concept of the "ideal self," and the degree of congruence between the two
- degree of self-awareness and self-acceptance
- defense system—the particular ways the individual escapes conflict by forms of temporary adjustment known as defense mechanisms
- relative strength and availability of effective coping behaviors, as opposed to a system of defense mechanisms
- role repertoire demanded in the individual's life and his or her effectiveness in those roles
- perception of the roles of each session participant and the individual's specific expectations about the encounter
- awareness of the communication process and the individual's sensitivity to verbal and nonverbal behaviors; his or her ability and willingness to engage in turn-taking behaviors necessary in interpersonal communication
- interpersonal behavioral and communication style and the individual's basic life position in regard to others
- nature and extent of the individual's stereotyped responses
- experience with and willingness to engage in self-disclosure

Given the possible combinations of all these and other organismic variables, is it any wonder that no two human beings (including clients and clinicians) are alike?

Basic Human Needs

One organismic variable listed above is so important that it warrants further discussion: the *basic need structure* of the individual. This includes the degree to which needs were met in the past and the extent to which any one of the needs is currently frustrated or satisfied. Many psychologists support the view that human functioning consists of primary organismic needs that must be met in order to ensure continuation in one's environment. Behavior is prompted by frustration of one or more of these needs and attempts to satisfy them. To many authorities, happiness is the emotion that accompanies satisfaction of a need.

Motivation theorists generally agree that deprivation of the primary biological needs of air, food, water, sex, and sensory stimulation motivates behavior. However, theorists have also proposed additional needs that they consider universal. They feel that these needs must be met if an individual is going to function fully and effectively as a human being.

One of the most popular lists of basic human needs is that proposed by Abraham Maslow (1956, 1968). Maslow made an influential contribution to our understanding of human behavior. Many of the earlier needs theories, or tension-reduction theories, were developed by researchers who worked almost exclusively with animal species other than human. Their applications to human behavior tended, therefore, to emphasize needs and frustrations common to human and other animal species. Maslow's work was concerned more directly with humans as social creatures who manifest some distinctly human developmental characteristics and behaviors in addition to their more primitive, biological ones.

Maslow arranged his list of basic human needs in a hierarchical form. Even though all of the needs must be met in order for a human to function at his or her highest level of effectiveness and capability, Maslow felt that the needs gradually emerged developmentally. The most basic level of the hierarchy contains needs that are prepotent to all others as far as actual physical survival.

Maslow's Hierarchy of Basic Human Needs can be summarized as follows:

Level I   Biological needs
Level II   Safety needs
Level III Love and affection or "belonging" needs
Level IV   Esteem needs (including self-esteem)
Level V   Self-actualization needs

In recent years, Maslow and other humanistic needs theorists have been criticized for promoting the self-centeredness and selfishness that critics claim are rampant in today's society. Other scholars laud the needs theorists for contributing to this century's progress in forwarding human rights issues. No doubt there is evidence on both sides of the controversy. However, it has been the authors' experience that the understanding and application of basic human needs theories can contribute greatly to satisfying and successful interpersonal relations.

In children and in adults, frustration of any level of the needs will motivate behavioral attempts to meet those needs and will tend to occupy the person's energies. Some adults can stand extreme deprivation of a lower level need in order to satisfy a need at a higher level. For example, a speech-language pathologist may drastically cut her food budget in order to accumulate money for a down payment on an office to start a private practice. An audiologist may neglect his private life to conduct a large number of audiological examinations for the data needed to complete his doctoral dissertation.

Maslow's theories served to highlight the importance of basic human needs in motivating and sustaining behavior. Although the needs are universal, the ways in which people endeavor to meet those needs (their goal selection) are highly varied, and may be vastly different from our preferred ways. Three men may be hungry. One may attempt to satisfy his hunger by a handful of seaweed and some grains of rice. Another may sit down to a meal of herring and boiled potatoes. The third may relish his hot dog and French fries. Three women may be frustrated in their need for esteem and respect from others. One may invite her friends to an elegant party. Another may enroll in an assertiveness training course. The third may devote three years of nights and weekends to writing a book.

According to homeostatic theory, a psychological drive, with its subsequent resulting activity aimed toward meeting a frustrated need, stems from a personal, internal disequilibrium. In organisms as complex as humans, a variety of needs can be aroused at any one time; goal selection and the organization of behavior to meet those goals, therefore, can be a very intricate process. Understanding basic human needs and the variety of ways in which individuals try to meet those needs can be helpful to professionals trying to understand a client's behavior and to motivate cooperation and change. A client will be satisfied with his or her initial meeting with you if the encounter has satisfied some potent basic need and has not frustrated others.

Another thought-provoking formulation of basic needs was presented by Snell and Gail Putney (1966). In common with other theorists, they included basic physical needs, for example: oxygen, water, sleep, food, and bearable temperatures. They also listed needs that are not absolutely essential to physical survival but that they felt also have an innate biological basis, such as the needs for muscular, mental, and sexual activity. They mentioned the tremendous inter- and intra-cultural variations in the ways people try to meet these needs, and discussed the extent to which various cultures make it easy or difficult to attain necessary satisfactions.

A major contribution the Putneys made to the understanding of human needs as they motivate behavior lies in their description of what they termed the "self-needs." They felt that certain needs common to all humans are the result of the basic process of socialization rather than of actual physical structure. The Putneys pointed out that all over the world young children learn how to be social beings, and in the process, they develop consciousness of themselves as separate, distinct beings.

The Putneys, and many other psychologists, believe that tension or unhappiness results from frustration of a basic need. They pointed out that a person is often aware of tension, but does not recognize the frustrated need that is provoking the tension. Misinterpretation of needs and misdirected energies in attempting to meet needs or reduce tension cause much human unhappiness.

Eric Berne (1961, 1963, 1964; 1972), well-known psychotherapist and founder of the therapeutic method known as transactional analysis, postulated his version of basic human needs. He was particularly concerned with the ways in which those needs are reflected in an individual's day-to-day behavior. Berne pointed out that time can be spent in any one of a number of ways. The ways people spend their time represent their attempts to satisfy three drives or "hungers": stimulus or sensation hunger, recognition hunger, and structure hunger.

Stimulus or sensation hunger reflects the human organism's need for constant communication with its environment. This communication is necessary to maintain relative homeostasis and effective functioning. Highly developed sense organs require a baseline amount of varied stimuli to process. Without sufficient stimuli, a person becomes lethargic or bored, or in case of more extreme sensory deprivation becomes highly disturbed and even begins to hallucinate.

A person, as a social animal, also requires at least some acknowledgment and acceptance by other living beings. Berne felt that this *recognition hunger* is an outgrowth or derivation of the particular forms of sensory stimulation provided early in life. These include social handling and being physically cared for by another. As the infant grows, and as conditioning processes occur, the child learns to make do with less actual physical mothering, settling for more subtle and even symbolic forms of recognition; a brief pat on the head, a smile, or a wave of greeting from across the playground, for example. As people mature, their need for recognition by another continues to influence their behavior.

The third type of hunger, *structure hunger*, that Berne postulated seems to reflect what many investigators feel is a universal human need to make sense of the world around us. People need to impose some organization or order upon the multitude of stimuli that bombards their central nervous system. This need for some type of organization extends to filling waking hours with an assortment of behaviors, some of which hopefully help to meet our other basic needs. Berne described this need to structure time, noting our various time-filling behaviors: pastimes, rituals, games, activities, and intimacy. Berne also described ways in which habitual and preferred behaviors assist in fulfilling various needs, particularly the overriding need to be recognized by others.

We see then that each participant in a first meeting will arrive with his or her own unique mixture of organismic variables, including a particular constellation of met and unmet needs. This amalgam will affect each individual's selection and perception of stimuli in the particular situation. It will also determine each individual's responses to the situation and to the other participant(s). In other words, organismic variables determine ways of relating to others, known as interpersonal style. The interpersonal style of each participant, in turn, will influence the nature of communicative interactions during the course of a professional session.

Dynamics of Interaction

Speech, language, and hearing specialists are well versed regarding communication models and the basic principles of communicative interaction. We will not spend time on those basics. Instead, let us review briefly a few theories that may help clinicians evaluate their own relationships with clients.

Research investigations have shown that certain types of behavior on the part of one person in a social interaction tend to elicit particular types of behavior on the part of the other person. An attacking, critical manner, for example, tends to provoke hostility. A sarcastic, unkind manner has been found to provoke passive resistance. A dependent, helpless manner often results in assistance by the other person. A competent, friendly manner often engenders trust. People who usually act hurt or suspicious or distrustful of others often find themselves rejected by companions. These reciprocal types of interactional behavior have been termed *interpersonal reflexes*. You may find the concept of interpersonal reflexes and complementary interpersonal behaviors helpful in understanding why you behave as you do with some people. It also can help you to understand why people often react to you in certain ways.

Transactional analysis, mentioned earlier as popularized by Eric Berne, employs another way of interpreting behavior in human interactions. Therapists trained in the system of transactional analysis analyze human interactions on the basis of three ego states (Parent, Adult, and Child) that comprise our personality. According to the theory of transactional analysis, all social interactions (*transactions*) originate from one of the ego states of the initiator of the transaction (known as the *agent*). They are addressed (verbally and/or nonverbally) to one of the three ego states of the recipient of the communication (known as the *respondent*). Interactions are described as *complementary* or *crossed* transactions depending on whether the ego state from which the respondent responds to the received message is the same ego state that was addressed by the agent (a complementary transaction), or whether another ego state originates the response (a crossed transaction).

Complementary transactions tend to encourage communication, while crossed transactions can cause the interaction to be frustrating and even terminated.

Many professionals have found that the study of complementary and crossed transactions, life-positions, life-scripts, and other fundamental concepts of transactional analysis can be very helpful. Interactional diagrams developed through transactional analysis techniques may help to explain why a session or relationship is effective and productive or stormy and unsatisfying.

Another popular method of explaining and analyzing human behavior and interaction involves application of the principles of *role theory* as discussed and applied, for example, by Ackerman (1958), Goffman (1959), Satir (1967, 1972), Berne (1972), Minuchin (1974), Steiner (1974), Argyle and Henderson (1985), and Bernstein (1985). Much of interpersonal behavior is prescribed by the life-roles people are called upon to play, or deliberately choose to play. For example, in each of the world's cultures, mothers are supposed to exhibit certain behaviors with young children. There are certain behaviors expected in the courtship rituals of young men and women in particular tribes. Clients often come to a meeting with a professional with the expectation of listening respectfully and receiving information, in keeping with their perceptions of how to act the role of a "patient."

A number of research studies have been conducted to identify dimensions on which interpersonal behavior can be described or measured. Robert Carson (1969) summarized the findings of several research studies on this topic. He concluded that human interaction involved variations on two independent, bipolar dimensions: dominance-submission and hate-love.

Several more recent investigators of dimensions of human interaction have agreed upon the dominance-submission and hate-love dimensions. Myron Wish (1979) reported research he and fellow investigators had conducted in which five dimensions of interpersonal communication were revealed. The five dimensions were described as follows:

Dimension 1 Cooperative versus Competitive
Dimension 2 Intense versus Superficial
Dimension 3 Task versus Nontask Oriented
Dimension 4 Dominance versus Equality
Dimension 5 Impersonal and Formal versus Personal and Informal

There are certainly elements of dominance-submission and hate-love (unfriendliness-friendliness) dichotomies in these dimensions. However, they also provide additional ways of viewing interactions. For example, you may be most comfortable as a clinician when your professional interactions are: (1) cooperative, (2) serious, (3) business-like, (4) egalitarian, and (5) relatively informal. You will consequently be more comfortable working with clients or colleagues who likewise favor similar operating points along the five dimensions. Because of your preferences along the dimensions, you may find yourself routinely frustrated by a ten-year-old client who wants to play and visit with you rather than devote energy to correcting his severe misarticulations (discrepancies along dimension 3). Or you may decline when another client insists that you contact her employer to arrange that she be transferred to quieter surroundings because you are the professional and therefore in complete charge (difficulty along dimension 4). It may be interesting and useful to you to consider your sessions with clients from the perspective of these different dimensions.

SUMMARY

Keeping in mind the various topics discussed in this chapter, we can summarize the requisites of an effective first meeting with a client as follows:

- The physical setting reflects the professionalism of the clinician and facilitates comfortable, uninterrupted conversation and/or interaction between clinician and client.
- The appearance and manner of the professional reflects competence, experience, and a genuine interest in the client.
- Special needs or known limitations of the client in regard to communicative ability have been considered and, if possible, met.
- Needed materials are at hand and provisions for recording pertinent data have been made.
- The professional is aware of the various purposes that initial meetings can serve.
- The speech-language pathologist or audiologist is alert to verbal and nonverbal clues that provide information regarding the stimuli to which the client is responding, the nature of his or her responses to these stimuli, and the organismic characteristics that appear to be influencing those responses.
- The clinician is knowledgeable regarding basic human needs and is alert to expressions of frustration of those needs on the part of the client.
- The clinician keeps in mind the dimensions of human interaction and endeavors to establish a facilitative atmosphere.
- The client, caretaker, or guardian must be able to receive and attach meaning to the messages of the clinician.
- The client, caretaker, or guardian and the clinician have to be willing to talk, to listen, and to share at least a portion of themselves.
- The client, caretaker, or guardian and the clinician must be willing to communicate what they expect from the professional contact.

- The client, caretaker, or guardian and the clinician must be willing to cooperate in working toward agreed-upon goals.

You must be aware, however, that even if the above requisites are met, any meeting may be disrupted or become ineffective because of the behavior of one or both of the participants. It takes an astute professional to establish and continue an effective therapeutic relationship. The next chapters will examine how to maintain and encourage cooperation and positive change in the clients with whom you work.

REFERENCES

Ackerman, N. (1958). *The psychodynamics of family life*. New York: Basic Books, Inc.

Argyle, M., & Henderson, M. (1985). *The anatomy of relationships*. New York: Viking Penguin, Inc.

Berne, E. (1961). *Transactional analysis in psychotherapy*. New York: Grove Press.

Berne, E. (1963). *The structure and dynamics of organizations and groups*. Philadelphia: J.B. Lippincott Co.

Berne, E. (1964). *Games people play*. New York: Grove Press.

Berne, E. (1972). *What do you say after you say hello?* New York: Grove Press.

Bernstein, P. (1985). *Family ties, corporate bonds*. Garden City, NY: Doubleday.

Carson, R. (1969). *Interaction concepts of personality*. Chicago: Aldine Publishing Company.

Cho, E., & Lueders, H. (1982). *Looking, working, living terrific 24 hours a day*. New York: Ballantine Books.

Goffman, E. (1959). *The presentation of self in everyday life*. Garden City, NY: Doubleday.

Maslow, A. (1956). Personality problems and personality growth. In C.E. Moustakas (Ed.), *The self: Explorations in personal growth* (pp. 232–246). New York: Harper & Brothers Publishers.

Maslow, A. (1968). *Toward a psychology of being* (2nd ed.). New York: Van Nostrand Reinhold Co.

Minuchin, S. (1974). *Families and family therapy*. Cambridge, MA: Harvard University Press.

Molloy, J.T. (1977). *The woman's dress for success book*. New York: Warner Books.

Molyneaux, D., & Lane, V.W. (1982). *Effective interviewing: Techniques and analysis*. Boston: Allyn & Bacon.

Pavlov, I.P. (1927). *Conditioned reflexes: An investigation of the physiological activity of the cerebral cortex*. Translated and edited by G.V. Anrep. Oxford University Press: Humphrey Milford.

Putney, S., & Putney, G. (1966). *The adjusted American: Normal neuroses in the individual and society*. New York: Harper & Row.

Satir, V. (1967). *Conjoint family therapy* (rev. ed.). Palo Alto, CA: Science and Behavior Books, Inc.

Satir, V. (1972). *Peoplemaking*. Palo Alto, CA: Science and Behavior Books, Inc.

Skinner, B.F. (1938). *The behavior of organisms: An experimental analysis*. New York: Appleton-Century-Crofts.

Skinner, B.F. (1953). *Science and human behavior*. New York: Macmillan.

Steiner, C.M. (1974). *Scripts people live*. New York: Grove Press.

Wallach, J. (1986). *Looks that work*. New York: Viking Penguin, Inc.

Wish, M. (1979). Dimensions of dyadic communication. In S. Weitz (Ed.), *Nonverbal communication* (pp. 371–378). New York: Oxford University Press.

3

The Assessment Process: Fostering Trust and Cooperation

Learning how to conduct speech-language and hearing evaluations constitutes an important part of the professional's role. As a professional, you must have a clear understanding of exactly what is to be accomplished in a particular diagnostic evaluation. You need to consider the questions to be asked and answered, the assessment tools to be used, how materials are to be presented, how the information will be recorded, how the results will be reported and to whom—to name a few. Most university training programs place heavy emphasis upon methods of assessment and diagnosis. Requirements for professional certification and licensure are designed to ensure that a considerable amount of experience is obtained in evaluating clients prior to receiving a license or certificate.

In any professional contact, professional acumen and personal interaction skills each play a part in determining the outcome of the session. All professionals readily acknowledge the importance of selecting appropriate instruments and measures and administering them efficiently and accurately. Equally as important are the techniques used in interacting with clients. Barbara Hutchinson (1979, p. 1) asserted that: "Of all the skills required for speech clinicians, there are none so important as the skills needed for interviewing, taking case histories, and counseling. Everything else clinicians do depends upon how well these have been done."

Many excellent publications provide details regarding assessment of communicative problems (Hutchinson, Hanson, & Mecham, 1979; Peterson & Marquardt, 1981; Meitus & Weinberg, 1983; Nation & Aram, 1984; Emerick & Haynes, 1986; and Schiefelbusch, 1986, among others). Our emphasis in this chapter is not on specific diagnostic procedures but rather on the manner in which the assessment session is conducted. We will first discuss the clinician's principal goals for the evaluation process. We will then consider some important aspects of clinician behavior that contribute to effective evaluation sessions.

GOALS OF THE ASSESSMENT PROCESS

What are the goals for an evaluation session or sessions? Six important goals are as follows:

1. to determine if there is a communication problem and, if so, the nature and extent of the problem
2. to determine contributing causal factors, particularly those that are remediable
3. to determine the direction and procedures to be followed in alleviating the communication problem
4. to strengthen the relationship between the client and the clinician so that future sessions will be productive
5. to encourage the involvement of the client in accepting the necessity and desirability of change
6. to facilitate the client's cooperation in procedures designed to produce needed change

In the following paragraphs, we will consider further some factors involved in each of these goals.

Determining the Nature and Extent of the Communication Problem

To this end, the clinician will carefully select tests or other evaluative procedures that are designed to provide needed information. Necessary data regarding the client can be obtained in a variety of ways: observation, formal and informal testing, interviewing, and reviewing documents pertaining to the client. As mentioned in Chapter 2, some information may be obtained prior to the evaluation session.

Five reminders prompted by clinical experience in administration of diagnostic tests are as follows:

1. Make certain the tests you give are suitable for the age level of your client.
2. Make certain that the tests selected are appropriate for the cultural and ethnic background of your client.
3. Make certain the value of the information obtained warrants inclusion of the particular test in the diagnostic session.
4. Make certain you know the test well enough to administer it smoothly and accurately.
5. Make certain you are not providing clues to the correct answer through nonverbal or paralinguistic cues.

Determining Contributing Causal Factors

Sometimes the etiology of a communication problem is evident. There may be a visible physical anomaly (such as cleft lip and/or palate, agenesis of the ear canal, ankyloglossia, or laryngectomy). Or there may be an abnormal organic condition that has pervasive effects upon multiple areas of functioning (cerebral palsy, Down syndrome, amyotrophic lateral sclerosis, parkinsonism, for example). Other times, the etiology of a communication problem (stuttering, for example, or some articulation or language problems) is more difficult to ascertain.

Some of the etiological conditions causing communication problems are remediable through medical or surgical means; others require a different approach. Part of professional wisdom is making the distinction. Another part is ascertaining the appropriateness of professional involvement at a particular time. It is unprofessional for a communicative disorders specialist to spend weeks or even months working with a client to modify a problem (for example, using blowing exercises to alleviate hypernasality due to a submucous cleft) that could be markedly reduced in a much shorter time by medical, surgical, or prosthetic means. It is also unprofessional to cause a client to spend hard-earned money unnecessarily (as in fitting a hearing aid for a mild loss due to severely impacted cerumen).

Tragic results may occur when professionals attempt to diagnose conditions about which they have little or no knowledge. This is illustrated in the following excerpt from an interview of the mother of a deaf three-year-old boy talking with the child's speech-language pathologist. In it, the mother recounts her experience with a psychologist who had evaluated her child but was apparently unskilled in working with hearing-impaired children. This lack of skill and knowledge led the psychologist to misdiagnose the child's condition and to recommend an inappropriate educational placement.

In all of the interview excerpts contained in this and following chapters, the letter *C* will be used to designate the clinician and *R* will designate the respondent—in this case, the client's mother. Names of all interview participants have been changed to preserve anonymity.

Interview Excerpt 3-1

R: I had Bobby evaluated psychologically, and I was not pleased with how it came out because I didn't think it was accurate. Yeah, and so I was talking to Bobby's teacher in the infant deaf program, and I showed her the report and she goes "You're kidding!" You know, because the psychologist was recommending a TMR [trainable mentally retarded] over a hearing impaired program. Yeah, and I said to the psychologist,

"You've got to be kidding," and he said, "No, even with a hearing aid he will still need the TMR class." I shut my mouth. I just, you know, I'm not going to talk to this man. So I told his preschool teacher, and she read the report and she said, "I don't believe that. What are you going to do about it?" And I said, "Well, you know, what can I do?" She said, "Well, would you like him re-evaluated?" And I said, "Yeah," and she said, "Well I know a man that does evaluations on the hearing impaired—that's his background." And so I'm having Bobby evaluated by him now. We went up yesterday for the first time and just in 15 minutes he passed all the tests that he gave him, up through the three-year-old level, and it looks like he might go beyond that.

Determining Therapeutic Direction and Procedures

As you conduct the evaluation session, you will gain information that will enable you to plan appropriate procedures for alleviating the communication problem. Insofar as possible, select tests that provide baseline data against which results of therapy may be measured. Also select tests that provide information helpful in planning therapy activities. In addition to ascertaining and specifying the problem through evaluation procedures, you also gain valuable information regarding the client's personality, learning style, cognitive ability, interests, and possible compensatory behaviors. This information will also provide guidelines for you in planning and preparing for initial therapy sessions.

Strengthening the Client/Clinician Relationship

Much of what was discussed in Chapter 2 regarding first impressions is pertinent to this goal. Ideally, your behavior during the evaluation session will instill confidence on the part of the client and the client's family in your professional abilities. Your behavior will attest to your respect for and genuine interest in the client. You also want to convey your desire to assist in the client's achievement of satisfaction in communicative relationships.

Encouraging Client Involvement

Effective behavioral change requires the realization by the person involved that change is necessary and desirable. Some clients will come to an evaluation session eager to make recommended changes. In other cases, the client may be reluctant to put forth the needed effort and/or expense. On some occasions, clinicians may find themselves faced with a client who resists change, and perhaps even the diagnostic process, for a variety of reasons. If a client attends the diagnostic session not by his or her own volition but because of someone else's decision, it is especially important to determine whether the client is personally aware of the problem and is amenable to change.

Facilitating Client Cooperation

An effective diagnostic evaluation concludes by sharing—usually with the client and/or the client's family—data obtained regarding the communication problem. This is often followed by a preview of what the client can expect if therapy is initiated. The clinician's manner while discussing recommendations and prognosis plays an important role in determining the client's attitudes toward future therapy. This will be discussed further in a later section of this chapter.

FACILITATING THE ASSESSMENT PROCESS

In addition to setting and working toward goals for the diagnostic session, there are other important clinician skills that influence the assessment process. These include the following, which we will list here and then discuss in further detail:

- conforming to requirements of the work setting
- adapting to the age of the client
- helping the client/family feel at ease
- previewing the evaluation procedures
- making the most of available time
- supporting clients' self-esteem
- minimizing unproductive behavior
- sharing evaluation results and recommendations
- understanding the grief process

Conforming to Requirements of the Work Setting

In Chapter 1, we discussed the variety of settings in which speech and hearing professionals work: schools, clinics, hospitals, private practice, colleges and universities, and a number of business and community agencies. In any particular work setting, there will be certain rules and regulations (often in written form, but sometimes unwritten) regarding the form, content, and timeframe of diagnostic assessments and evaluations. In some agencies, for example, specific diagnostic tests or procedures are required. In all agencies, certain record-keeping procedures must be followed. It behooves the professional to conform to those requirements, and to work to change any that seem outmoded, inefficient, or unrealistic.

Sometimes, circumstances at a particular setting make it necessary for the professional to settle for less than ideal diagnostic procedures. For example, the clinician who sees patients in a hospital ward will have to work within the limitations imposed by the setting and by the client's physical condition. The patient may be under heavy medication and/or still suffering from the immediate effects of recent trauma. The interaction may be only a few minutes, may be interrupted by the patient's physical needs or the ministrations of hospital personnel, and is usually lacking in privacy. Formal testing in such circumstances is often not possible.

The speech-language pathologist working in the school setting must obtain written parental permission to conduct a diagnostic evaluation. The explanation of proposed procedures can be made available at the time this permission is secured. Experienced school professionals will attest that there is tremendous variation in parental interest in diagnostic procedures. In some instances, the clinician expends considerable energy in merely obtaining a parental signature consenting to the procedure. In other instances, parents not only wish to be present at the evaluation but may request that they have the opportunity to preview the test questions.

In almost any agency, the clinician may be faced with constraints upon maximally effective functioning. For example, an unrealistically short timeframe may be allotted for a diagnostic evaluation; a hired interpreter may call in reporting car trouble; a new interdisciplinary team member may view all communication disorders as requiring psychotherapy; preferred diagnostic materials may not be available; or needed equipment may not be functioning and funds may not be available for repair. To paraphrase W.B. Prescott: In the communicative disorders profession, as in everyday life, we are all continually faced with a series of great challenges brilliantly disguised as insoluble problems.

Adapting to the Age of the Client

In addition to the nature of the presenting communication problems, the client's age has important implications for assessment. Table 3-1 shows the age groups in the typical caseload of a speech-language pathologist and of an audiologist, as reported by Cynthia M. Shewan (1988, p. 29), in her report of the 1988 Omnibus Survey conducted by the American Speech-Language-Hearing Association.

Table 3-1 Age Groups in Typical Caseloads

Age	Speech-language pathologist caseload (%)	Audiologist caseload (%)
Birth to 2 years	4.6	8.7
3 to 5 years	19.3	13.9
6 to 17 years	44.7	12.5
18 to 64 years	17.6	28.9
65 to 84 years	11.6	29.0
85+ years	2.2	7.0

From these estimates, it can be noted that nearly 70 percent of speech-language pathology clients were 17 years of age or younger, while almost 65 percent of audiology patients were age 18 or older. The table also points out that the typical speech-language pathologist or audiologist will be called upon to work with clients of a wide age range. Some general remarks concerning work with elderly clients are presented here.

Elderly clients may well make up a greater proportion of a clinician's caseload in the future. Demographic studies have shown that the percentage of people over the age of 65 has grown from 4 percent in 1900 to 12 percent in 1988. The prediction is that the percentage will increase to approximately 22 percent by the year 2050. D.J. Fein (1983) predicted that by the year 2050, 39 percent of individuals aged 65 or older will have speech and language impairments; 59 percent of this age group will have hearing impairments. Speech-language-hearing professionals can thus expect even more requests for their services from this age group.

The position paper entitled "The Roles of Speech-Language Pathologists and Audiologists in Working with Older Persons," prepared by the American Speech-Language-Hearing Association's Committee on Communication Problems of the Aging (1988, p. 80), states the following:

> Older persons are a unique group whose characteristics must be appreciated in order to design appropriate and adequate services. . . . Multiple health problems and specific disabilities contribute to and are influenced by the older adult's increasing frailty, social isolation, mobility restriction, dependence on drugs, and susceptibility to mental impairment (such as confusion, memory changes, and depression), along with diminishing financial resources and altered sensory functions. Many of these age-related changes reduce or modify the nature and frequency of communicative interactions engaged in by older persons.

The committee that prepared the position statement also noted (p. 82) the following:

> . . . effective service delivery to older persons must arise out of a comprehensive understanding of the aging process and of the social, psychological, and physiological characteristics of older individuals in this society. This understanding leads logically to the recognition that older persons are at risk for deterioration in their daily communication interactions because of the presence of one or more specific communication disorder combined with more general age-related changes in individual functioning and social expectations. Speech-language pathologists and audiologists are uniquely qualified to provide interventions addressing communication interference and thus must be prepared to assume professional roles that are responsive to the total communication needs of older persons.

In the following sections exploring other aspects of the assessment process, consideration will be given to working with various age groups.

Helping the Client Feel at Ease

Several factors are important in helping the client feel as comfortable as possible in an inherently uncomfortable situation: the physical setting in which the evaluation takes place; the welcome and attention accorded to the client; the structuring of the session by the clinician so that the client knows what to expect and feels able to ask questions about the procedures; the use of active listening techniques by the clinician and his or her attention to the client's basic needs; and adaptation by the clinician to any particular circumstances affecting the evaluation of the client.

Professionals are aware that the demeanor of the client during the assessment process provides a great deal of information. The client's initial poise and the way he or she copes with the assessment procedures are likely to reflect the way the client meets other interpersonal situations in everyday life. Lon Emerick & William Haynes (1986, pp. 83–84) point out that the clinical examination is performed to provide a working image of the client. They state that "an important aspect in acquiring a working image of an individual is determining how he perceives himself and his situation."

Previewing the Evaluation Procedures

Clients have a need and right to know what you hope to accomplish in an evaluation session and what they will be expected to do. This orientation by the clinician to the situation and to the procedures to be followed is called *structuring* and often is an important factor in helping the client feel more at ease. Sometimes the structuring will include the clinician's sharing with the client the rationale for each test as it is administered. The extent of structuring in any session will be dependent upon the complexity of the planned activities and the client's degree of familiarity with them. It will also depend upon the age and personality of the client.

When it comes to previewing the evaluation procedures planned for a child client, the clinician relies on verbal and nonverbal clues regarding the degree of detail sought or preferred by the parent. A brief explanation of what you hope to accomplish in the session is always appropriate. A description of the procedures to be used is also of interest to most parents. Some parents come to a diagnostic session with definite ideas of what needs to be done. Others leave those decisions entirely to the professional. In any diagnostic session, it is important that the clinician tell the child (if the child is able to understand) what to expect during the evaluation. This structuring can be in very simple terms, but it establishes certain ground rules that will be followed in the session. Two examples of structuring are given below:

1. I have some pictures and toys that I want to show you. Let's sit down here and see what I have. (for a very young child)
2. I'm going to show you some pictures now, and I'd like you to tell me the name of each picture. Then, we're going to look at some puzzle pieces, and I'll ask you to do certain things with them. (for an older preschool child)

The extent of your structuring with child clients will be dependent upon the age and cognitive abilities of the child and the tasks that you wish to have the child complete during the diagnostic session. Some children are very aware that this is a testing type of session; others are not. You do not know exactly what the parents have told the child in anticipation of the visit. It may be helpful to ask the parent about this prior to beginning the actual testing. Children need an explanation of the testing procedures and what they will be expected to do.

With clients of any age, it is important that instructions be given in a manner that ensures understanding of the procedures to be followed. Language limitations, as well as physical and cognitive limitations, must be considered. It is important to remember that, no matter how much time and patience is required for necessary instruction, all clients must be treated with respect, and adult clients must be treated as adults.

Making the Most of Available Time

When conducting a diagnostic evaluation, an important consideration for the professional is how to allot most effectively the available time. The age and abilities of the client naturally play an important part in that consideration. In the following paragraphs, we will consider time allotment as it relates to various client age groups.

When conducting a diagnostic evaluation with a young child, the professional must determine how much of the session will be conducted with the child; how much information will be obtained from the parent; and what percentage of time will be devoted to observing the parent-child interaction. Most professionals will attempt to obtain information via all three sources.

For example, an audiologist testing a very young child may first introduce noisemakers to obtain some useful preliminary information regarding reflexive arousal and orientation responses. This may be followed by procedures involving sound localization and perhaps by immittance audiometry. The inclusion of more complex procedures may require an additional appointment. During the first session, the parent or caretaker may be enlisted to aid in the testing, providing an opportunity for the clinician to observe parent-child interactions. The audiologist will also have to decide how much time should be allowed for interviewing the parent regarding the child's background and history as well as current behaviors observed at home regarding response to sound.

In a speech-language evaluation, the focus in most instances will be primarily working directly with the client. An efficient use of time when testing a child may be to have the parent complete a questionnaire while the child is being tested. If an observation room is available, the parent may be invited to observe the test session and provide comments later. The clinician may wish to observe the parent(s) and child in an assigned or impromptu activity.

No matter what the age of a client, it is vital that the clinician know what information is to be obtained during the session. With older clients, the test selection and procedures can often be laid out in advance with some detail. With young children, appropriate tests and materials will no doubt be preselected by the clinician with the understanding that some may prove ineffective. With very young children, the only preparation may be the placement of various toys and pictures around the room. In any event, the materials and procedures are only means to an end.

Much can be learned from using play activities with young children. Carol Westby (1980) discussed the assessment of cognitive and language activities through play. She stated (1980, p. 154) that "formal psychometric tests yield an estimate of some specific skills, but they do not assess all of the cognitive, representational, and thinking skills necessary for the use of language for communicative purposes." Westby commented that often a very young child's play will indicate certain uses of symbolic representation that are requisites for verbal language development. Language and "pretend" play both require that the child mentally represent reality; however, actual language is more complex and requires rule-governed grammatical relationships that need not be present in pretend play.

The language used by older children during pretend play often furnishes a realistic picture of their language abilities. Appendix A of Westby's 1980 article contains a Symbolic Play Scale Checklist that can be useful in assessing the play of children from nine months to five years of age.

Formal testing might not secure the greatest amount of information, even if a child is mature enough to participate in it. You often learn as much from observing how a client responds to tests and procedures as you do from the obtained score. You may get more information from the side comments of the child regarding the tests and activities than from the test procedures themselves. Such comments often give realistic information about the child's abilities and about the child's pragmatic development. They also provide information on how the child functions, his or her learning style, and strategies he or she uses to formulate answers.

Doris Allen, Lynn Bliss, and Jack Timmons (1981) studied how scores on three standardized tests of language development compared to clinicians' judgment of normal or impaired language behavior in the children observed. They concluded that the final decision concerning the language status of a child should take into consideration both the objective test data and the experienced clinician's subjective evaluation. Depending on the circumstances and the child's response to formal testing, the decision may be more affected by clinical judgment than by formal test results. For example, the authors state (1981, p. 68) that "children who are not good test takers may have abnormally depressed test scores due to behavioral and not language problems. Clinical judgment will be more heavily weighted than test scores for such children."

As knowledge has increased regarding adolescent language development, more tests have been developed to evaluate this age group. Again, it benefits the clinician to be aware of these tests and to select those most appropriate for his or her teenage clientele. Tests should be administered in a straightforward manner. With this age group, digressions and diversions must be discouraged so that the tests can be completed in an efficient manner, allowing time for conversation at the end of the testing session.

In addition to working with a variety of adults who are capable of understanding and dealing directly with their communicative problems, professionals may also find themselves working with adults who are cognitively impaired, either through developmental disabilities or through head trauma, progressive brain deterioration, or a cerebral vascular accident. The clinician needs to consider carefully how much time to spend in the diagnostic session or sessions with the client as opposed to time spent with family members. This holds true in therapy sessions as well. The therapist must decide how much time will be spent working directly with the client as opposed to how much time will be spent counseling family members and perhaps training them to carry out therapy activities.

Elderly clients sometimes need special time and attention, in addition to physical assistance. The position statement on working with older persons published by the American Speech-Language-Hearing Association's Committee on Communication Problems of the Aging (1988, p. 82) emphasized that speech-language pathologists and audiologists "must exercise flexibility in implementing appropriate adaptation of assessment and intervention techniques to the needs of older clients." Such adaptations include larger than normal pictures and printed materials, well lighted diagnostic and therapy rooms, allowance for reduced mobility and/or motor dexterity, consideration of need for increased response time, and sensitivity to indications of fatigue.

For clients of all ages, procedures must be followed carefully when administering standardized tests. However, most children—and many adults—will lose interest if the clinician needs time to read the test instructions regarding procedures. In addition, much valuable time is lost because of the clinician's ineptitude. For these reasons, it is important to have a familiar repertoire of evaluative activities and/or tests. On the basis of this extensive experience, the clinician may be aware of items in a particular test that do not seem valid or reliable for a particular clientele and can view performance on those items with skepticism. Having a repertoire of familiar tests does not preclude examination and review of new test materials and procedures as they appear on the market; however, it ensures that selected tests will be known so well that the clinician can administer them easily and efficiently.

Much attention has been drawn in recent years to the need for culturally nonbiased assessment materials. A clinician working with particular ethnic groups must review all tests administered to make certain that they are appropriate for the clientele. Assessment of bilingual, bicultural clients and limited-English-speaking clients is a focus of several recent publications (for example, Erickson & Omark, 1980; Cole & Snope, 1981; Bilingual Education Office of the California State Department of Education, 1986; and Cheng, 1987; among others). Communication disorders specialists should also be familiar with the position paper on Clinical Management of Communicatively Handicapped Minority Language Populations published by the Committee on the Status of Racial Minorities of the American Speech-Language-Hearing Association (1985).

In apportioning available time, the clinician will also want to provide opportunities for spontaneous speech to occur—not only to obtain information about the client's abilities in this area but also to provide opportunities to learn more about the client's interests and activities. These data can be important in planning future therapy sessions.

It is important to use a minimum amount of time previewing procedures in order to allow the greatest possible time for discussion of findings and recommendations later in the session. The clinician has to make the final decision regarding time allocation, and may often have to point out time constraints to the client or parent either in a conversation prior to the appointment or early in the diagnostic session.

James Nation and Dorothy Aram (1984, p. 201) remind clinicians of two other important considerations in making the best possible use of available diagnostic time.

> When doing speech mechanism examinations with children, never assume that you will get to look in their mouths as often as you would like. Make every observation count.

and

> Knowing when to discontinue using a tool is as important as knowing when to use a certain tool. It requires knowing when enough details about the behaviors under study have been obtained or when a patient no longer is performing adequately or with interest.

Supporting Clients' Self-Esteem

Inability to communicate effectively often leads to a low level of self-esteem. Consequently, speech and hearing professionals are likely to meet with many clients whose interpersonal experiences have been unsatisfying or even traumatic. An important part of the therapeutic environment, therefore, is the clinician's effort to engender confidence and willingness on the part of the client to engage in communicative interactions and to work toward change. Many of the suggestions we have made thus far are designed to promote growth of self-esteem.

Keeping the client's self-esteem in mind when conducting a diagnostic evaluation, the clinician needs to consider carefully the order in which he or she presents tests. For example, it is often reassuring to a language-delayed child if a receptive test that requires only nonverbal responses is administered first. As the test session progresses, more difficult tests can be introduced. Since many tests require continuing until failure (often on several consecutive items), the clinician may want to have a few stock "passable" items with which to close the testing. The scores on these items are, of course, not included in the test results. Closing the test session with success rather than with failure allows the child to maintain self-esteem.

The older the children and the more aware they are of their communicative problems, the more you will treat them independently during the session. They will come to the test room unaccompanied by parents. You will provide an explanation for why the evaluation is being conducted. You will discuss the procedures that you are planning to follow. You will encourage them to share their feelings with you regarding their social relationships and interpersonal communication. You will invite them to participate in discussion of the results of the evaluation and recommendations for the future. As children reach adolescence, their active participation in all these aspects of the evaluation becomes even more crucial.

The clinician's efforts to preserve the client's self-esteem are especially important when working with adolescents. Teenagers are extremely sensitive to any differences from peers. Whereas younger children sometimes enjoy the stimulation of a new situation and the individual attention received in an evaluation session, adolescents may find this very same situation repugnant. They may also be very aware of the nature and extent of their communication problems; any tests that emphasize these may result in uncooperative behavior. Familiarity with the local teenage culture, lexicon/language, and communication style can be very helpful when conducting evaluation sessions and therapy with this age group. The clinician does not have to *use* the current adolescent terminology, but it is important to understand it.

Many of the suggestions given in Chapter 2 in regard to meeting a client for the first time relate to preserving and often boosting the self-esteem of adult clients. Your verbal and nonverbal behavior during the diagnostic session will be perceived and responded to—either consciously or subconsciously—by the client and other involved participants. It is important to realize that your verbal and nonverbal behavior may indicate the following to your clients:

- whether you consider yourself inferior, equal, or superior to them
- whether you wish to dominate them or work as equals with them
- whether you like or dislike them
- whether you accept or reject them
- whether you are spending time with them willingly or resentfully
- whether you believe that what they have to communicate is important or unimportant
- whether you are willing to try to understand the client's problem or viewpoint
- whether you are willing to suspend judgment or evaluation of the ideas or feelings expressed by the client and/or other interested participants
- whether you are willing to share (appropriately) your thoughts and feelings with clients or prefer to keep your thoughts and feelings hidden

Your clients' self-esteem will be either bolstered or lowered by their contacts with you in both diagnostic and therapy sessions, depending on what they sense in you regarding some of these fundamental beliefs or attitudes.

Minimizing Unproductive Behavior

Due to increased attention to parent education and early intervention, speech-language pathologists and audiologists often see children at a very young age.

Some audiologic procedures (behavioral observation audiometry, immittance audiometry, and electrophysiologic audiometry, for example) permit the testing of infants without their voluntary participation. (See, for example, Finitzo-Hieber, 1982; Jerger, 1984; Northern & Downs, 1984; Pappas, 1985; and Martin, 1987.) Some procedures for very young children require minimal participation that is encouraged through the use of tangible reinforcers. A parent or guardian may serve as an assistant to the audiologist in these procedures. If that is the case, it is important for the clinician to provide careful instructions regarding the procedures and to caution the assistant against anticipating or cueing the child's behavior.

James Jerger (1984, p. xii) stated that

> In spite of the impressive advances provided by electro-acoustic and electrophysiologic techniques, it is well to remind ourselves that behavioral audiometry is, and will probably always be, the method of choice for evaluating total auditory function.
>
> . . . The key to the successful exploitation of all these advances in our routine clinical work lies, perhaps, in the development of newer strategies for using them in judicious combination.

In regard to speech-language evaluation, the clinician also uses behavioral observation to assess prespeech behaviors in very young children. Currently, although electrophysiologic techniques are available to measure brain response during communicative activity (positron emission tomography and magnetic resonance imaging, for example), the employment of these measures is not typically available or practicable for speech-language pathologists nor are the measures typically used with infants or young children unless severe neurological disorders are diagnosed or suspected.

The majority of assessment procedures require at least minimal cooperation on the part of the client. It is generally preferred that a child above "toddler" age come to the test room unaccompanied by a parent. A common fear of clinicians is the specter of a screaming child clinging to the mother's skirt refusing to take one step anywhere without the parent. Each clinician has a method of choice in handling such a situation. Some clinicians are adept at picking up the child, moving quickly to the test room, and providing an interesting toy for distraction. Some clinicians take a toy or interesting gadget right to the waiting room to entice the child to follow them to the test room. Others opt to invite the parent to accompany the child and clinician to the test room, hoping that as the child becomes involved in the interesting diagnostic activities, the parent will be able to leave the room or at least move into the background. Most parents can suggest a strategy that will appeal to the child and encourage him or her to accompany the clinician. How insistent you are on the separation will depend to a great extent on the age of the child and your personality. It is important to realize that an exceptional fear on the part of the child to leave his or her mother provides valuable diagnostic information.

In addition to fear of separation and of the unknown, other factors can trigger uncooperative behavior: lack of interest on the part of the clinician, inadequate structuring of the session, boring and monotonous test items and activities, and consistent overtaxing of the client's abilities. You must be aware that the diagnostic setting itself, as well as the level of anxiety and trepidation it engenders in the client, will have an effect upon performance. Emerick and Haynes (1986, pp. 83–84) remind us that, although for the examiner the testing situation may be very familiar and routine, for the client it is a novel experience and must be recognized as such. They further state that

> Behavior is a function of the individual and the situation. We should be aware that our test results reflect not just the client's abilities but also his performance *in* the diagnostic setting.
>
> . . . Our diagnostic activities should include an assessment of a client's larger social context; the younger the individual, the more important this aspect of the evaluation becomes.

James Nation and Dorothy Aram (1984, pp. 200–201) give a number of helpful suggestions for working with children. Five of the suggestions are listed below.

1. Remember that most children are easy to test. They go through the paces in a remarkably matter-of-fact manner. Take a hint from this. Make your manner likewise. Assume that "here is something we are going to do." It may be enjoyable but that is really secondary. In most cases, time is saved and the actual creation of emotional reactions is avoided if the diagnostician does not approach the testing as a thrilling, exciting game that the child is going to "just love." . . . You are securing a representative sample of the child's speech. The more simply and efficiently this can be done, the less wear on the diagnostician and child.
2. Administer the tools quickly and efficiently. For most children the process must move along at a reasonably good rate in order to hold their attention and to prevent prolonging the testing beyond its maximum usefulness. But do not push the child too fast. . . .
3. Allow children to have temporary diversions during the testing. They should be able to make comments, ask seemingly irrelevant questions, and get up and move around without being made to feel guilty. . . . The diagnostician should maintain control of the testing

situation. This control can be gentle though insistent. In most cases it is sufficient to direct attention to the testing materials after brief diversion.

4. Be careful of asking the child if he wants to do something. This often sets off negativism, and what if the child says "no" to a task you had every intention of doing. . . . Negativism cannot usually be reduced by prodding to respond and certainly not by displaying disapproval of his "uncooperative" behavior. When a child is thrust into a potentially threatening (to his way of feeling) situation, he has a right to be negative until such time as he can evaluate the situation. Negativism is often acceptable behavior that does not need to call forth any particular emotional reaction on the part of the diagnostician.

5. The use of reinforcement must be considered carefully for maintaining continued participation. Verbal reinforcement usually works, but in some instances other primary and secondary reinforcers will be needed. But the reinforcing device should not impede the flow of testing. . . .

With young children, a clinician often finds that a few interesting, manipulable toys will set the stage for pleasant interactions. The clinician then notes the toys that evoke attention and interest on the part of the child. Those toys then serve as a basis for further interaction. In this way, the child determines the activity.

An experienced clinician will be able to learn a great deal even from a nonverbal, minimally cooperative child using nonstructured, informal means. The use of "self talk," (in which the clinician states aloud in simple terms what the clinician is noticing or doing at the moment); "parallel talk," (in which the clinician states aloud in simple terms what the child is noticing or doing at the moment); and "silence" (during which the clinician provides periods when the child may vocalize or verbalize if he or she is so inclined) are often the techniques of choice and the only ones that may be effective.

The school-aged child should feel relatively comfortable accompanying the clinician to the test room. Resistance to the testing situation is liable to take more subtle forms if it is present. The child may verbalize his impression of the test items as "dumb" or "boring." He or she may introduce nonrelevant items for discussion to avoid completing the test. Some children will respond to most test items by saying "I don't know" and may need encouragement to take a guess or try to answer the item.

Since uncooperative behavior sometimes results from fear of the unknown, school-aged children need an explanation of the testing procedures and what they will be expected to do. The extent and amount of details provided in this structuring will be dependent upon the age of the child and his or her ability to comprehend. As with the preschool-aged child, it is important that the clinician be expert at administering the selected tests so that time will be profitably spent and so that the child will not lose interest because of the slow pace of the session. The clinician must take the cue from the child's early responses to determine how quickly items can be presented.

In comparison to preschool clients, children of school age are much more aware of their abilities and shortcomings and naturally prefer situations in which they can do well. The astute clinician provides such opportunities throughout the test session to encourage the child to participate. Positive reinforcement needs to be handled carefully: you do not want to distract the child with too much praise, and you also do not want to interfere with the test results. It is best not to reinforce the child's answers; rather, the clinician should respond to the child's efforts. For example, suitable comments might be the following: ''I like the way you listen when I ask the questions and then think about your answer'' or ''You are doing a good job on these—there are only three more questions to answer.''

It is the clinician's responsibility to have in his or her repertoire tests that have proven inherently interesting to children. If a usually popular test is not interesting to a particular child, it is often because the items are beyond the child's capabilities. Although some tests are long and tedious, the clinician may have particular reasons for wishing to administer them. In that event, it can be helpful to acknowledge the difficulty to the child to assure him or her that you know the items are hard to answer but that it is important to try.

Adolescent clients sometimes pose special challenges to the diagnostician. It is not uncommon for a teenager with a communication problem to have experienced many diagnostic evaluations and even many years of therapy. The clinician's challenge in this situation is to explain adequately the rationale for another diagnostic evaluation to the client and to provide sufficiently interesting materials to maintain cooperation and participation. One of the particular characteristics of adolescence is the vacillation between dependence and independence. Experienced clinicians have found that the more they deal directly with the client in an adult manner the more likely they are to secure cooperation in testing.

Professionals who work frequently with the 20- to 50-year-old adult population find that personal motivation for evaluation and therapy is usually higher than in the school-aged population. Many adult clients seek out help because they feel their vocational and/or social life will be more satisfying if their ability to communicate is improved. Their motivation to cooperate and make changes can be high if the perceived ''pay-off'' is desirable. Sometimes they have been encouraged to obtain help by employers, friends or relatives, or physicians who are concerned about a physical condition such as vocal nodules due to vocal abuse.

As more foreign-born adults take their place in the American workforce, achieving intelligible speech production in English can be a significant step in career advancement. The speech-language pathologist with specialized training in foreign accent modification may find work with this clientele productive and satisfying. It is important for the clinician to respect the client's abilities in his or her native language while reinforcing the client's conviction that proficiency in English is a worthwhile and achievable goal.

Audiologists are likely to have adult clients with hearing problems such as noise-induced loss, otosclerosis, tinnitus, or drug-related loss. It is in this age group that gradual losses become severe enough to cause occupational or social difficulties. Close communication with physicians and other medical personnel is often necessary for a complete diagnostic evaluation. Adult clients may require hearing aid evaluation and instruction in maximal use of amplification. Some of these clients may be highly motivated to make use of all the technology that is available; others may resist. If the audiologist feels that amplification could be very beneficial to the client, he or she will have to be adept in countering such resistance. Techniques for dealing with resistance will be discussed further in Chapter 4.

Sharing Evaluation Results and Recommendations

Many clinicians are skilled at administering informal and formal tests to children, but have difficulty relaying their findings to parents and other professionals. Others are better at imparting information to family members than they are at testing and working with young children. Most clinicians can profit from evaluating and improving their techniques in both areas.

A positive, honest, and realistically optimistic approach on the part of the clinician is likely to be the most effective when sharing the results of the evaluation with a client and/or family members. Professional jargon should be avoided when possible and explained when necessary. A supply or library of appropriate explanatory pamphlets, brochures, charts, and so forth can be a source of useful visual aids to make information more meaningful and useful to session participants. Even though results are shared orally at the close of the evaluation session, a written summary should also be provided as soon as possible to the client and other appropriate individuals.

Clinicians vary in the amount of information they can gain from testing/ observing a young child. They also vary in their ability to share their findings in a positive light, as noted in the following examples:

Example of Clinician 1
I can't really tell you anything. Johnny refused to talk to me and spent most of the session sitting under the table pouting.

Example of Clinician 2

Johnny was a little shy with me this first time. I noticed that he seemed interested in the pop-up book and the jack-in-the-box. When I played with them while he watched me from under the table, I noticed that he knew what to expect. When we were finished, he led me right to the room where he knew you would be.

In talking with parents following a diagnostic session, the clinician must always consider how much should be discussed in the presence of the child. Never underestimate the degree of listening and understanding of which the child is capable. Part of this depends upon whether your comments are positive or negative. A few positive, but honest, comments made in the presence of the child can often promote self-esteem and future pleasant relations with the child. Often parents are so concerned and eager for discussion that they overlook the effects it might have upon the child. Therefore, you must determine the extent to which a child's condition is discussed in his or her presence.

In summarizing the evaluation results, the clinician must again decide how much information will be discussed in the presence of the child; how much information will be presented orally and how much in writing; and how much time will be available for discussion of the test results and recommendations for the future.

Experienced clinicians stress the importance of including the adolescent client in the discussion of the results of the evaluation and in planning future therapy. You run the risk of alienating the adolescent and losing his or her cooperation by talking only with the parents and ignoring the fact that it is the teenager who must participate in future therapy and actually make needed changes. Problems arise when parents do not acknowledge the teenager's responsibility for change and instead try to mandate exactly what the teenager will do.

Adult clients are often involved in many different activities and have many responsibilities. Although they may be highly motivated to change, time constraints may be a factor in their ability to follow through on therapy activities. Recommendations for remediation must clearly define what will be necessary to make desired changes in communicative abilities, with particular emphasis on time commitments.

Unless the client's comprehension abilities are impaired to such an extent that he or she cannot understand, the professional will share the evaluation results with the individual and secondarily with family members as appropriate. Even in situations of severe impairment, it is important to relate to the adult client as an adult.

Sharing evaluation results and recommendations with family members can be as important in working with older adults as it is in working with children. In many cases, family members are asked to assume responsibility for aging parents at the same time that they are coping with the responsibilities of raising a growing family and fulfilling job commitments. Very often, the responsibility for arranging for and transporting the older client to the diagnostic session is assumed by a daughter or daughter-in-law (or, less occasionally, a son or son-in-law) who must fit this into an already crowded work and home schedule. In making recommendations for therapy, the professional needs to be sensitive to the time demands of therapy activities and the impact upon family members. At the same time, it is also important to treat the older client as an independent individual, capable of answering questions regarding his or her life and activities and making his or her own decisions regarding follow-through on recommendations.

Understanding the Grief Process

Why is it necessary to include a section on the grief process in a chapter on assessment of communicative abilities? Professionals naturally hope that their contacts with clients will be positive and pleasant. However, there are occasions when the information they need to impart is not positive or pleasant and may be something the client does not want to hear. Before clients come to you, many of them have experienced the loss of former abilities or skills. They may be grieving over that loss. Sometimes, you may have to define or confirm a problem that may have been suspected but never acknowledged. It is your professional role to be able to recognize characteristics of the grieving process so that you may better understand some of your clients' behaviors and, when possible, assist them in working through their grief.

The concept of "grief work" has been extended to include the reactions of people to all types of loss, such as the loss of a limb in amputation; the loss of the voice through laryngectomy; the loss of the use of the body in spinal cord injury; and the loss of the "perfect child" when a child is handicapped. At any time in the professional's caseload there may be

- a terminally ill patient whose speech problems are severe but secondary to the fatal condition
- clients who are trying to learn to accept the loss of sensory capabilities, such as a progressive hearing loss
- a head-injured adolescent whose high school sports career has been abruptly ended by a motorcycle accident
- a man with aphasia who can no longer assume the role of business executive and/or husband and father
- several children in the professional's caseload whose parents are mourning the loss of the "ideal" child they had envisioned as they planned their family

- an elderly person seen in a rest home who is mourning the loss of independence and the ability to maintain a home

In addition to these special cases, any client may at times experience feelings of grief and loss as a part of the human condition. You must consider that the energy clients devote to grief work will not be available for other aspects of therapy. It is useful for you to understand what is happening to the client as he or she works through grief.

Much has been written in recent years regarding the grief process. Elisabeth Kübler-Ross (1969) described various stages through which a person passes in coping with death and dying: denial, anger, bargaining, depression, and, finally, acceptance. These stages have been corroborated by other researchers, although they may use different terms to describe each stage. Researchers agree that it is unhealthy to block or repress emotions felt in any of the phases of grief. The phases do not last for any prescribed length of time; in fact, at any one period of mourning, some people may exhibit behaviors characteristic of several of the stages. Some people may skip one or more stages while others may seem to be arrested at a particular stage and may not be able to reach the level of acceptance. When confronted with a particularly difficult or poignant situation, a person may even temporarily revert to an earlier stage.

It is important to realize that children as well as adults experience loss and grief and, therefore, may be in a stage of mourning. Children can lose a loved one through death or through parental divorce or separation. They can be deprived of necessary experiences, friendship, and love because of their difficulties in communicating. Children can experience a loss of self-esteem when they cannot meet the expectations of their parents, teachers, or peers. Cathleen Postel (1986) commented that children can progress through the stages of grief if information is shared with them and they are permitted to discuss the situation. However, when kept in ignorance or denied opportunities for expressions of grief, children, like adults, will rarely grow beyond the initial stages of denial, anger, or depression.

When sharing the results of an evaluation confirming the presence of a significant communicative problem, the clinician must be prepared to encounter expressions of the grief process. The client, parent, spouse, and/or other family members may find that the reality of a serious problem is too difficult to accept. Their first reaction may be one of denial that can be manifested in refusal to discuss the problem or efforts to prove the clinician's diagnosis wrong. In many instances of severe communicative disorders, the parent or spouse may already be immersed in the grief process and may be evidencing one of the stages of grief beyond denial.

Dennis Tanner (1980, p. 916) discussed grief as the natural human reaction to loss and related it to speech, language, and hearing problems.

An integral part of behavior patterns of individuals with communication disorders is their reaction to the loss of the speech and hearing functions.

Loss is a fundamental aspect of any disability which requires rehabilitation; the patient or client has lost a function. Grief is a natural and predictable reaction to that loss. The patient's reaction, regardless of the dimension or degree of the disability, may have an influence on the course and direction of rehabilitation.

A clinician's interaction with the patient who is grieving over loss of speech or hearing capabilities can have significant influence not only on the patient's ultimate acceptance of the disability, but also on motivation and the desire for therapy. Ultimately, the clinician's interaction with the grieving patient can affect the overall prognosis for recovery of function.

The uninformed clinician's actions in the ongoing process of rehabilitation can interrupt, postpone or break down the grieving process and thus reduce the probability that the patient will accept the disorder and its implications. Interruption of the normal grieving process can reduce the patient's motivation for therapy and interfere with the client-clinician relationship; alter, postpone and interfere with the short-term and long-term goals of rehabilitation; and contribute to the maintenance of counterproductive behaviors. For example, the angry patient may remain angry or the depressed patient may remain depressed.

For those patients with irreversible disorders, the clinician's actions may facilitate or assist the normal grieving process. To do this, the clinician must be acutely aware of the patient's loss and the stages of grief which are, for the most part, ordered and predictable. Ultimately, the clinician will assist the individual in reaching a stage of acceptance of the disability and its implications. A client in the acceptance stage of grief is likely to improve as a result of therapy because more energy can be devoted to rehabilitation and reacquisition of function.

Following is an excerpt from an interview between a staff worker (speech-language pathologist) in a child development clinic and the mother of a four-year-old developmentally disabled son. In this excerpt, the mother exhibits both denial and anger, and expresses strong negative feelings toward professionals evaluating her son and the procedures used in this evaluation. In one utterance, she even says that some of the procedures used to help her son may in fact be harmful. From a psychiatric standpoint, this utterance could be seen as the mother's unconscious attempt to rationalize her son's condition if she will no longer be able to repress or deny it.

As in our other interview excerpts, *C* is used to designate the clinician, and *R*, the respondent.

Interview Excerpt 3-2

C: We are recommending placement of Ronnie in the Developmental Center preschool program.

R: I won't agree to that. Ronnie is just fine, and you people are making some big deal out of these tests. First the pediatrician, then my in-laws, and now you!

C: We're all just trying to find out what would be best for Ronnie— to give him the best possible chance to develop.

R: You act like he's some kind of moron. My husband didn't talk until he was almost two years old and there's nothing the matter with him! Taking him around to these places; sitting and waiting until somebody gets good and ready to see us. It's damned annoying!

C: Well, you had to wait because there are several parts to the test and different people administer them.

R: I hope they know more than that pediatrician does. With all the shots and vaccines and vitamins and now these tests—before you know it, there *will* be something the matter with Ronnie!

C: Mrs. Monner, your son is mentally retarded. There's no doubt about that. But if he's going to get the best possible training, we want to have as much information about his condition as we can.

R: What do you mean, retarded? That's a terrible thing to say about a little fellow only four years old. He's a lot smarter than some of the people we've come across in the last six months.

C: It's foolish for you to act this way about the situation. People are trying to help and you refuse to face the facts.

R: Nobody has given me any facts. They're too busy playing God!

The clinician in this excerpt begins by giving the mother information regarding the son's evaluation and the recommended placement. She continues to give information despite the mother's expression of feelings and rejection of the diagnosis and recommendation. Before any constructive action can take place, some of the feelings must be confronted. In her continuing attempt to clarify the information, the clinician uses a term that is likely to be emotionally highly charged ("mentally retarded"). We cannot tell if the clinician is aware that the mother is evidencing mourning; we do know that the clinician makes no attempt to deal with the feeling. She identifies the feeling as ''foolish,'' passing judgment on the mother's behavior. If she had been more alert to expressions of the grief process, the clinician might have used more appropriate terminology.

In reviewing the grief process and factors that might trigger it, we must not overlook a very important loss that many clients suffer: the loss of self-esteem. Clients whose communicative problems prevent them from participating in a variety of professional, business, and social interactions may feel diminished in self worth. Parents of a disabled child experience loss of self-esteem in many different ways. Audrey McCollum (1985) commented on this loss.

> From the time we begin thinking of conceiving a child, most women and men have doubts about the outcome. But these are usually dispelled by the assumptions we make about our capabilities, often without much conscious thought.
>
> Most of us expect to contribute unflawed genes to the embryo which will cause it to develop into a healthy baby. Both parents expect themselves to surround their child with a cocoon of care and protection to ensure its happy and healthy development, to ensure the fulfillment of at least some of their daydreams. A child's impairment, whether inherited or acquired, confronts us with a sense of having failed to live up to our expectations. We are helpless to undo the faulty development and our sense of competence and self-regard can be shaken drastically.

Knowledge of the grief process can help clinicians to understand the reactions and behaviors of their clients to the losses they are experiencing. It can also help clinicians to understand that a client's expressed anger is sometimes part of the grief process rather than related to any actions on the part of the therapist. In addition, knowledge of grief work can be helpful to clinicians in dealing with periods of loss and grief in their own lives. However, it is important to realize that, although there is much we can do to help the grieving client, there are some things we cannot do. Grieving people have to find their own answers in their own ways and times.

SUMMARY

This chapter has been concerned with aspects of the assessment process. Six goals were suggested as appropriate for a diagnostic session. In light of these goals, some questions you might ask in evaluating a particular diagnostic session are as follows:

- Did I determine if there is a communication problem and, if so, the nature and extent of the problem?

- Have I determined contributing causal factors, particularly those that are remediable?
- Did I determine the direction and procedures to be followed in remediating or alleviating the communication problem?
- Did I strengthen my relationship with the client so that future sessions will be productive?
- Did I encourage the involvement of the client in accepting the necessity and desirability of change?
- Did I facilitate the client's cooperation in procedures designed to produce needed change?

In conducting a self-evaluation of some personal skills essential to effective assessment and diagnostic sessions, you may also find the following questions helpful:

- Did I meet the requirements of my agency in the conduct, reporting, and follow-up of the assessment session?
- Were my materials and methods suitable to the age and condition of my client?
- Did I help the client and accompanying family members or caretakers feel at ease?
- Did I structure the session appropriately and preview the procedures to be followed?
- Did I make the most of the available time?
- Did I try to conserve and even enhance my client's self-esteem?
- Did I minimize unproductive behavior by respect and consideration for my client, appropriate and interesting materials and activities, awareness of my client's basic needs, and attention to the principles of behavior modification?
- Did I communicate the results of my evaluation and my recommendations in an understandable and considerate fashion, using appropriate visual aids and tape recordings when appropriate? Did I follow up the session with a written report to the client and/or other appropriate individuals?
- Was my understanding of the grief process reflected, when appropriate, in my interactions with my client or members of the family?

REFERENCES

Allen, D.V., Bliss, L.S., & Timmons, J. (1981). Language evaluation: Science or art? *Journal of Speech and Hearing Disorders, 46*(1), 66–68.

Bilingual Education Office, California State Department of Education. (1986). *Beyond language: Social and cultural factors in schooling language minority students*. Los Angeles: Evaluation, Dissemination and Assessment Center, California State University, Los Angeles.

Cheng, L.L. (1987). *Assessing Asian language performance: Guidelines for evaluating limited-English-proficient students*. Rockville, MD: Aspen Publishers, Inc.

Cole, L.T., & Snope, T. (1981). Resource guide to multicultural tests and materials. *Asha, 23*(9), 639–649.

Committee on Communication Problems of the Aging. (1988). The roles of speech-language pathologists and audiologists in working with older persons. *Asha, 30*(3), 80–84.

Committee on the Status of Racial Minorities. (1985). Clinical management of communicatively handicapped minority language populations. *Asha, 27*(6), 29–32.

Emerick, L.L., & Haynes, W.O. (1986). *Diagnosis and evaluation in speech pathology* (3rd ed.). Englewood Cliffs, NJ: Prentice-Hall.

Erickson, J.G., & Omark, D. (1980). *Communication assessment of the bilingual, bicultural child*. Baltimore: University Park Press.

Fein, D.J. (1983). Projection of speech and hearing impairments to 2050. *Asha, 25*(11), 31.

Finitzo-Hieber, T. (1982). Auditory brainstem response: Its place in infant audiological evaluations. *Seminars in Speech, Language, and Hearing, 3*(1), 76–87.

Hutchinson, B.B., Hanson, M.L., & Mecham, M.J. (1979). *Diagnostic handbook of speech pathology*. Baltimore: Williams & Wilkins.

Jerger, J. (Ed.). (1984). *Pediatric audiology: Current trends*. San Diego: College-Hill Press.

Kübler-Ross, E. (1969). *On death and dying*. New York: Macmillan.

Martin, F.N. (Ed.). (1987). *Hearing disorders in children: Pediatric audiology*. Austin, TX: PRO-ED.

McCollum, A.T. (1985, May/June). Grieving over the lost dream. *The Endeavor*.

Meitus, I.J., & Weinberg, B. (1983). *Diagnosis in speech-language pathology*. Baltimore: University Park Press.

Nation, J.E., & Aram, D.M. (1984). *Diagnosis of speech and language disorders* (2nd ed.). San Diego: College-Hill Press.

Northern, J.L., and Downs, M.P. (1984). *Hearing in children* (3rd ed.). Baltimore: Williams & Wilkins Co.

Pappas, D.G. (1985). *Diagnosis and treatment of hearing impairment in children: A clinical manual*. San Diego: College-Hill Press.

Peterson, H.A., & Marquardt, T.P. (1981). *Appraisal and diagnosis of speech and language disorders*. Englewood Cliffs, NJ: Prentice-Hall.

Postel, C.A. (1986). Death in my classroom? *Teaching Exceptional Children, 18*(2), 139–143.

Schiefelbusch, R.L. (Ed.). (1986). *Language competence, assessment and intervention*. San Diego: College-Hill Press.

Shewan, C.M. (1988). 1988 Omnibus survey: Adaptation and progress in times of change. *Asha, 30*(8), 27–30.

Tanner, D.C. (1980). Loss and grief: Implications for the speech-language pathologist and audiologist. *Asha, 22*(10), 916–928.

Westby, C.E. (1980). Assessment of cognitive and language abilities through play. *Language, Speech, and Hearing Services in Schools, 11*(3), 154–168.

4

Motivating Clients for Effective Therapy

In Chapters 2 and 3, we discussed the importance of the first meeting, assessment of the client, and the expectations of the client and the clinician. The natural outcome of early interactions is often the enrollment of the client in therapy; if appropriate, you may be the therapist. This chapter is concerned with motivating clients for effective therapy.

INITIATING AND MAINTAINING EFFECTIVE THERAPY

The decision to enroll in therapy with you is dependent upon several conditions.

- The individual and/or the individual's family agrees there is a communication problem.
- The individual and/or the individual's family believes the problem can be modified and that you are the person to help.
- The individual and/or the individual's family believes the problem is serious enough to warrant the efforts needed to make the required change(s).
- The scheduled time and fee for therapy is manageable.

Once the client enrolls, several additional factors motivate the client's continuation in therapy.

- The relationship that the client and clinician have developed is pleasant, productive, and satisfying to the client.
- The perceived gains continue to justify the efforts the client and his family must make. If progress is apparent, there is motivation to continue.

- In some settings (as, for example, school settings or the military), the client is obliged to complete a prescribed period of therapy.

If you, as the clinician, feel there is a sufficiently severe problem to warrant therapy and that you are the best professional to accomplish this, what techniques can be helpful in securing the client's cooperation? First, a well-planned therapy program with clear goals and objectives and interesting activities and materials is vital. Second, the client must sense your respect and regard for him or her, no matter how severe the problem or the extent to which it interferes with other interpersonal relationships. This genuine respect for the client is often referred to as "unconditional positive regard" on the part of the therapist (Rogers, 1951). Clinicians also need to develop empathy with each client; that is, to perceive the situation from the client's viewpoint and to consider the client's basic needs. One way you can develop empathy with your client and convey unconditional positive regard is through *active listening*. Active listening can be summarized as consisting of four characteristics:

1. attentiveness to the speaker
2. desire to understand the speaker's viewpoint
3. willingness to suspend judgment or evaluation of the ideas or feelings expressed by the speaker
4. willingness to check your understanding by putting into words what you feel the speaker has conveyed

Thomas Gordon (1977, p. 72) emphasized that active listening conveys acceptance rather than evaluation of the client's statements.

Active Listening communicates, "I hear what you're feeling," neither agreement or disagreement, no judgment whether the feelings are right or wrong. The listener only conveys acceptance that the feelings exist. This kind of acceptance can be very disarming because people so seldom encounter it.

Walter Rollin (1987, p. 29) made the following comment.

One of the difficulties novice therapists, and perhaps a few professional ones, frequently have is not only listening actively but understanding what their clients are communicating. Instead of focusing on the feeling state being expressed, they attend only to the content or the problem being communicated. Our concerns as counseling speech-language pathologists and audiologists are not to solve the client's problem per se but to try and understand the feeling state that underlies the problem.

Naturally if the client is struggling to adjust to the output of a hearing aid, it is incumbent on the audiologist to provide the necessary informative guidelines. But if that same client complains of difficulty in adjusting to wearing an aid—embarrassment, feelings of inadequacy— the counseling therapist must be prepared to switch gears and reflect back to the client those feelings the audiologist is experiencing from that person.

Making use of active listening does not imply that you do not critique or judge your client's performance on specific therapy items. For example, you certainly would evaluate the client's production of a phoneme or appropriate pitch or use of syntactic construction when attempting to achieve therapy goals. You would use active listening in discussions with the client involving his or her life experiences, perceptions of the problem, frustration of basic needs, and so forth. As clients realize that you are trying to understand their viewpoints, frustrations, and experiences, they will be more ready and inclined to accept your evaluations of their communicative performance. In other words, you will be emphasizing the distinction between the person and the behavior. In this manner, you promote the client's self-esteem, thus motivating the client to continue in therapy.

ESTABLISHING THERAPY GOALS

Questions that need to be addressed in establishing therapy goals are as follows.

- What does the client/family most want to happen as a result of therapy?
- Are these expectations realistic?
- Is the communication problem the result of a stable medical condition, or will there be a progressively worsening state of health?
- Are the goals agreed upon by the client, family members, and clinician, and are these goals achievable?
- Are the goals, if achieved, going to have a significant impact on the client's communicative effectiveness?

Let us expand briefly on each of these questions, utilizing brief excerpts from clinician interviews to illustrate pertinent points. Note that the clinicians in some of these excerpts use techniques of active listening known as *restatement of content* (repeating or summarizing actual material or data expressed verbally by the client) and *reflection of feeling* (verbalizing current emotions expressed either verbally or nonverbally by the client). As in all of the interview excerpts, *C* denotes the clinician and *R* the respondent.

What Does the Client/Family Most Want To Happen As a Result of Therapy?

The following is an excerpt from an interview between a speech-language pathologist and the mother of a seven-year-old language-delayed son. In this excerpt, the mother is describing her desire that speech therapy will enable her son to develop as "a whole person" and "in an age-appropriate way."

Interview Excerpt 4-1

R: From the very beginning, when it became clear to us that Shawn needed some help with his speech development, I think our motivation has been just for him to gain that competence in order to be a whole person.

C: Yes, you'd like to have him speak the same as any other person.

R: Yes, we were afraid that it would really hinder his social development to, um, to not be able to speak clearly, and that was our primary concern, you know, rather than worrying about how he'd do in school.

C: Well, you felt perhaps that the speech problem would keep him from the same sort of social skill development that the other kids have.

R: That's right. Also, having been a child myself and remembering back then, I know that children can be very hard on anyone who's different in any way. So we want to continue to pursue speech therapy so that he can develop in an age-appropriate way.

In the following interview excerpt, the mother of an eight-year-old girl with articulation problems describes how she views her child's speech problem and what she hopes to learn from the speech-language pathologist with whom they have just enrolled the child for therapy.

Interview Excerpt 4-2

C: How would you describe Ellen's speech?

R: For the family relationship its basically . . . um, we describe her as Sylvester the cat . . . too much saliva in her mouth, and it escapes through the side of her mouth. I have no training at all with speech to technically say. Her first grade teacher thought we should try to get it corrected at this point.

C: So what are you looking forward to in bringing her here?

R: To help me decide if it's a physical problem, if it could be corrected eventually, if it's something we could work on with her at home, or if it's something that really needs lots of your help.

Interview Excerpt 4-3 is an interchange using both manual and oral communication ("total") between a clinician and a 30-year-old deaf man who has enrolled for speech-language therapy. Although he is proficient in sign language, he wishes to improve his oral communication.

Interview Excerpt 4-3

C: Are there times when you have a problem communicating?

R: When I go to a restaurant and order food, I point. I can't say the words in the menu. They are hard to say.

C: So you don't feel comfortable pronouncing the words in the menu.

R: Right. I feel embarrassed to use my speech, but it is easy to point.

C: Do you think it is a problem?

R: Yes, it is a communication problem. I need language practice and role playing to communicate in everyday life. Also, some special problems in speech, how to say, pronunciation of words.

In each of these excerpts, the client or a member of the client's family is verbalizing what he or she hopes will be accomplished in speech-language therapy. These expectations are sometimes stated in general terms and, at other times, in more specific terms. It is the clinician's responsibility to pay close attention to these expectations and translate them into manageable therapy goals.

Are the Expectations Realistic?

Speech-language pathologists and audiologists occasionally find themselves talking with clients or parents whose expectations, in the best judgment of the clinician, may not be attainable. This places the clinician in a situation that can be both a dilemma and a challenge. The dilemma: should expectations be lowered, or is the client actually capable of more than the clinician perceives? The challenge: to structure therapy goals in such a way that the client will be led to develop to his or her maximum potential yet not be exposed to continual frustration because of failure to succeed in therapy tasks. Usually, unrealistic expectations are revealed early in therapy. Sometimes, however, such expectations may develop later in therapy after some progress has been made, leading the client to assume that the progress will continue indefinitely at the same rate. If that is an unrealistic assumption, the clinician will have to discuss this with the client so that false hopes do not lead to frustration and anger.

Interview Excerpt 4-4 is taken from a discussion by a speech-language pathologist with the mother and father of a 26-year-old man with Down syndrome. The parents are trying to be realistic in their expectations regarding their son's communication abilities, but find it difficult to assess his capabilities.

Interview Excerpt 4-4

Father: I wish we could understand his speech a little better. I don't expect him to make sentences like we sure would like, but just to speak a word or two words together, clear enough where you could know what that word is. Then you can kinda put two and two together and you can almost guess what he is talking about. I wouldn't expect him to carry a conversation with nouns or pronouns.

C: Some words would be too difficult for him.

Father: Yeah, because I don't see none of it, not a bit of it, as much as I hate to say that. You know without his speech, he is a lost duck. That's the main thing, to try to be able to get him to say a few things that are understandable.

C: I know that speech is very important to all of us. That's the best way we may all communicate, but let's say if he is having a lot of problems with the way that he is saying words, how about using sign language?

Mother: That's what we're gonna have to do for Donald. He's probably gonna have to learn to use sign language.

C: Do you think that will help?

Mother: I think so.

Father: I don't think he'll pick it up. Well, I would like to see *any* improvement—but that's still not helping his speech.

Mother: Well how are you going to do it? When you can't go any further, what are you gonna do? His doctor said that we must accept it, which I did.

In the following excerpt, the mother of a 13-year-old autistic girl describes the evolution from unrealistic hope to more realistic expectations.

Interview Excerpt 4-5

C: What types of suggestions would you give to parents whose child has recently been diagnosed as "autistic?"

R: Try to have patience, be a little optimistic. I mean, as much as now I can say that I've accepted Sandra, there was a long time when my optimism got me through. My thinking that she would be okay is what got me through. And okay, maybe the teachers thought it was impractical; it got me through the day to think that someday Sandra would be okay. And when I was ready to accept the fact, that was when I was ready. Don't give up and be pessimistic right at the beginning when your kid is little. Some of these kids do come out of it. Some of them turn out fine, but not too many. Be optimistic, have patience, and try and get help. Use your respite. I felt guilty sending her off to camp or having someone else taking care of her at times. And then I realized that I needed it, and she needs it.

C: That's true.

R: With these kids, you can't expect too much, but little accomplishments—they mean so much. You get so much. If you set your mind to it, to enjoy each milestone with these kids. When you wait so long, it does mean a lot. So many people just walk through life expecting things and taking them for granted. And I don't do that anymore.

Is the Communication Problem the Result of a Stable Medical Condition, or Will There Be a Progressively Worsening State of Health?

When a clinician is working with a client who has a deteriorating physical condition, goals for therapy must be regularly modified or revised to adapt to reduced capabilities. In the interview excerpt that follows, the wife of a 69-year-old male stroke victim relates to the speech-language pathologist the recent occurrence of another stroke. It is evident from this interchange that the clinician must reevaluate the client's performance and make adjustments in therapy objectives.

Interview Excerpt 4-6

R: Ernie tried to finish this worksheet at home that you gave him last Tuesday. He was very upset. He had a lot of trouble and couldn't do it. When I looked at it, it looked like the ones he had done three weeks ago and he didn't have any trouble finishing them then.

C: So you noticed that Ernie seemed to be having more difficulty? How has he been feeling the last few days?

R: Not too good. In fact, I had to call the doctor Tuesday night. Ernie really scared me. We were eating dinner and he got this funny look on his face and tried to talk to me and nothing came out. The doctor came by the house. By then, Ernie looked better and talked a little but was real tired. The doctor said he probably had another stroke but that it wasn't a big one. He changed Ernie's medicine and told him to stay at home for several days. He said for us to call him if there was any more trouble, but Ernie seems about the same as before now—except he couldn't do that worksheet no matter how hard he tried.

C: Martha, Ernie may well have had another small stroke. He may look about the same as before, but this new stroke may have made it harder for him to read or figure out things. I'll check up on some of these things in our therapy session today. I surely appreciate your mentioning this to me. It's important that we don't overtax Ernie by expecting him to do more than he can reasonably handle.

In the following interview excerpt, the clinician is working with a 57-year-old woman who has been diagnosed as having parkinsonism. The therapy goals, therefore, have to take into account the progression of the disease. In view of the likelihood of further deterioration of the client's voice and articulation capabilities, the clinician is having the client practice techniques that will be useful now and as speech becomes more difficult. The client had indicated earlier that she is having more difficulty making herself understood. The clinician is responding to that previously expressed concern.

Interview Excerpt 4-7

C: Norma, you've mentioned that sometimes your friends comment that they can't hear everything you say, especially at the ends of your sentences. You say that you seem to run out of energy.

R: Well, the doctor told me that I might notice being more tired and not have much energy. I didn't realize it takes so much energy to talk.

C: It does take quite a bit, and some days are probably better than others for you. We want to make all your efforts pay off. That's why we've been practicing with these sentences using special ways to say them so that you can be heard but you don't use all your energy to do it.

Are the Goals Agreed upon by the Client, Family Members, and Clinician, and Are These Goals Achievable?

Interview Excerpt 4-8 illustrates the agreement of parent and clinician regarding the speech therapy goals for a nine-year-old girl with articulation problems. The clinician initiated the interchange by asking the mother what she most wants to have happen in therapy. The mother's goals are viewed as appropriate and realistic by the clinician and agreement is quickly reached.

Interview Excerpt 4-8

C: Mrs. Hankin, tell me where you'd like to see Sarah's speech therapy lead.

R: Well, what we ultimately had in mind was for her speech to be clear. And she's real shy, I'd like to see her become more outgoing with other kids.

C: Do you feel that her communication problems are interfering with her relationships with other children?

R: Yeah. She tends to stay to herself and not play with other kids because she has trouble being understood.

C: So, if she were able to make herself understood, she'd be more willing to approach other children.

R: Yes, I think so. I think, also, that other children have trouble getting to know her because they have trouble understanding her. She has problems with "s." I noticed in particular because it's hard for her to pronounce her name. She has trouble with "r," too, and "l." She says things like "wain" and "wike."

C: Yes, "r," "l," and "s" are the three sounds she had trouble with when I tested her. Those will be the three sounds we'll be working on in therapy. I believe that when her speech improves, you will find that she will be more outgoing with her friends.

It is rare for a professional speech-language pathologist or audiologist to begin a course of therapy without having discussed, at least in general terms, therapy goals with the client or appropriate members of a child client's family. Misunderstandings can arise, however, when more specific therapy goals and objectives are not shared and/or when no estimate is given of the time that will probably be involved in achieving the goals.

In the following interview excerpt with the mother of a seven-year-old girl with multiple articulation errors, it is evident that the parent initially did not realize the severity of the problem. The parent is disappointed because large gains in intelligibility are not apparent after five weeks of twice-weekly therapy sessions.

Interview Excerpt 4-9

C: Megan is doing well.

R: I'm glad someone thinks so.

C: You're not happy with her progress?

R: I don't see any results. When I watch her in therapy, she says her sounds; but when she speaks regularly, there is no difference. I don't see any change. Maybe I was also—maybe I had quite an illusion that it's not a hard problem and that it could be taken care of quite easily.

C: How a child does in therapy is up to the individual child and upon a lot of other factors. For instance, it depends on her motivation, her homework, and especially on the problem that the child has.

R: But the way her speech sounds, I don't see a difference. And the homework that I do with her, she's willing to do it, but I don't see how doing it in homework and then in speaking is going to help.

C: Megan has difficulty with quite a few sounds. She has improved several of them already, but she needs more practice before she can say them easily in everyday speech.

It is obvious that the mother does not have a clear understanding of what is involved in the therapy program for this child with multiple articulation problems. The ultimate goal of intelligible speech is no doubt agreed upon by the clinician and the child's parents. However, realistic intermediate goals and timeframe for duration of therapy have apparently not been discussed.

Are the Goals, If Achieved, Going To Have a Significant Impact on the Client's Communicative Effectiveness?

The therapy goals for some clients are clear-cut and easy to define. In other circumstances, clients with multiple problems will require extensive therapy and careful prioritizing of therapy goals. A major factor in such prioritizing is consideration of the impact of achieving a goal on the client's communicative effectiveness. For example, clients with aphasia who have difficulty in producing single word utterances would not profit from a therapy goal that concentrates on raising their pitch. Children who are considerably delayed in language development will naturally have many articulation errors; however, the goal of expanding their expressive vocabulary usually takes precedence over requirements for correct pronunciation of all the phonemes.

Sometimes physical problems affect communicative abilities and need to be addressed before speech-language therapy is initiated, or concurrently with speech-language therapy. In the interview excerpt that follows, the clinician agrees with the mother of a four-year-old boy with Down syndrome that placement of binaural pressure equalization tubes is of high priority in achieving maximum benefit from the child's therapy program.

Interview Excerpt 4-10

R: You know I've been talking with the doctor about having tubes put in Matthew's ears again. She said she could do it next Wednesday, but that's our next therapy session. I hate to have him miss therapy, but if he doesn't have tubes, the audiologist said his hearing is quite a bit reduced, about 60 dB less; but with the tubes, his hearing is within the acceptable range.

C: It's very important that Matthew get as much information from hearing as he can.

R: Yes, because if you can't hear it, it means you can't process that information. You're just going to be that far behind.

C: I agree with you that placement of the tubes is a high priority. Let's reschedule next week's therapy for another time.

In Interview Excerpt 4-11, the parents of the 26-year-old man with Down syndrome discussed in Excerpt 4-4 are discussing their reaction to an increased attention to syntactical goals on the part of the clinician. The father is concerned that too much time is being spent on activities that will not be helpful in increasing his son's communicative effectiveness.

Interview Excerpt 4-11

C: I have Donald's homework, and I hope you will be able to spend some time with him going over it.

Father: I sure hope it doesn't have a lot of sentences in it for him to try to say. The heck with sentences. I don't hear any words—much less sentences.

Mother: Oh, I understand him better than Dad does.

Father: You should spend more time teaching him words for things rather than worrying about sentences.

Mother: The homework last week was teaching him words. It was a picture of a plate and stuff and he was to color it and name the food that he had eaten. Poor guy, he still can't say onion rings clear enough. But I know what they are, so I tell him look at my mouth and I'll say "onion ring" and he says them. Another person wouldn't understand him, but I do. He is trying.

C: We spend a lot of time on vocabulary, Mr. Moore—on everyday words that are important for Donald to know. The short sentences we are working on could help him express himself better to other people. I wanted to have Donald try those.

In summarizing our thoughts on establishing therapy goals, we wish to emphasize the importance of setting long-range and intermediate therapy objectives. These objectives must be clearly stated and agreed upon by all participants in the therapy process. Children, at as early an age as possible, should participate in goal-setting and should understand the objectives of each therapy session and of any homework that is assigned. We have stressed the importance of prioritizing goals to achieve maximum communicative effectiveness. This does not imply that only one goal at a time should be addressed. Working on several goals at one time can give variety and interest to therapy sessions and, even more importantly, can actually facilitate more rapid achievement of communicative success.

If a client is being seen by more than one professional, it is critical that goals are communicated to all the persons involved. It is important that the therapy goals of the speech-language pathologist or audiologist are compatible and congruent with those of the other professionals. This is particularly crucial if the client is being seen by more than one speech-language pathologist or audiologist. Currently, speech-language pathologists sometimes find themselves acting as coordinators for clients' multidisciplinary therapeutic programs. They are thus responsible for ensuring that goals and objectives are communicated to all participants. Working as a member of a team will be discussed further in Chapter 9.

We must not lose sight of the fact that the ultimate goal of any therapeutic intervention is to enable the client to satisfy his or her basic needs more effectively and efficiently. Since these needs are often met by interactions with others, the role of the speech-language pathologist or audiologist in maximizing communicative effectiveness cannot be overestimated.

MOTIVATING BEHAVIORAL CHANGE

Therapy focused on maximizing communicative effectiveness involves behavioral change. The clinician's goal, therefore, is to be an agent for change. All of us know from experience that it is not always easy to motivate people to change their behavior. Some factors encourage change, and others mitigate against it. In this section, we will discuss factors that encourage change; in the subsequent section, we will consider counterproductive factors.

As mentioned previously, people do not ordinarily change unless they are displeased or dissatisfied with some condition in their lives. In some instances, significant others perceive some aspect of the individual's life or behavior as a problem. Significant change does not usually occur in this circumstance unless the individual agrees with the perception. In the case of young children or cognitively impaired individuals who are not able to perceive the actual problem or the ultimate rewards of altered behavior, change must be motivated by more immediate and often tangible rewards. The understanding and use of techniques of behavior modification are of proven value. Experienced professionals in our field are well aware of these techniques and utilize them appropriately with all clients.

In all effective therapy situations, the client must experience a positive "payoff" for efforts expended for change. The client must feel that there is more to be gained, either immediately or in the future, by change than by maintaining the status quo. The clinician plays an important role in confirming and supporting these feelings on the part of the client. This is true in early appointments when decisions regarding initiating therapy and setting therapy goals are being made. It is also true in every ensuing therapy session. It is the clinician who suggests workable therapy objectives and points out the relationship of the short-term objectives to the long-term goals. It is the clinician who devises a data-recording or record-keeping system so that even small amounts of change can be documented and called to the client's attention when progress is slow and discouragement ensues. It is the clinician who arranges appropriate and interesting therapy activities and outside assignments for the client to practice and refine new communicative behaviors. And it is the clinician who provides opportunities for the client to report outside experiences of his or her personal communicative success since therapy began.

Individual therapy sessions that are satisfying and motivating encourage continuation in the program. As the clinician plans each therapy session, it is helpful to consider the three hungers described by Eric Berne (1961) and mentioned in Chapter 2: *stimulus or sensation hunger, structure hunger,* and *recognition hunger.*

Stimulus hunger—the need for our sense organs to receive sufficient and varied input from the environment—can be met in the therapy session by providing therapy materials and activities that (1) pique the client's interest, (2) are sufficiently varied, and (3) challenge the client to use emerging skills rather than merely repeating firmly established behaviors. Research has indicated that goals perceived to be difficult to achieve can actually lead to better performance than less challenging goals, provided that the individual agrees with the goals and that they are ultimately attainable.

Structure hunger—the need to make sense of the world around us—can be met by ensuring that the client understands what he or she is expected to do in the therapy session, what constitutes successful performance, and how the activities relate to therapy goals. It is important to remember that structure hunger is also met by establishing a regular therapy schedule, meeting with the same clinician in familiar surroundings, and participating in a general therapy routine. However, there is a fine line between comfort and boredom—in other words, satisfying structure hunger at the expense of stimulus hunger. Making the distinction is critical when working with children, particularly those who have difficulty coping with change.

Recognition hunger—acknowledgment and acceptance by others—is met in the therapy situation by the attention of the clinician (and other participants in the session) and by the use of other reinforcement techniques. Attention given during the session by the clinician or other participants may be positive (for example through active listening, verbal praise, a smile, a desired tangible reinforcer) or negative (criticism, a frown, withholding a desired reinforcer, or causing actual physical discomfort). Research has shown that positive attention is more effective than negative in producing desired behavioral changes. Experience has shown that persons deprived of positive attention will often provoke negative attention to meet their recognition hunger rather than endure repeated situations where their existence is not acknowledged. Sometimes the clinician needs to consider obnoxious behavior by a client from the standpoint of possible deprivation of the client's recognition hunger or other basic needs. A word of caution is necessary in regard to praise and positive recognition: praise must be based on accurate observation of specific behavior or performance; must be authentic and not feigned; and must be positively reinforcing to the client.

In our discussion of S-O-R variables in Chapter 2, we discussed how organismic variables can affect an individual's behavior and the responses he or she makes. These organismic factors can enhance or impede a client's progress from setting goals to achieving them. The clinician who is attentive to organismic needs and the special characteristics of each client can often utilize that knowledge in promoting behavioral change. This attentiveness may also lead to awareness of factors that might cause resistance to change. Some of these factors will be considered in the following section.

DEALING WITH COUNTERPRODUCTIVE FACTORS

Physiological Factors

Clients may have difficulty in participating fully in a therapy session or program because of physiological factors such as illness, weakness, fatigue, or even hunger. Some of these conditions can be easily remedied. Others cannot be alleviated or removed and may even be the cause of the communication problem. At times, conditions can be circumvented. Distinguishing among these conditions can be a concern for the clinician. A therapy session may have to be postponed if a client is ill. If a client's condition is such that he or she has more energy or alertness during a particular time of day, it makes sense to schedule therapy for that time. It is also best to avoid scheduling therapy during a child's regular nap time.

Sometimes it is beneficial to provide snacks for a child client who may have therapy scheduled close to or during his or her usual mealtime or who does not receive adequate daily nourishment. If the clinician is concerned about the client's physiological condition, a medical referral may be necessary.

Many professional caseloads include clients who have serious physical problems that affect the vocal mechanism and/or speech musculature. Frequently, these communication problems are secondary to systemic conditions that have serious implications. Speech-language pathologists working with clients with conditions such as multiple sclerosis, amyotrophic lateral sclerosis, or acquired immune deficiency syndrome (AIDS) are well aware that other symptoms and concerns can affect clients' motivation and available energy for speech therapy.

Speech-language pathologists and audiologists working with AIDS patients, for example, are likely to be concerned with the neurologic manifestations of the disease as well as the effects of the disease on the tympanic membrane, tongue, larynx, or nasal mucosa. We are now familiar with the effects of AIDS upon the central nervous system and the accompanying dementia. Flower and Sooy (1987, p. 26) state

> Typically, patients have difficulty concentrating, slowing of thought, word finding difficulties, slowing of speech, personality changes, and occasional gait difficulties. . . . ENT manifestations can be the presenting complaint for about half of all AIDS patients.

Not only the client but the therapist may be affected by the unfavorable prognosis of serious medical conditions. Depression must be recognized as a factor in how therapy proceeds. The various aspects of depression as they affect the client-clinician relationship and the therapy process will be discussed later in this chapter.

Resistance

Changing communication habits is often seen as changing aspects of one's person and, thus, involves changes in self-concept. This can be frightening. When faced with frightening situations, the tendency is to retreat or resist. One way clients retreat is to withdraw from therapy. Another is to be absent repeatedly from scheduled therapy sessions. This is not to say that all absences from therapy are forms of resistance. There can be transportation problems, financial problems, scheduling problems, or exacerbation of medical problems that prevent the client from attending therapy. On occasion, however, absenteeism may be a form of resistance to therapy. This may become apparent only after other possible reasons for absenteeism have been considered and eliminated.

Resistance can be defined as reluctance on the part of a client to abandon old patterns of thought and/or behavior. Resistance can be classified as *overt* if it is manifested by observable verbal or nonverbal behavior, or *covert* if the resistance is internalized and not readily apparent to an observer. Overt resistance is usually easy to determine. A child may clamp his lips tightly closed just as the clinician begins a speech mechanism examination. A client with aphasia shakes his head and pushes the therapy materials away. A client regularly comes to therapy with unfinished homework assignments.

Covert resistance is more subtle, because it is not readily observable and is often overlooked by inexperienced clinicians. A mother agrees to make an appointment with a counselor regarding her child's emotional problems and repeatedly forgets. A young girl receiving therapy for a lateral lisp fails to make any progress because she believes her father thinks her speech is cute. A hearing-impaired client expresses interest in attending an aural rehabilitation class but later states that she was "too tired" to attend the sessions. A clinician delays writing a requested report because of "other demands" on his time.

What can we do when faced with resistance? We can confront it. We can discuss with the client the observed behaviors or subtle indications that lead us to believe that the client is reluctant to participate fully in therapy. We can encourage the client to express any feelings related to the proposed changes. Expression by the client of negative and ambivalent feelings often enables us to determine possible reasons for the client's reluctance to change. Discussing those feelings can also clarify for the client the causes of the resistant behavior. It is important that this discussion be conducted in a nonjudgmental manner by a caring, empathic clinician. The use of active listening techniques—open questions, restatement of content, and reflection of feelings, for example—is important during this process of understanding and neutralizing resistance. Problem-solving techniques (to be discussed in Chapter 8) are also useful in working through resistance.

Much resistance can be prevented. Factors that counteract and assist in preventing resistance include: attention to the basic needs of the client, client participation in setting and prioritizing therapy goals, practical and achievable therapy objectives, stimulating and interesting therapy activities from which the client is able to choose, use of positive reinforcers during therapy sessions, use of formal or informal contracts and other methods of documenting progress, and positive rapport established between the client and clinician.

Defense Mechanisms

Resistance to change is often caused by fear or anxiety. Sometimes a person can alleviate anxiety by direct action known as *coping behavior*, through which the situation causing the anxiety will be changed in a less overwhelming or ego-threatening direction. When people cannot alleviate anxiety through direct action, they tend to employ *defense mechanisms*—subconscious ways of avoiding painful realizations. Defense mechanisms do tend to reduce anxiety, at least temporarily. The unfortunate aspect is that the use of defense mechanisms necessitates distortion or denial of the realities of a situation. In that sense, defense mechanisms are self-defeating, energy-consuming, and do not address the crux of the problem. They deter clients from realistic identification and appraisal of the anxiety-producing situation. Defense mechanisms prevent clients from directing their energies into effective coping behavior. Sigmund Freud (1927) was a pioneer in describing defense mechanisms, some of which clinicians are likely to face in therapy and in other professional contacts. Common defense mechanisms include

- *denial:* refusing to acknowledge the reality or existence of something
- *displacement:* shifting negative impulses and feelings about one person or object to a safer or less dangerous person or object
- *identification:* taking on the thoughts, feelings, and/or actions of another person who is seen to have greater worth or power
- *intellectualization:* divesting an anxiety-producing thought of all emotional content to permit the thought to remain at a conscious level
- *projection:* attributing unacceptable feelings or ideas to others rather than accepting them as one's own
- *rationalization:* justifying an unreasonable or illogical idea, impulse, or act to make it appear reasonable
- *reaction formation:* transforming anxiety-producing or painful impulses or urges into their opposite forms, often in an exaggerated way
- *regression:* reverting to a less mature level of behavior
- *repression:* excluding from consciousness unacceptable feelings, ideas, or impulses
- *sublimation:* modifying and channeling unacceptable impulses into socially acceptable forms

As a clinician, you will occasionally meet with examples of defensive behavior on the part of a client or the client's family. In some individuals, particular defense mechanisms operate so consistently that they are present in most of that individual's interpersonal contacts. With other clients, your comments or nonverbal communication during the therapy session may actually prove anxiety-producing. Defense mechanisms may be triggered in the client as a direct result of your behavior. Many clinicians are convinced of the importance of providing an atmosphere in which clients can express their innermost feelings with a minimum of defensive reactions. In such an atmosphere, the coping responses of clients will be heightened and facilitated so that clients will be able to choose more effective ways of behaving in their environment.

You, as a clinician and as a human being, can also fall prey to fear or anxiety and the possible consequences. If this happens, it is helpful to become consciously aware of specific anxiety-producing situations, or existing conflicts between your beliefs and your behaviors. It is helpful to bring your energies to bear directly on the anxiety-producing situations rather than to deny or distort their existence. You will then be able, either with or without professional assistance, to explore your needs and new ways of meeting them. If these new behaviors are more effective and more compatible with your self-confirmed beliefs and values, they will be less anxiety-provoking.

Skilled clinicians, then, will be alert to defensive behavior in clients and in themselves. They will be prepared to work through and modify such behaviors, perhaps with the assistance of other professionals. As we have mentioned, defensive behavior is often the result of fear or anxiety—emotional reactions precipitated by the body's stress response. Let us now examine the mechanisms of stress and stress management.

Stress

The human body is designed to cope with fear-producing and anxiety-producing situations. Every living being exists in an environment, a small portion of the universe in which the organism must survive at any particular moment. Continued existence depends on coming to terms with the external environment. Air, food, water, and a variety of other substances for bodily utilization must somehow be obtained from the environment. Waste products must be eliminated. In the latter half of the nineteenth century, Charles Darwin (1859), a naturalist, and his contemporary Claude Bernard (1865), a physiologist, investigated phenomena of animal environmental adaptation. Bernard described physiological mechanisms that operate to assist an organism in maintaining the relatively constant internal state that is necessary for physical survival.

In the 1930s, Walter Cannon, another physiologist, used the term *homeostasis* to describe this process of maintaining internal balance. Cannon (1939) pointed out that when homeostasis is upset or thrown into disequilibrium, the body initiates certain reactions to remedy the situation. If insufficient oxygen is available, breathing will speed up; if body temperature is rising beyond the safe limits, perspiration occurs in an attempt to cool the body; and so forth. Any information perceived by the sense organs that signals a possible threat to survival will trigger a response in the central nervous system. The response prepares the body for immediate action and heightened physical activity. The heart rate increases; more blood is pumped to the peripheral muscles and less to the digestive tract. Attention to the impending danger is heightened and the body stands ready to do battle with the intruder or leave the scene as quickly as possible. This *fight-or-flight response*, verified and described by Cannon, is also known as the *general adaptation response* or *stress response*.

The fight-or-flight response was studied extensively by Hans Selye. Selye (1974, 1976) pointed out that this automatic bodily response to a sensed threat to homeostasis and survival can be triggered by a wide range of incoming stimuli in the modern human being. The response, with its accompanying emotions of fear and excitement, can be triggered not only by the approach of a ferocious animal or menacing fellow human, or being trapped in a tunnel with insufficient oxygen; it can also, through conditioning processes, be triggered by the sound of a dentist's drill, a frown on a clinician's face, the score on a diagnostic test, or even the approach of a mild-mannered client.

Fighting or fleeing is necessary in some situations as a short-term emergency adaptive response. Modern society, with its many anxiety- and fear-producing possibilities, may arouse the body's defenses over long periods of time. This frequent and long-lasting arousal of adaptive responses can lead to physical ailments and emotional disturbances. The fight-or-flight response is a universal one, but some of the sensory messages that trigger it vary greatly among humans because of individual experience and conditioning. What may trigger the stress response in one person may have negligible effect upon another. It should be noted that not all situations that trigger the bodily reactions of stress are negative ones. A person can be excited by the prospect of a pleasant social event or by the arrival of a surprise gift. Selye termed this positive "revving up" of our system *eustress*. This type of positive bodily response is not one that causes concern.

Research has shown that high levels of stress can be a problem at any age or life stage. Some investigators (for example, David Elkind, 1984, 1988) are concerned with the demands and pressures placed upon children growing up today. Others (for example, David Fletcher, 1984) are concerned that the elderly are especially vulnerable to the negative effects of stress because of poorly functioning homeostatic mechanisms and because the elderly are often denied instruction in stress management. *Universal stressors* affect people of all ages: deprivation of oxygen, prolonged lack of adequate food, exposure to injury, insufficient protection against a perceived threatening environment, deprivation of positive feedback needed for self-esteem, and a host of others that result in severe deprivation of basic human needs. However, specific stressors tend to vary not only with the individual but within various age groups. Listed below are a few stressors that are important to consider when working with clients in particular age groups.

- childhood: separation from parent; beginning school; premature responsibility for self-care; pressure to succeed academically, athletically, and socially; mistreatment by parents or peers; pressures toward drug usage; physical illness and hospitalization

- adolescence: pressure to succeed academically and socially; conflict between family values and peer values; unsatisfactory relationships with peers; ambivalence between dependence and independence related to family; career decisions; frustration of sexual urges; hormonal changes and accompanying bodily changes; parental divorce or death; death of peer
- young adult: establishment of a career; search for a mate; search for satisfactory housing; raising of a family; divorce or separation; balancing of marriage/family and career demands; male and female role conflicts; achievement and maintenance of financial solvency; overcoming dependencies; time overcommitments
- mid-life adult: declining physical abilities; conflicts with children; responsibilities for aging parents; disappointment with levels of achievement; heightened awareness of one's mortality; divorce or separation; time overcommitments
- older adult: death of spouse and/or peers; change in standard of living; change of residence; declining health; retirement; increasing dependency upon others; isolation and feelings of loneliness; lack of stimulation

Along with the possible stressors listed above, individuals with speech, language, and/or hearing problems often experience additional stress related specifically to communication difficulties in interpersonal relations. People depend on others to assist them in meeting basic needs. Those individuals who have difficulty in communicating find themselves at a great disadvantage in our society. Dissatisfying and unsuccessful communicative interactions thus contribute to high degrees of stress. Speech-language pathologists and audiologists will have clients in whom the stress response is often triggered during communication experiences, sometimes to such a high degree that it must be dealt with as part of the therapeutic program. Some clients may have speech or voice disorders actually resulting from or exacerbated by chronic stress. Clinicians will also see clients whose environment and life circumstances contain an astonishing number of stressors. In many instances, the clinician may wish to include techniques of stress management in the therapy program to assist clients in achieving maximum communicative effectiveness.

How can you identify those clients whose reactions to stressors are interfering with progress in therapy? You can be alert to some of the symptoms of severe and prolonged stress. Physical symptoms include the following: tremors; easy fatigability; restlessness; palpitations; dizziness; faintness; sweating; frequent urination; unexplained body aches, pains, and itchings. Emotional signs of stress include the following: feelings of futility, inadequacy, alienation; loss of motivation; distractibility; poor interpersonal relations; and drug use and abuse. You may notice certain facial characteristics often associated with stress: a furrowed brow; tense facial muscles; frequent licking of the lips, tongue movements, and swallowing; fleeting eye contact, frequent shifting of gaze, and eye blinking. Occasionally, a client will be so tense in the jaw and throat area that you may observe a rapid neck pulse.

Once you identify a client as suffering from severe or prolonged stress, you will need to decide what further steps should be taken. If stress symptoms are noted, but the stress does not appear to be directly related to the client-clinician interaction or to be directly interfering with communication, you may decide that it is unnecessary or inappropriate to spend therapy time on stress management. If there is concern about high levels of stress, appropriate referrals may be investigated. Make appropriate referrals if you are not comfortable assisting the client in dealing with stress because of lack of time, severity of the problem, or your limited background and experience in stress management.

If you and your client agree that an appropriate goal for therapy is acquisition of stress management skills, the following suggestions for managing stress may be helpful.

- **Assist the client in identifying his or her personal stressors.** There are several self-rating scales (for example: Holmes & Rahe, 1967; Farquhar, 1977; Lazarus & Folkman, 1984; Nathan, Staats, & Rosch, 1987) any of which can be used to identify current client stressors. Often, direct questioning of the client, coupled with active listening techniques, will provide more than sufficient information.

- **Assist the client in identifying stressors that can be eliminated or lessened.** There can be optional activities, responsibilities, and/or chores that cause stress and could readily be removed from the client's schedule. Others that cannot be removed may be revised to lessen stress. Some people simply have to learn how to say "no" to other people's excessive demands. Others have to learn to modify their own unreasonable demands upon themselves.

- **Assist the client in learning relaxation skills.** Most clinicians are familiar with techniques for deep muscle relaxation and mental relaxation (for example, those of Jacobson, 1938, 1976; and Benson, 1975). Researchers have found that moderate exercise is relaxing for most people. Some people find that imagining ("imaging") themselves as relaxed, comfortable, and in control of a feared situation enables them to handle it more effectively when it actually occurs. Progressive desensitization can also prove helpful in lessening stress in unpleasant situations. Biofeedback methods are also used to assist in relaxation.

- **Assist the client in budgeting stress energy.** People sometimes overreact to situations that do not warrant that degree of attention and stress. It can be helpful to think of available energy as money in a bank account. There is a limited amount available, and it is wise to expend it judiciously; in other words, don't spend 10 dollars worth of energy on a 10 cent problem. Reevaluating a situation may convince the client that the situation does not warrant the emotional energy expended.

- **Encourage the client to consider other stress management techniques not directly related to communication therapy.** Experts (for example, N.L. and D.A. Tubesing, 1983, 1984, 1986) have many other suggestions for stress management, including the following: eat right; make time for hobbies, light exercise, and other leisure activities; cultivate light-heartedness and a sense of humor; avoid chemicals such as nicotine, alcohol, caffeine, and hard drugs; clarify your value system and learn time-management skills; cultivate friends and support groups; and learn and use problem-solving techniques. Many people also find prayer, meditation programs, yoga, or tai chi helpful in stress management.

In considering factors that can be counterproductive to effective therapy, there is one other that merits discussion and that often results from inability to deal with stress: depression.

Depression

The human condition of depression was discussed by ancient Egyptian, Greek, and Roman writers who often used the word *melancholia* to identify depressed states. Descriptions of individuals suffering from depression have changed surprisingly little over the centuries. Today's investigators report a dramatic increase in cases of depression in modern society, and identify depression as a major public health problem.

In working with individuals with communication problems, you are likely to encounter clients suffering from varying degrees of depression. Depression may actually be causing some of the client's communicative difficulties. Or depression may be the result of impaired interpersonal communication. In any case, depression can interfere with the client's progress in therapy. It is useful for you to recognize the symptoms of depression and to make appropriate referrals when necessary.

According to the National Institute of Mental Health [NIMH] (1981), possible signs of depression include the following:

- changes in appetite
- shifts in sleeping patterns

- fatigability or lack of energy
- agitation or increased activity
- loss of interest in daily activities
- decreased sex drive
- inability to concentrate
- feelings of sadness, hopelessness, worthlessness, guilt, or self-reproach
- thoughts of suicide

NIMH recommends that if an individual manifests at least four of these symptoms, and the symptoms have lasted for at least two weeks, professional help should be sought. It is recommended that an individual combatting symptoms of depression start with a physical check-up, because some physical illnesses and/or medications used in their treatment may actually cause depression. If physical illness is not diagnosed, a mental health specialist should be sought for evaluation and therapy.

In a scientific exhibit at an annual meeting of the American Psychiatric Association, Dr. Ronald C. Smith (1975) presented profiles of depression. Excerpts of conversations with depressed patients were included in the exhibit and some are listed below. Phrases used by the patients describing their symptoms give voice to the symptoms of depression discussed in the preceding paragraphs. During the course of working with a client, you may hear similar phrases.

Behavior Disturbances

"can't talk right" . . . "don't want to do anything" . . . "shake physically, can't calm down" . . . "sleep and watch T.V. all day" . . . "no energy or interest in doing anything or being with people" . . . "avoid people" . . . "haven't been able to work for nine months, just can't" . . . "don't care about bathing, haven't washed for two or three weeks" . . . "don't care about things I used to enjoy" . . . "just don't know what to do" . . . "angry at what's happening, take it out on other people."

Psychosomatic Complaints

"shake all over" . . . "no interest in sex at all" . . . "throbbing headaches" . . . "constipation" . . . "a headache every other day" . . . "heart pounds like wild."

Affective Disturbances

"feel lousy, rotten" . . . "very sad, but don't know why" . . . "afraid of the day starting, don't want to face people" . . . "dread everything;

dread living" . . . "feel like a big blob" . . . "want to hide under the covers" . . . "cry an awful lot" . . . "worry about everything" . . . "everything seems so hopeless" . . . "why is it happening to me?" . . . "feel agitated, tense, all tight inside" . . . "angry at others but really at myself" . . . "feel all alone, no one to help or care" . . . "body is still but mind goes 90 miles an hour" . . . "mind just keeps going, can't concentrate on anything" . . . "keep thinking, worrying" . . . "don't know how I'll feel from minute to minute" . . . "can't get myself together."

Disturbed Self-Esteem

"disgusted with myself, self-contempt" . . . "seriously considered suicide" . . . "don't care if I live or die" . . . "don't feel like living, easier to die" . . . "feel unloved" . . . "don't like myself or my body" . . . "lost my self-confidence" . . . "angry at self" . . . "feel totally empty" . . . "tried to kill myself before" . . . "I feel helpless, all alone" . . . "don't know who I really am."

Appetite Disturbances

"no appetite, food tastes like sawdust" . . . "not hungry at all" . . . "eat more than usual; that's all I do—eat."

Sleep Problems

"sleep most of the day to avoid the world, to hide" . . . "can't sleep at all" . . . "fitful sleep, no rest, have scary dreams" . . . "prefer to sleep but wake up often during night" . . . "can't sleep when I'm alone" . . . "it's hard to fall asleep" . . . "just doze, off and on."

If you hear phrases like these from clients who also exhibit other described symptoms, the possibility of depression should be considered. Donald F. Klein (1977) in a physician's handbook on depression noted that the major symptom of depression is an individual's inability to enjoy the things of life that previously brought pleasure.

In recent years, there has been more recognition of the fact that depression knows no age boundaries. Frederick Goodwin, a psychiatrist and scientific director of NIMH, stated in an article by Joseph Alper (1986, pp. 37–38) that

Until maybe 10 years ago, we believed that severe depression was solely an illness of adults. . . . Now, however, we know that idea is dead wrong. Adolescents, even children, suffer from major depression as much as adults do.

Alper (1986, p. 38) pointed out that

> . . . estimates vary of how many young people suffer from major affective disorders, which include depression and manic-depression, an illness characterized by elation, hyperactivity, or irritability, alternating with depression. Depending on the age of the youngster and how his illness is defined, the estimates can range from one to six percent. There is no question, however, that the problem is serious and that it is growing. One study indicates that the percentage of older teenagers with major affective disorders has increased more than fivefold over the past 40 years.

> . . . there is mounting evidence that a constellation of harmful behaviors that accompany depression—suicide attempts, drug abuse, anorexia, bulimia, and juvenile delinquency—may be methods that young people use to try to cope with the anguish they feel. So if depression can be curbed, many of these disorders might disappear as well.

We have already discussed the many symptoms of depression as they occur in adults. Many of these symptoms also occur in children and adolescents suffering from depression. We will briefly note some variations and special considerations associated with young children, adolescents, and the elderly.

It is interesting that researchers Jeffrey Cohn and Edward Tronick (1983) found that infants as young as three months old actually responded to depressed states in their mothers by more crying, fussing, and grimacing than was evidenced in the infants' behavior when the mothers were in happier moods. Other studies have also indicated that mood states of mothers can have definite negative effects upon a child's emotions and behavior. Thus, as the incidence of depression among young mothers, particularly single parents, increases, we are likely to see a concomitant increase of depression in their children.

Often the symptoms in young children are very similar to those found in adults. However, the child may not be able to describe verbally his or her feelings; thus, the depression may go unrecognized and untreated. This is particularly true of the child with delayed speech and language development. Sometimes childhood depression is *masked*, manifested in aggressive behavior rather than in the symptoms of depression more easily identified. A child may evidence psychosomatic illness, may be a "troublemaker" in school, may run away from home, or may evidence delinquent behavior. A common symptom of depression in children is decline of academic performance. As with adults, treatment for childhood depression may involve use of antidepressants and/or psychotherapy.

Dealing with adolescents can be difficult under the best circumstances. Dealing with depressed adolescents can be an even greater frustration and challenge, and frequently requires the assistance of psychiatrists specializing in the treatment of teenagers. Suicide or attempted suicide is often the outcome of adolescent depression. Closely following accidents and homicides, suicide is the third leading cause of death in young people. As with children and adults, depression in adolescents can be *endogenous* (having no apparent external cause and probably resulting from a neurochemical imbalance within the central nervous system) or *situational* (also known as *reactive*). Situational depression most often follows a severe life disappointment such as loss of a loved one, a sudden distressing role change, or a traumatic experience involving loss of self-esteem. It can also result from prolonged deprivation of basic physical needs. These circumstances are depressing to most people; however, symptoms continuing for prolonged periods and sometimes even after circumstances have changed for the better are diagnosed as situational or reactive depression. Some cases of depression appear to be *mixed*; that is, they appear to have both endogenous and reactive components.

A common cause of depression in adolescents is the feeling of not being appreciated or understood by their families. Also, parental pressures for high academic, athletic, and/or social achievement can lead to feelings on the part of the teenager that he or she can never "measure up." Reactions to such pressures may lead to difficulties in school, rebelliousness, running away, rash or impulsive behaviors, and drug and alcohol abuse. Abrupt and radical changes in personality may also be indicative of depression. As mentioned above, eating disorders can also be a problem among adolescents, and their link with depression is now well established. Norman Rosenthal (1985) mentioned the growing body of evidence that suggests that the brain systems that regulate mood and eating behavior are intimately related. He found that approximately 60 percent of bulimic patients and 30 percent of anorexia nervosa patients are depressed. Trials with various antidepressants in patients with eating disorders demonstrated that drugs that increase central nervous system levels of serotonin (a neurotransmitter connected with emotional states) reduce binge eating by about 70 percent in bulimic patients.

Family members and others who work with adolescents must be sensitive to symptoms of depression, both the apparent and the more subtle or masked. They must also take seriously any talk of suicide, since statistics have shown that approximately 75 percent of suicide victims have actually mentioned their suicidal intentions prior to killing themselves. If you are working with an adolescent client in whom you note depressive or suicidal symptoms, consultation with family members and recommendations for professional help in overcoming the depression are certainly warranted.

Elderly people may be more vulnerable to stress and depression because of higher incidence of physical illness and effects of medication used to treat those illnesses. There is also evidence that the hypothalamus and the hormonal system function less efficiently in the elderly. Diminution of sensory acuity, such as hearing and vision, can deprive the individual of necessary stimulation from the environment and can also interfere with interpersonal contacts. In addition to these physiological factors, changes in life situations and loss of supportive relationships can lead to depression in older people.

As a professional, it is likely that you will see elderly clients whose communication is affected by depression, particularly if you work in geriatric units or long-term care facilities. One of the marked symptoms of depression is a slowing of mental and physical responsiveness to the environment. This often manifests itself in very slow, mumbled answers to questions; delayed responses to items on diagnostic tests; an apparent state of listlessness or disinterest in response to therapy activities; and an inability to make decisions relevant to therapy.

Clinicians may confuse the symptoms of depression with those of senile dementia (of the Alzheimer or other types) because often they appear similar. Both depressed and senile patients may exhibit unresponsiveness, apathy, confusion, short-term memory loss, and poor self care, in addition to reported anorexia or insomnia. Often the only way the distinction can be made between the two conditions is by careful observation of a variety of behaviors, by investigation of the individual's history, and/or by initiation of a trial period of antidepressant medication supervised by the patient's physician.

Lawrence Lazarus, John Davis, and Maurice Dysken (1985, p. 45) commented that

> In general, depressions have a sudden onset, whereas degenerative dementias such as Alzheimer's disease and multi-infarct dementia manifest themselves gradually. The demented patient confabulates to cover up his cognitive impairment and becomes angry when his memory is tested. On the other hand, the depressed but cognitively intact elderly patient may simply refuse to communicate.
>
> It should be noted that many elderly demented patients have a concomitant depression that makes assessing the relative contribution of dementia and depression a difficult diagnostic task.

The authors (pp. 45–46) further state

> During the diagnostic interview, the physician establishes rapport by empathizing with the patient's perceived sense of loss, depletion, and

hopelessness. Yet the physician should convey a hopeful, helpful attitude.

The elderly often feel that being depressed is a sign of moral weakness and may therefore feel ashamed. By explaining that depression is a medical illness caused, in part, by biologic and biochemical factors, the physician may relieve the elderly person's shame and help him accept treatment. Also, by carefully working through the reluctance of the patient and family to comply with treatment or to be referred to a psychiatrist, the physician can enhance the chances of a successful outcome.

These comments are appropriate not only for physicians but for speech-language pathologists and audiologists to consider when working with clients exhibiting these behaviors.

The clinician may find it helpful to become acquainted with several of the self-rating questionnaires that are available to assist in identifying depression in clients of various ages. One that is commonly used is the *Beck Scale* (Beck, 1967). Others include the *Hamilton Rating Scale for Depression* (Hamilton, 1960), the *Zung Self-Rating Depression Scale* (Zung, 1965, 1975), and the *Geriatric Depression Scale* (Brink et al., 1982).

SUMMARY

In this chapter, we have considered many factors that facilitate effective therapy. These can be summarized into a series of guidelines for successful client/clinician interpersonal relationships.

Guidelines for Client/Clinician Interpersonal Relationships

- Cultivate empathy: the ability to view life and therapy from the client's point of view.
- Form a "therapeutic alliance" with the client: the client as the principal worker and you as the facilitator for change.
- Consider the basic needs of the client and try to fulfill rather than frustrate those needs throughout the therapy program.
- Basically, it is the client's needs that are to be met during a therapy session. If the clinician is depending on the client and the therapy session for need satisfaction, energies may be misdirected and mixed messages may be sent.

- Consider your first responsibility to be toward your client, regardless of your client's age. Family members are important but secondary to the clinician-client relationship.
- Make every moment of your time with your clients count. Get "maximum mileage" from each diagnostic and therapy session.
- Prioritize therapy goals and objectives so that most time and energy (both the client's and yours) are spent on those that are likely to produce the largest "payoff."
- Make certain the amount of available time spent in talking by the clinician and by the client is in a proportion conducive to improvement and change by the client.
- Be prepared to be flexible in therapy without sacrificing therapy goals.
- Remember that fear, anxiety, stereotyped responses and prejudices, self-absorption, and compulsion to talk can all interfere with productive listening. This holds true for both client and clinician.
- Be alert to nonverbal and verbal clues to physiological conditions that affect progress in therapy, including symptoms of deterioration, stress, or depression.
- Be alert to signs of defense mechanisms that may interfere with coping behavior and progress in therapy.
- Cultivate listening techniques: both the acute, unbiased, trained listening necessary in diagnosing and critiquing speech and voice characteristics that need to be changed; and the equally important "active listening" ability that facilitates awareness of the client's thoughts and feelings—positive, negative, and ambivalent.
- Remember the importance of respect and courtesy in all contacts with people, no matter what their age, disposition, or human condition.
- Whenever possible, don't "tell"—"demonstrate."
- In every way practical and possible, help your client to feel in control of his or her own actions and ultimate change and success.
- Remember and use appropriate principles of behavior modification, keeping in mind that positive reinforcement is more effective than negative reinforcement or punishment in changing behavior.
- Foster a therapeutic atmosphere that will encourage the client to take the risks involved in change without fear of ridicule or blame.
- Accept resistance with understanding, and try to work through the client's apprehensions.
- Retain a pleasant and positive approach without denying the seriousness of a client's presented problems.
- Review and abide by the American Speech-Language-Hearing Association's Code of Ethics (ASHA, 1986).

REFERENCES

Alper, J. (1986, May). Depression at an early age. *Science*, pp. 37–42.

American Speech-Language-Hearing Association. (1986). Code of ethics of the American Speech-Language-Hearing Association. *Asha, 28*(4), 55–57.

Beck, A. (1967). *Depression: Causes and treatment*. Philadelphia: University of Pennsylvania.

Benson, H. (1975). *The relaxation response*. New York: William Morrow and Co.

Bernard, C. (1865). *An introduction to the study of experimental medicine*. Republished in 1927. New York: Macmillan.

Berne, E. (1961). *Transactional analysis in psychotherapy*. New York: Grove Press.

Brink, T.L., Yesavage, J.A., Lum, O., Heersema, P.H., Adey, M., & Rose, T.L. (1982). Screening tests for geriatric depression. *Clinical Gerontologist, 1*(1), 37–43.

Cannon, W.B. (1939). *The wisdom of the body* (rev. ed.). New York: Norton.

Cohn, J., & Tronick, E. (1983). Three-month-old infant's reactions to simulated maternal depression. *Child Development, 54*(1), 185–193.

Darwin, C. (1859). *The origin of species*. London: John Murray.

Elkind, D. (1984). *All grown up and no place to go: Teenagers in crisis*. New York: Addison-Wesley.

Elkind, D. (1988). *The hurried child: Growing up too fast too soon* (rev. ed.). New York: Addison-Wesley.

Farquhar, J. (1977, Fall/Winter). Stress and how to cope with it. *The Stanford Magazine*, pp. 50–55, 71–75.

Fletcher, D. (1984, November/December). Stress management for older patients. *Geriatric Consultant*, pp. 27–29.

Flower, W.M., & Sooy, C.D. (1987). AIDS: An introduction for speech-language pathologists and audiologists. *Asha, 29*(11), 25–30.

Freud, S. (1927). *The ego and the id*. London: John Murray.

Gordon, T. (1977). *Leader effectiveness training (L.E.T.)*. New York: Bantam Books.

Hamilton, M. (1960). A rating scale for depression. *Journal of Neurology, Neurosurgery and Psychiatry, 23*, 56–62.

Holmes, T.H., & Rahe, R.H. (1967). The social readjustment rating scale. *Journal of Psychosomatic Research, 11*, 213–218.

Jacobson, E. (1938). *Progressive relaxation* (2nd ed.). Chicago: University of Chicago Press.

Jacobson, E. (1976). *You must relax* (5th ed.). New York: McGraw-Hill.

Klein, D.F. (1977). *The physician's handbook on depression*. New York: Pfizer Laboratories.

Lazarus, L.W., Davis, J.M., & Dysken, M.W. (1985). Geriatric depression: A guide to successful therapy. *Geriatrics, 40*(6), 43–53.

Lazarus, R.S., & Folkman, S. (1984). *Stress appraisal and coping*. New York: Springer Co., Inc.

Nathan, R.G., Staats, T.E., & Rosch, P.J. (1987). *The doctors' guide to instant stress relief*. New York: G.P. Putnam's Sons.

National Institute of Mental Health. (1981). *Causes and treatment of depression*. Rockville: National Institute of Mental Health.

Rogers, C. (1951). *Client-centered therapy: Its current practice, implications, and theory*. Boston: Houghton Mifflin.

Rollin, W.J. (1987). *The psychology of communication disorders in individuals and their families.* Englewood Cliffs, NJ: Prentice-Hall.

Rosenthal, N.E. (1985). Depression, eating disorders biochemically tied? *Internal Medicine News, 18*(6), 50.

Selye, H. (1974). *Stress without distress.* New York: J.B. Lippincott Co.

Selye, H. (1976). *The stress of life* (rev. ed.). New York: McGraw-Hill.

Smith, R.C. (1975). *Profiles of neurotic depression.* Scientific exhibit presented at 128th annual meeting of the American Psychiatric Association, Anaheim, CA.

Tubesing, N.L., & Tubesing, D.A. (Eds.). (1983, 1984, 1986). *Structured exercises in stress management* (Vols. I, II, III). Duluth, MN: Whole Person Press.

Zung, W.K. (1965). A self-rating depression scale. *Archives of General Psychiatry, 12,* 63–70.

Zung, W.K. (1975). *The measurement of depression.* Columbus, OH: Charles E. Merrill Publishing Co.

5

Working with Family
Members To Expedite Therapy

In spite of changing mores and shifting family patterns in today's world, the speech and hearing professional will often be working not only with clients, but with family members or significant others. There is no doubt that the accomplishment of speech and language improvement goals can either be facilitated or inhibited by the attitudes and behaviors of important persons in the client's environment. This chapter will address aspects of a clinician's work with family members.

CONTEMPORARY FAMILY PATTERNS

In some ways, family life has changed dramatically within the last few decades. Survival of family units is more unstable than in previous generations. In 1986, *U.S. News & World Report* gave the following statistics regarding recent family patterns in the United States. One out of every two new marriages in the United States is destined to end in divorce. Sixty percent of two-year-olds are now expected to live in a single-parent household at some time before their eighteenth birthday. The picture of the American family as consisting of a father fulfilling the role of breadwinner, a mother as homemaker and responsible for child care, and one or two carefree children is no longer the norm. Today fewer than one in five families fits that picture. More than half of women with children under the age of five work outside the home. In addition to changing lifestyles, families all over the world are being torn apart or threatened by natural disasters, disrupted living conditions, and wars and revolutions.

However, in spite of changes that have occurred, the family still meets some very basic human needs. The family is the place where the most intimate of relationships are formed and nourished. The traditional passing on of cultural history and mores occurs within the family. Although concern is voiced about the future of marriage and family life in America, there appears to be a trend towards reestablishment of the importance of these institutions. Sandy Dornbusch, Director of the Center for the Study of Families, Children and Youth at Stanford University, stated in an interview with Bob Beyers (1988, p. 2) that he remains very optimistic about the future of families and children in America.

> The entire society, including young people who are getting married, is becoming more aware of the importance and symbolism of marriage. Simultaneously, society as a whole is becoming more aware of the symbolism and importance of children. If we fail to care about kids, we're all going to suffer. Of course, families are changing. Whenever there's social change, there's tension.

Today's parents are confronted with a number of stressors, as were those of previous generations. With all the demands and conflicts facing families today, it is difficult to follow optimal parenting guidelines. Not only must parents (or often just one parent) provide food, shelter, and clothing for themselves and their children, but they are also expected to provide their children with education; recreational opportunities; orthodontia and other cosmetic improvements; and moral guidance in the face of teenage pregnancies, alcohol and drug abuse, and a burgeoning crime rate. Mere survival as a family is not enough in many modern cultures. There are also standards of family life and accomplishment that parents and children are expected to achieve. The added factor of a communication disorder in one or more members of the family system can certainly complicate and sometimes prevent the achievement of those desired standards.

TYPES OF INTERACTIONS WITH FAMILY MEMBERS

We have already noted in Chapter 2 that, along with activities involving diagnostic evaluation and therapy procedures, sessions with clients or family members often fulfill one or more of the following goals:

- information getting
- information giving
- expression and exploration of feelings
- problem solving
- planning for future action

Many interactions with parents, siblings, or spouses of clients are designed to accomplish these purposes. Early meetings and diagnostic evaluations often devote considerable time to obtaining information regarding the client and the communication difficulties that bring him or her to therapy. However, at any time during the course of therapy, the clinician may feel the need for obtaining more information. In any therapy session, the clinician may be called upon to share information with the client, explore feelings that have surfaced during therapy, or engage in problem solving. In this section, we will examine some excerpts of conversations between clinicians and members of clients' families illustrating these purposes.

Interactions Obtaining Information

In getting information from a client, you must decide what information would be helpful to you in the work you are trying to accomplish. Sometimes you may use case history forms or intake forms that you or other professionals have compiled or that are required in the agency where you work. These forms include topic areas that have proven to be important. A rapid give-and-take of questions and answers may be quite appropriate in responding to some of these questionnaires. For example, questions securing factual information such as name, address, birthdate, and so forth can be asked and answered very quickly. Some questions take more time to respond to because they are not strictly factual. The answer depends more on how the respondent feels or interprets the questions.

You must be alert to whether or not the information you are getting is really important. It is easy to start asking questions. The respondent's answers can then trigger more questions. The conversation can continue in that fashion, and it may be quite a while before you realize that the information you have obtained is not all that significant. The clinician who does not keep the goal of the session in mind may reach the end of the time allotted for the session and find that many important questions have been left unanswered. Thus, in an information-getting interview, structuring is very important.

Often, a clinician can expedite achievement of the goal by sharing with the respondent reasons he or she needs certain information. Sometimes a clinician simply fires questions at a respondent and receives answers. However, the answers might be much more meaningful or significant if the respondent understood why the information was necessary. Clinicians often assume that a person is going to understand the reasons for curiosity in certain areas. A parent, for example, might feel that the clinician is prying unduly into personal subject matter; the parent may not realize these details are crucially related to the child's condition.

A respondent will often look to you for assurance that the information he or she is giving to you is appropriate. According to the principles of behavior modification, behavior that you approve is likely to recur or become more frequent. You, then, can encourage information-giving through use of approval. What you have to beware of, though, is *what* you approve. If the respondent is giving you a variety of information, and obviously one type of information or certain facts are meeting with your approval, he or she is likely to give more similar facts. The respondent is likely to refrain from giving any contradictory information or something that might throw a different light on the matter, and yet you want him or her to keep sharing information with you. The trick in approval is to approve the attitude of the respondent—his or her willingness to share with you—without actually voicing positive or negative judgments about the specific statements or information he or she is giving.

The following interview excerpt is an example of information getting during an interview with a mother of a four-year-old boy with delayed language. As in previous chapters, *C* is used to indicate the clinician, and *R* is used to designate the respondent in the interaction.

Interview Excerpt 5-1

C: The first question I wanted to ask was, as a mother how did you pick up on Gregory's language, his slower language?

R: First of all, Gregory is the third child so I had some expectations about words they should be saying and when he was, when he was approaching two years old, he was not saying the words. He was not even saying "Mommy" and "Daddy," not even "Ma" and "Da."

C: Mm-hm.

R: At that time, I was seeing my pediatrician with my newborn baby and asked him about Gregory. So he checked Gregory and tried to talk to him but, of course, Gregory didn't say anything. At that time my pediatrician said, "Why don't you try having him evaluated at the University Speech and Hearing Clinic?"

C: So he referred you here.

R: Yes, he gave me the telephone number. We came out here right after that.

Interactions Giving Information

When giving information to a client or family member, it is important that you present it in a clear manner, that you are accurate in the information you present, and that you are comfortable in acknowledging when you do not have the necessary information. Sometimes, the information you give will be readily accepted by clients or family members. At other times, strong emotions associated with the topic, or aroused by you, may interfere with the listener's ability to process and accept the information offered. You must be alert to emotional reactions on the part of the respondent. These reactions cannot be ignored if you hope to get the message across. In some situations, the emotions may have to be explored and dealt with before information giving can proceed. In other circumstances, a modification or rephrasing of the information may be sufficient.

The following interview excerpt with the wife of a patient who has suffered a stroke provides an example of what can go wrong in an information-giving session. There is no doubt that the clinician is giving information. However, much of the information provided does not readily address the wife's needs. At one point, the wife is asking for a clarification of terms that she does not understand—a request that is ignored by the clinician. At another point, the wife is requesting information as a result of her emotional state: negative feelings toward her husband's condition and progress. Here again, the clinician's responses do not really address the wife's concerns.

Interview Excerpt 5-2

C: Bob had a good session today. He was able to go through most of the activities without getting frustrated.

R: That's good. He gets so upset and angry at home.

C: We also worked on the dysarthria. He had some difficulty with the lingual alveolar phonemes but many of the plosives were correct.

R: Dysar . . . ? Plosives?

C: Yes. . . . Well, you know we did spend most of the time on those, but I was so pleased that he was doing so well that we worked on that longer than I originally planned.

R: How long do you think it will take 'til he's back to himself? I just don't know how much longer I can go on like this; we can't even talk to each other.

C: Well, today was a good session. We have to be thankful for every step forward.

R: How can you tell when there's progress? I get so discouraged.

C: That's natural. Most people in your situation feel like that.

The errors in the above interview speak for themselves. A similar situation occurred in Interview Excerpt 3-2 where the clinician gave information and completely ignored the mother's negative feelings aroused by the diagnosis.

In the following excerpt, the older sister of a 20-year-old male with a severe stuttering problem is explaining to the clinician why she has taken the initiative in seeking help for her brother. She explains that ever since her brother began to stutter severely at the age of five, her parents have refused to seek any help for him because of a cultural belief that a problem is "God-given" and therefore should be endured.

This excerpt provides an example of both information getting and information giving on the part of the clinician. The sister shares information regarding her family's cultural background and the reason for the parents' nonparticipation in the therapy program. At the same time, the clinician is aware that the older sister has a tendency to assume responsibility for some of her brother's communication, especially in situations that are difficult for him. The clinician wishes to emphasize the importance of allowing the client to assume responsibility for his communication needs.

Interview Excerpt 5-3

C: So you're the one who encouraged Jed to come here for therapy. Has he had previous help with his stuttering problem?

R: No—none at all. You see my parents are totally almost illiterate. They were only educated in religion and a little bit to read and write their own language but nothing in a broad sense.

C: Mm-hm.

R: People in the community where they lived say "Oh, this thing— this is God-given"; they think it should not be corrected. So when illiterate people give this kind of feeling without knowing anything, then the parents, my parents, sort of say "Oh yeah, nothing will be done to his speech." And that's where they close the case.

C: But you feel that something should be done for Jed.

R: Yeah, yeah, it was my initial idea, and I want to give him support. It's so important that he communicate and associate with people, friends and everything, so he won't shy away from conversing.

C: Your helping your brother get started in therapy has really benefited him. I'm happy to see that now he is taking the initiative in working on the steps of our stuttering program. He has been doing his homework assignments faithfully. The more situations he can be in to practice his contracts (that's what we call his homework), the better off he is.

R: Yeah, for a while I used to make phone calls for him and make appointments for him, and now he is doing this most of the time himself.

C: Yes, one of the most important things in the program that we emphasize is that the client takes responsibility to become fluent and that he has the capability to do so. It's his decision to become fluent or not to become fluent.

R: Yes, I don't know why I didn't think about it before. I felt sorry for him and kept doing things for him.

C: Well, it's good that you realize that now, because the more that he can do for himself, the better off he is. He is capable of taking responsibility for whatever his needs are. But it's nice to know that he has the support of his sister.

Interactions Expressing and Exploring Feelings

The expression and exploration of feelings can be the major goal of a session with family members. It may be difficult to accomplish other goals in an interpersonal relationship until certain feelings are verbalized, acknowledged, and dealt with. As mentioned in Chapter 2, many counselors and psychotherapists feel that the free-flowing expression of emotions is in itself therapeutic.

In Interview Excerpt 5-4, the wife of a 63-year-old stroke victim is describing her view of the changes that have occurred in her life because of her husband's illness. Throughout a lengthy interview, she repeatedly expressed feelings of frustration caused by the amount of help and attention her husband now needs. The clinician used active listening techniques to encourage the wife's expression and exploration of these feelings.

Interview Excerpt 5-4

R: The snare I've run into is that Wally doesn't want me to go any-place and leave him alone. He's so possessive now, you know. Before, I could just go anyplace—but I can understand his situation. I think at first he was afraid. But now, I don't know—I don't think he's afraid now to be by himself but, uh. . . .

C: He's gotten used to you being there.

R: Right. Just for him. He doesn't want me to go anyplace.

C: So it's been a big change for you.

R: Oh yes, a very big change, because before I could go where I wanted to go. 'Cause I had my car and I could just go. But now, in the morning I give him exercises. Then I get his shower, get him ready to go wherever. And get the breakfast and then maybe I'll take him to his therapy or to his swimming. And when we get back, it's lunchtime, so I get lunch. And then there's his homework and grocery shopping, and then it's time for dinner. So I get dinner together. I'm doing something for him all the time because, you know, there's no one 'cept me to do it.

C: Does it get you down sometimes?

R: Well, yes. When I, when I feel that I've really done, you know, too much, I'll go somewhere and put my legs up and turn the TV on, or get a book or something and relax.

C: Well, good. You need some time to yourself.

R: Maybe I have to stress that to Wally. Maybe I have to say that right out.

The life change for this woman as a result of her husband's stroke entailed quitting a job she enjoyed and eliminating some leisure activities that she found stimulating. She was committed to the care of her husband. What she needed was the opportunity to air her frustrations without being considered selfish or uncaring. She also needed to be encouraged to seek some respite for herself. The clinician was in a good position to address both of these needs.

Interactions Involving Problem Solving

Although the excerpt given above was concerned with expression and exploration of feelings by the wife, it also touched on a problem: the limited opportunity for the wife to have some time for herself. Chapter 8 will be devoted to a discussion of helping clients and families become effective problem solvers. Specific procedures for analyzing and solving problems will be discussed in that chapter. However, there are two considerations we wish to mention here. One is that the client or family member may identify a current problem but not always be aware of the cause of the problem and/or possible solutions. Part of the professional's role is to take available information, postulate some contributing causal factors, and make suggestions for the client's and/or family members' consideration. This will be illustrated in Interview Excerpt 5-5.

Another consideration involves the concept of ownership of a problem. A person "owns" a problem when his or her needs are being frustrated or not met, or when his or her behavior or circumstances are personally unsatisfying. When clients admit ownership of a problem, they can become motivated to solve it by changing their behavior. Difficulties often arise when a client wants another person to change his or her behavior because it bothers the client. A person who will not admit ownership of a problem regarding behavior will not be motivated to change. This will be illustrated in Interview Excerpt 5-6.

In the following interview excerpt, the mother of a four-year-old daughter with delayed language is discussing her concerns about her child's reluctance to talk at home and in other situations outside the therapy session. The mother and the clinician discuss some techniques the mother can use at home to encourage her daughter to verbalize more.

Interview Excerpt 5-5

R: If Sally doesn't start talking more, she'll never be ready for kindergarten next year. When I observed her I noticed that she said more to you than she ever says at home.

C: Well, I try to make the activities interesting and use things that I know Sally enjoys. What sorts of things does she like to do at home?

R: She likes to do play-dough and puzzles. She likes to make mudpies, too. She stays outside by herself quite a bit. And that's all right with me; I have so much to do I can't entertain her all the time.

C: Does Sally ever help you or watch you while you're working around the house?

R: Well, sometimes. I've noticed something about myself lately. I quite often don't listen to her if I have something on my mind.

C: So you've noticed that you tend to be preoccupied, sometimes you don't really listen?

R: Yes. I don't know whether I've noticed that more so since I've been observing here at the clinic and, you know, things came to my attention. I'm not really sure why I'm noticing more now, maybe because I've been so busy at home that I haven't been paying attention, and I know I haven't. I must work on that too, listening when she's talking. But I want to help her talk more if I can.

C: Two of the best ways I know of are by using parallel talk and self talk. Do you remember when we talked about those last week at the parents' meeting? When you're with Sally, you can put into words what she's doing if she isn't talking about it herself. Or you can explain what you're doing when you are working around the house and she is with you.

R: Mm-hm, that's self talk, right?

C: That's right, self talk.

R: I've been trying to remember to do that even though it's hard to get used to doing it.

C: Good. It doesn't really matter what you talk about, anything, folding the laundry, cooking. For instance, "I'm peeling carrots; I'm going to put the carrots in the soup." And then give Sally time to talk to you about it if she wants to.

R: Mm-hm, right.

C: The reason parallel talk and self talk are so effective is that Sally knows that you are interested in what she is doing, that you like having her with you, and that it's fun to talk together. That's why really listening to her is important too.

R: I'm going to work on doing that more at home, now that I see
what a difference it makes when you do it.

In the next interview excerpt, the mother of a six-year-old son (Brian) with
learning disabilities is expressing her concern about her husband's tendency to
favor an older son (David) and ignore the younger boy. She is discussing this with
her child's clinician because she feels her husband's behavior is detrimental to the
client's development. The clinician points out that, although the wife views her
husband's behavior as a problem, unless the husband agrees that it is a problem, he
is unlikely to change his behavior.

Interview Excerpt 5-6

R: Brian's teacher told me that he needs more attention and
praise at home. I told my husband that, but he doesn't seem to
think it's very important.

C: How does Brian get along with his father?

R: (long pause) Well, he gets . . . they get along okay. But I think
his father favors David, which I've told him. Well, not that he
means to, but it's like, if he's going to take one of them, he'll
always take David.

C: Uh huh. Why do you think that is?

R: Well, for one thing, David will stay out all day with him. If they're
going to be out a couple of hours, Brian will get bored and want
to come home within an hour.

C: Mm-hm.

R: I, I, well, I told him, I said, "It's not fair." I said, "You should take
Brian off by himself, or at least the two of them together." I
know my husband has trouble understanding Brian, but
Brian's speech is getting better now. I think it's mostly that
David is older and more mature, and that's why my husband
favors him.

C: Well, I can understand that you're concerned that Brian
doesn't have more time with his father. And you have let your
husband know how you feel about that. Basically, he's the one
that will have to see it as a problem, too, and make efforts to
include Brian. Perhaps some outings with all the family
together would help.

R: We haven't tried that for quite a while. Brian's older now, and it might work out.

Interactions Planning Future Action

Sometimes an interaction with a family member is for the purpose of planning an action that the clinician feels is important to the accomplishment of therapy goals. Interview Excerpt 5-7 is with the mother of a three-year-old boy with delayed language. During a routine recheck of the boy's hearing, the audiologist has noted impacted cerumen and is suggesting a plan of action. The mother is being advised to have the child's pediatrician check his ears and remove the wax if she deems it necessary. The child will then have his hearing rechecked.

Interview Excerpt 5-7

C: Mrs. Andrews, what I found is that Justin's hearing is basically the same as it was last year. Although in the lower frequencies, his hearing has decreased slightly in the left ear. What I would like to have you do is to have Justin go back to his doctor and have the doctor check his ears. As I was examining them, it looked like a heavy buildup of hardened ear wax. So I would like for you to have it checked.

R: I have some solution for his ears. Do you think I should use it?

C: What I would suggest before doing anything like that is to check with the doctor and let her decide what she would like you to do.

R: Okay, I'll do that. She's taken care of that hardened ear wax before.

C: I can then recheck Justin's hearing to see if the wax was causing the decrease in hearing in his left ear.

In planning for more complex and extensive future action than a check with a client's pediatrician, it is desirable to establish long-range and intermediate goals. The nature of these goals will, of course, depend on circumstances prompting the action. Speech-language pathologists and audiologists have had considerable practice in such goal setting. Clinicians routinely emphasize the planning, practice, and evaluation of new behaviors by clients as they progress in therapy. Clinicians also realize the importance of helping clients develop insight into problems that may arise in trying to carry out planned actions.

Nena and George O'Neill (1974) have done considerable work assisting people in acquiring new behaviors and changing their lifestyle. The O'Neills referred to these significant changes in life direction as "shifting gears." One of their major points was that a person must take the risk of new behavior in order to grow. They pointed out the paradox of the human being's need for security (which implies maintenance of the familiar) and the need for change (which implies going into the unknown and taking risks). They also indicated that significant life changes can be made in a series of small, achievable steps. Family members as well as clients often have to be reminded of these truths.

In each of the interview excerpts we have presented, the client-clinician relationship has been cordial. There were no indications of hostility, unfriendliness, or competitive behavior. As we discussed in Chapter 2, dimensions of interactions may include situations that are less than ideal. The clinician is usually aware of these situations as they occur in professional practice. Some sessions are more effective than others, and the clinician must face that fact. The goal is to analyze the interactions that are less effective and try to determine what caused them. In this way, similar situations can be prevented or handled differently in the future.

What causes unsatisfactory relations between clinicians and family members? Jane Schulz (1985, p. 5), a college professor of special education and the mother of a developmentally disabled son, has written about factors that influence parent-professional cooperation. She mentioned that parents often appear to professionals as either overprotective or uncaring. However, she pointed out that many parents have skills that could be positive contributions to their child's education. Schulz felt that there has been reluctance on the part of professionals to admit that they need help, and also a reluctance on their part to accept and utilize the abilities of parents. Schulz stated

> . . . there appear to be two factors crucial to effective parent-professional interaction: communication and respect. While these elements are essential to any good relationship, they seem to be missing in many of our parent-teacher confrontations.

Philip Roos (1985, pp. 254–255) suggested the following guidelines for fostering productive work between parents and professionals. Although his intended audience was parents of mentally retarded children, the guidelines can apply to all parents and/or appropriate family members of clients with communicative handicaps.

> Parents should be accepted as full-fledged members of the multidisciplinary team. They should be considered as colleagues, and their contributions should be treated with respect.

Parents and professionals should recognize that they may have pre-conceived notions about each other that may interfere with working together. Destructive stereotypes and negative expectations should be openly discussed whenever possible.

Professionals should try to accept parents where they are . . . and develop a listening skill that encourages full disclosure. Most effective counselors, I am convinced, have learned to develop good ears while restraining their tongues. Professionals should resist the temptation to criticize parental attitudes so as not to stifle free expression of feelings or reinforce feelings of guilt and worthlessness. Before parents can develop constructive attitudes toward their handicapped child, they must come to grips with whatever negative feelings may exist.

Professionals should be particularly attuned to the existential anxieties experienced by parents . . . , and they must be willing to listen to expression of these anxieties.

Professionals should share with parents all relevant information that is the basis for planning and decision making. Information should be furnished as soon as it becomes available to minimize parents' anxieties resulting from ambiguity and threat of the unknown. Unless there are compelling reasons to withhold specific information, parents should be furnished with the same data, including test findings and written reports, as other team members.

Clear two-way communication is essential to productive parent-professional interaction. Professional jargon should be avoided as much as possible, and technical terms should be simply explained. Parents as well as professionals should indicate whenever they suspect that they are not completely clear on what is being communicated.

In general, professionals should have the prime responsibility for selecting the methods and techniques to be used, and parents—or, when appropriate, the clients themselves—should be ultimately responsible for selecting goals and objectives. Whenever possible, these should be joint decisions involving parents, clients, and professionals. In reaching these decisions, parents and clients must be furnished all relevant information, including a description of available alternatives. . . .

Parents as well as professionals need support and encouragement as they try to cope with the problems and frustrations. . . . Mutual reinforcement, praise, and encouragement can be very useful.

Parents and professionals should guard against competing against each other. They need to be constantly aware of the possibility of competitive rivalries and of the temptation to use each other as scapegoats or to undermine each other's efforts. . . .

In Chapter 2, we mentioned some of the principles and vocabulary of transactional analysis and pointed out that it can be useful in understanding why sessions or relationships can be productive or unsatisfying. Pamela Grannis and Gary Peer (1985) have utilized transactional analysis techniques to analyze interactions between teachers and parents of handicapped children. Their premise is that parent/teacher partnerships are most effective when both parent and teacher are communicating from the Adult ego state. They note four attitudes that can be potential impediments to effective communication: (1) "The Know Nothing Parent," (2) "The Know Everything Parent," (3) "The Know Nothing Teacher," and (4) "The Know Everything Teacher."

The "Know Nothing Parent" is one who communicates complete helplessness to the teacher and relies heavily on teacher direction and guidance. The authors suggest that in working with this type of parent, it is important that the teacher help the parents recognize that they do have important knowledge about their child and can be actively involved in their child's education.

The "Know Everything Parent" appears to know more than anyone else about his or her child's abilities and needs. Such parents are often highly judgmental and critical of the professional and the professional's agency. These attitudes may be a reflection of feelings of anger, denial, hurt, or a result of past conditioning regarding interaction with professionals. It is important that the professional not react defensively or become intimidated by the "Know Everything Parent." The professional should respond to the parent in a rational, factual manner. In transactional terms, the professional should not allow his Child ego state to be activated by the Parent ego state of the respondent. The goal should be to initiate Adult-Adult interactions.

The "Know Nothing Teacher" is one who lacks self-confidence in his or her professional abilities and who often lacks professional experience. Such a teacher does not engender confidence on the part of the parents. The parents, therefore, are less likely to follow through on any of the teacher's instructions or suggestions. The authors caution that often the "Know Nothing Teacher" is operating from the Child ego state. The goal should be to initiate more Adult statements in parent-teacher interactions.

The "Know Everything Teacher" is the "expert" and assumes that the parents know nothing. A teacher with this attitude is likely to treat parents as ignorant, inept at parenting, and unable to participate in their child's educational program. Parents are likely to respond to this attitude by becoming frustrated, angry, or uncooperative in interactions with the teacher. Grannis and Peer recommend that teachers of this type reexamine their view of the parents' role in education, avoid "talking-down" to parents, and encourage parents to take an active role in helping their child.

The authors state that the ideal relationship is between the "Know Something Parent" and the "Know Something Teacher." They conclude (p. 174) that

> The most promising way to improve relationships between parents and professionals is to establish a view of parents and teachers as adult partners. . . .
>
> While striving for more Adult-Adult transactions with parents, the special education teacher has the added role of providing support and encouragement from the Parent ego state from time to time. The teacher needs to recognize and support parents' strengths. . . .
>
> Parent/teacher communication is affected by attitudes of both the parent and teacher. The "Know Nothing" and "Know Everything" attitudes are not conducive to an Adult parent/teacher partnership. Transactional Analysis with the P-A-C model is a relatively simple tool teachers can use to identify and change these attitudes. The "Know Something" parent and teacher attitude acknowledges both the parent's and teacher's role as Adults in the education of children. This is best accomplished when both parent and teacher communicate as Adult to Adult.

If sessions with clients and conferences with family members are tape-recorded, you can listen to the tape and analyze the session in the light of the purposes that the interactions were meant to serve. Listed below are some questions that you can consider when analyzing sessions intended for particular purposes.

When the goal is information getting:

- Did I secure the information I wanted?
- Is the information pertinent?
- Did the respondent appear to be cooperative and willing enough to provide me with honest, accurate information?
- Is the information obtained in this one session sufficient for my purposes, or should I validate or confirm it at other times and in other circumstances or with other means of information-getting at my disposal?

When the goal is information giving:

- Did I give the client or family member the information that I planned and wanted to give?
- Was I sensitive to the respondent's requests for additional information, even when those requests were framed in an indirect manner?

- Did I pay attention to feedback from the respondent to determine whether or not I was presenting information in a nonthreatening and understandable way?
- Did I furnish appropriate and professionally accurate information?
- If I was unable to answer a professional question, did I acknowledge that inability in a straightforward manner? If appropriate and practicable, did I offer to try to secure the information for the respondent?

When the goal is expression and exploration of feelings:

- Did I create an accepting, nonjudgmental atmosphere in which the client or family member could express negative and ambivalent feelings as well as more socially acceptable or positive ones?
- Was I alert to changes in facial expression, body movements, tone of voice, and other nonverbal cues that can indicate feelings not verbally expressed?
- Did I try to make the respondent more aware and more accepting of his or her feelings by acknowledging and verbalizing—in other words, reflecting— those feelings?
- Did I stay with exploration of the respondent's feelings even though I felt uncomfortable at times in a situation much different from everyday conversation and socially acceptable small talk?

When the goal is problem solving:

- Was I alert to signs or expressions of anxiety, depression, or general frustration that could indicate the existence of some serious, unsolved problem?
- Did I help the respondent to reduce a general problem to more specific behavioral terms?
- Were we able to reach an accurate answer to the question, "Who owns the problem?"
- Did we establish priorities among the stated problems, so that neither of us was overwhelmed by the magnitude of the problem-solving task?
- Did I help the respondent develop and examine alternatives to his or her present behavior, and were the proposed alternatives possible and practical?
- As a result of our work together, has the respondent learned to use some of the basic rules of problem solving so that he or she will be able to deal more efficiently and effectively with future problems?

When the goal is planning for future action:

- Is the planned behavior appropriate in light of the goal to be achieved?
- Is the planned behavior appropriate for this particular respondent, at this particular time, and in these particular circumstances?

- Have I involved the respondent in all stages of planning for future action, including the establishment of long-range goals, intermediate objectives, and the behaviors to be implemented?
- Are the goals, objectives, and behaviors described in clear, precise, and verifiable terms?
- How will we know when the planned behavior has been accomplished satisfactorily? What provisions are there for evaluation and feedback?

FAMILY PARTICIPATION IN THERAPY

No matter how often a speech-language pathologist or audiologist sees a client for therapy sessions, the time spent with the clinician is still only a portion, and usually a very small portion, of the client's day or week. If the client is highly motivated to change a communicative behavior and the change is an easily achieved change, the client may practice throughout the day what he or she has learned in therapy. The client may not need any encouragement other than the successful accomplishment of the therapy objectives leading to the agreed-upon therapy goals. If, on the other hand, the behavior to be changed is not so easily modified, the client may need assistance and encouragement from family members, friends, teachers, and others in his or her communicative environment.

How do family members participate in therapy? A key factor in participation is making certain that the client attends the therapy sessions. This involves ensuring that the client gets to the session, arrives on time, is in a condition to participate in therapy, and meets the costs of therapy. Another key factor is the encouragement of the client by family members to continue in therapy and to take risks involved in changing behavior. Family members can encourage the client in communicative attempts involving newly learned skills even when early attempts are not very successful. Often, family members can supply support and encouragement when clients become frustrated or pessimistic about their communicative abilities.

In addition to the general support noted above, family members often take a more active role in therapy procedures. The first stage of this participation is often in the determination of therapy goals after the diagnostic evaluation has been conducted. It is generally true that the more actively clients and/or appropriate family members have participated in formulating therapy goals, the more conscientious and cooperative they will be in the therapy program. In addition, family members will be less likely to complain or have reservations about the therapy process if they have been intimately involved in planning and prioritizing therapy goals.

If complaints do occur at any time during the therapy process, the clinician must first listen attentively and nonjudgmentally to the objections raised. Sometimes, the objections can be met rather easily. For example, perhaps the family member has not been given sufficient information regarding the nature of the communicative problem, the purpose of particular activities and use of materials, or the time element involved in achieving desired changes. In other instances, the complaints cannot be so easily resolved. If, for instance, the wife of a stroke patient is reacting to interpersonal difficulties with her husband that existed prior to the stroke and have been exacerbated by it, her unhappiness with therapy or the therapist may be a manifestation of her general unhappiness and frustration. Or perhaps the parents of a child with severe language delay have not accepted the degree and nature of their child's disability; consequently, defense mechanisms have been triggered that may result in blaming the therapist for the child's limited progress. The clinician cannot hope to resolve all of a family's problems. However, the clinician can certainly use all the opportunities available to make family members feel an integral and positive part of the therapy process, rather than feel "outsiders" or opponents.

Many clinicians encourage observation of therapy sessions by family members after discussing specific therapy objectives and activities with them. The clinician is careful to point out the precise behaviors that are being modified. This can be a crucial factor if the family member takes a more active role in therapy. A few words of caution are in order, though, when considering observation of therapy sessions by family members. Some family members use a client's behavior or remarks during an observed therapy session as a basis for criticism or reprimand of the client after the session. The clinician must be alert to this possibility, and, if such behavior by the observer is noted, that behavior should be discussed. The parent or family member should be cautioned about the possible negative effects of intruding on the privacy and privileged communication of the therapy session—on either the relationship of the participants or on the self-esteem of the client. Family members can be encouraged to discuss what they have observed with the clinician rather than with the client.

At times, the clinician realizes that certain activities would be beneficial for the client but for one reason or another cannot be accommodated in the therapy sessions. The clinician can recommend learning enrichment activities for children, more opportunities for socialization for both children and adults whose interpersonal contacts are limited, provision for physical activities such as integrating music and movement, and more opportunities for enjoyable interactive experiences for all ages. Family members can be encouraged to provide opportunities for such experiences.

Some family members are willing and able to carry out instructions given by the clinician concerning specific assignments outside the therapy sessions. When this is the case, the clinician must ensure that the family member—in addition to the client, unless the age or condition of the client makes this impossible—is well aware of what behavior is being addressed, the steps that are necessary to change it, and ways to evaluate the client's attempts. The clinician should also explain and demonstrate to the family member behavioral techniques for increasing, decreasing, shaping, and maintaining behaviors, including the appropriate use of positive reinforcers.

Parents of infants can benefit from instruction in such time-honored techniques as *mirroring* an infant's nonverbal behaviors as well as *imitating* any vocalizations made by the infant. Many parents, of course, do hold their child, play with their child, observe the infant closely, and pace their responses appropriately to the infant's early interactive and communicative attempts. Frequently, however, infants with special problems do not engage in this reciprocal behavior. Parents, then, need to be encouraged to continue their attempts at mutual interactions with the young child, with the understanding that they need to be alert to even minimal attempts by the child to initiate or respond to this turn-taking. These strategies are also useful for parents of older, severely impaired children.

When appropriate, reminders to parents of the importance of *self-talk* and *parallel talk* in stimulating verbal response and development can often produce amazing results. As the child's verbal capabilities increase, parents can be instructed in the techniques of *expansion* (in which the parent reframes the child's utterance into a syntactically more adult form) and *extension* (in which the parent acknowledges the child's comment and adds new but related semantic information). It has been our clinical experience that almost all parents can become more aware of and adept at using the above techniques when they realize the importance of such interactions with their children. However, in attempting to increase parent-child interactions and facilitate the child's verbal productions, the clinician needs to be aware of cultural variations in child-rearing, including the importance attached to child language acquisition and use.

Clinicians are utilizing parents as home therapy aides for school children with a variety of problems. Before such a program can be effectively executed, however, the clinician must ascertain that the parent is genuinely willing to help in that capacity, that the parent and child can work well together in the assigned activity, and that the parent and child understand the home procedures to be implemented.

Budd, Madison, Itzkowitz, George, and Price at the University of Nebraska Medical Center (1986) reported on the efficacy of a joint intervention approach in treating children with stuttering problems using the Shames and Florance (1980) stutter-free speech method. The intervention consisted of an intensive one-week treatment clinic for children, their parents, and their school speech pathologists. During the week of instruction, parents were instructed in the therapy approach, participated in observations and demonstrations, and practiced fulfilling therapy contracts with their children under supervision. The subsequent home therapy program entailed provision by the parent of several brief practice sessions each week during which the child implemented one to three contracts while visiting or playing a game with the parent. Both child and parent evaluated the child's performance of the contracts, and the parent rewarded completion of the contracts with agreed-upon positive reinforcers. The home therapy program was carried out in conjunction with continued school speech therapy. On the basis of their research findings, the investigators concluded that having parents act as "co-therapists" was effective.

Friends and relatives of adult clients with communication problems can also play a key role in the therapy process. Not only do they often help the client complete and evaluate homework assignments, but they also provide valuable encouragement and support of the client in his or her rehabilitative efforts. Nevertheless, the first obligation of clinicians is to the client. Consequently, clinicians must be certain to respect any wishes of the client regarding confidentiality of information or the nature and degree of family members' participation in therapy. To do otherwise is to run the risk of losing the client's trust and cooperation.

Whether or not the clinician will encourage a parent or family member to assist the client in specific therapy procedures must be dependent upon the clinician's professional judgment. Not all family members can participate in the therapeutic program to the extent of acting as "adjunct therapy aides." Not all have the capability, inclination, or time to be so actively involved in the therapy program. There is no doubt that, in addition to capability, inclination, and time, there are certain personality characteristics necessary to serve as a family member "therapist." Patience, objectivity, and a sensitivity to the client's frustration level are a few requisite characteristics. Even though family members do not participate directly as adjunct therapists, they can still be assured of the importance of their contribution to the therapy process. The clinician can remind them of other ways (discussed in this chapter) they can demonstrate their encouragement and support of the client.

Family members are often called upon to inform or educate others about the client's communication problem. Because of innate human curiosity, any condition that is out of the ordinary attracts attention. The more severe and visibly apparent the communication problem, the more likely the client is to be exposed to outsiders' inquisitiveness and often negative reactions. Family members find themselves in a position of protecting the client or acting as a "buffer" between the client and the outside world. If they can develop an attitude of pleasant matter-of-factness as they briefly explain the client's condition, family members find these buffer interactions less disagreeable and stressful than if they attack, criticize, or retreat from the curious observer. Often, the clinician can assist in the development of such an attitude, not only by the clinician's own behavior toward the client and family members, but by discussion, and possibly rehearsal, of appropriate responsive behaviors. When family members develop effective ways of dealing with such encounters, they provide models for the client to emulate in his or her own interactions with others.

The presence of a family member whose communication disorder is severe often requires that other family members alter their lifestyles or roles. For example, the parents of a child with a severe disability not only need to relinquish their image of the ideal child and learn to accept the child's imperfections; they also find themselves playing the role of "caretaker" longer than they had envisioned. The spouse of a client who has suffered a stroke must not only take on added responsibilities; the spouse may also find that other dimensions of the marital relationship have changed in significant and often disturbing ways.

Close relatives and friends of a child or adult client with a severe communication disorder may be working their way through the grief process described in Chapter 3. Myra Behmer (1976), the mother of two children with serious health problems, described her feelings as she worked through the stages of grief. She pointed out her feelings of guilt, shame, helplessness, and frustration as she attempted to adjust to the loss of the "perfect children" she had hoped to raise. In adjusting to their children's disabilities, she and her husband found four strategies helpful. The first was *matter-of-factness* about the disabilities (for example, using medical terms in speaking of the children's conditions and discussing the conditions openly within and outside the family). The second was conscious attention to maintaining *a sense of humor*. The third was maintaining *a balanced life*. The fourth was *self-acceptance*, indicating that parents will be better able to care for their disabled children if they accept their own imperfections and weaknesses, yet maintain their dignity. Behmer (1976, p. 37) cautioned parents against allowing the child's disability to overshadow all other aspects of family life and relationships.

> I once read that a child's toy held too close to the eye will block out the view of a mountain. If held too close to the mind's eye, a child's disability can negate the life of the whole family. It is essential to develop perspective toward it.

Speech-language pathologists and audiologists who work in school or preschool settings often find that major contacts with parents occur in connection with Individual Education Plan (IEP) meetings: meetings mandated by law in which parents and school personnel confer about the child's individual education plan. Witt, Miller, McIntyre, and Smith (1984) explored parental satisfaction with IEP meetings. Their research resulted in the following three suggestions for improving parental satisfaction in these meetings:

1. Allow enough time to share ideas.
2. Encourage and facilitate participation by parents by actively seeking their input and then using it in developing their child's educational program.
3. Arrange for contributions by professionals from a variety of disciplines.

The research confirmed the fact that parents are more likely to be supportive of their child's educational program if the parents have been actively involved in developing the program and if they are satisfied with the process by which it was developed.

Professionals working in school districts are often frustrated by the lack of contact with the parents of clients. Robert Fuqua, Susan Hegland, and Shirley Karas (1985) surveyed 185 teachers of preschool handicap classrooms to determine what types of parent contact methods they used and what type they found most satisfying. More than 95 percent of the special educators used the initial IEP conference as a principal parent contact, along with personal notes or letters, phone calls, or invitations to the parent to observe in the classroom. Sixty-five percent of the teachers occasionally used parent volunteers in the classroom, and 70 percent conducted occasional parent group meetings. As is often the case, the teachers indicated that lack of follow-through or commitment on the part of parents was a major problem.

In the study, the special education teachers reported concern about their own lack of skill in communicating professional information to parents and in discussing difficult and sensitive topics and feelings. The teachers also considered the lack of time provided for parent involvement activities to be a major problem area. It is interesting that interactions characterized as more direct, informal, and personal, such as personal notes and casual face-to-face contacts, were not only related to greater teacher satisfaction with parent involvement. They were also associated with teachers' reports of improved communication on the part of both themselves and parents.

In *Learning disabilities and the preschool child*, a statement of the National Joint Committee on Learning Disabilities (1987, p. 37), the ideal role of the family in preschool services to handicapped children is described. Note that the following points made by the committee apply to school services in general as well as to preschool services:

> The family serves as an important source of information about the child's status and needs. Similarly, it is essential that the family understand and help to implement the programmatic goals established for their child. Family members should have access to a range of support services, including the following:
>
> - assistance in recognizing, understanding, and accepting the child's problems;
> - assistance in developing effective ways to manage and facilitate the child's development in the home environment;
> - assistance in program selection; and
> - assistance in locating parent support networks and programs.

Direct family involvement in the preschool program is a major factor in effectiveness. The family has responsibility for the application and generalization of learned skills and adaptive behaviors into the home environment and will consequently require open communication with professionals who provide services to the child. They also need to be included in the development of program policy and advocacy efforts. . . .

Families should be assisted in participating fully in all phases of identification and treatment of a preschool child with specific patterns of deficits. In order to accomplish this, certain needs must be met.

a. Parental participation must be encouraged and welcomed.
b. Parents must be provided with support services that will enable their full and active participation.
c. Efforts must be made to develop parent education materials and programs that explain the child's needs and detail the intervention strategies to be implemented by the family.

As important as it is for clinicians and family members to talk together, it is equally useful for the clinician to provide materials for family members. These may take the form of written materials describing the client's particular condition, suggestions for assisting the client in everyday activities as well as in therapy activities, information regarding community and/or national resources, and any other pertinent materials. Speech-language pathologists and audiologists find it extremely helpful to develop a library of such information that can be made available to family members.

A number of publishing companies have noteworthy materials designed to provide information for family members. For example, *Parent Articles*, edited by Margaret Schrader (1987), is a series of reproducible handouts providing information on speech therapy and speech/language disorders. The handouts answer frequently asked questions and suggest related activities to enhance children's speech and language skills. Lesley Sitkin and Bruce Murdoch (1987) have published a book designed to provide information for relatives and friends of brain-injured patients. The book describes the causes and types of head injury and gives suggestions for relating to the brain-injured family member. There are a number of excellent books containing suggestions for families of developmentally disabled clients of all ages.

Professional and lay magazines are another source of information helpful to families. For instance, in an article addressed particularly to parents of hearing impaired children, but applicable to all families, Char Becker (1987, pp. 27–28) listed the following helpful guidelines for parents when working with their children:

1. Speech training through natural, enjoyable interaction will seem easiest when fitted into today's busy life-styles.
2. When your child tells you something, casually repeat the sentence back to him or her, using correct English or lengthened versions of the statements. Ask your child to repeat occasionally.
3. Integrating speech and listening, language cognitive skills (listing, grouping, labeling), social and academic skills in the course of your child's day will give the child the ability to perform real life skills on his or her own as growth and development progresses.
4. If you're a person who needs organized play, set up a schedule for you and your child, even if it is one activity each day or every other day. Think of ways to incorporate the integrated training into that activity. They can be washing dishes, reading nursery rhymes, or changing doll clothes.
5. If it becomes boring for you, chances are it will also be boring for your child.
6. It is important not to get too focused on one deficit. Look at your child as a whole person. Consider what he or she needs as a whole person, but include the special needs . . . so that your child can participate.
7. Include your . . . child in the details of the family's schedule and activities. This will show your child that he or she is definitely a part of all of the activity. It will also help build vocabulary.
8. The role of the parent as primary caregiver is a big responsibility for giving a good foundation for listening and verbalizing in a young . . . child. Remember to take time for yourself. You will feel better and be a better parent despite the busy schedules with work, school, lessons and housework if you feel good about yourself.

The above examples are a few of many publications on communication problems and related topics suitable for family members. Clinicians who are alert to available materials will assemble a suitable library in a very short time. National and international organizations specializing in particular disabilities (for example Speech Foundation of America, National Head Injury Association, International Association of Laryngectomees, Association for Children and Adults with Learning Disabilities, United Cerebral Palsy Association, American Speech-Language-Hearing Association, Council for Exceptional Children, Alexander Graham Bell Association for the Deaf, and the International Cleft Palate Association) routinely prepare and distribute brochures, pamphlets, and newsletters that provide up-to-date information regarding the disability.

Many school districts, local agencies, and some professionals in private practice have prepared their own brochures for family members. This enables them to target information and suggestions to their particular population and locale. It also enables them to stress considerations that are important in their professional philosophy. One example of a brochure prepared by speech-language pathologists in a school district was developed by DeMoss, Foster, Moore, Sekimoto, and Smith at the Evergreen School District in California (1984). The brochure is given to parents as they register their children for kindergarten and was developed to help parents recognize and develop adequate language skills in their children. The brochure concludes with the following ten suggestions to parents:

1. Talk about things you do.
2. Talk about places you go.
3. Answer questions.
4. Listen to your child.
5. Read and talk about books.
6. Tell stories together.
7. Play games with your child.
8. Play word games together.
9. Pretend with your child.
10. Praise your child.

Although the above reminders may seem simplistic to a professional, you cannot assume that all parents will be aware of or remember how important these interactions with their children can be. Having the reminders in writing highlights suggestions that may or may not be given verbally. Written materials are especially important for limited-English-speaking families. Usually a proficient bilingual family member or friend is available to clarify or translate written materials so that information can be conveyed and misunderstandings avoided.

It should be noted that some current materials available for family members provide information about child/parent rights regarding services. They also instruct parents and caretakers in ways to evaluate the services a child is receiving. One such example is the Project Next Step manual for parents (Tawney, 1983). In it, parents are instructed how to ask questions regarding the IEP process, including development, implementation, and evaluation. Parents are also instructed on how to register complaints, both at the local and national level.

ENCOURAGING ENVIRONMENTAL CHANGE SUPPORTIVE TO THERAPY

Earlier in this chapter we discussed contemporary family patterns, pointing out how the family structure has changed in recent years. These changes affect not only family members, but also the professional's interaction with the family. We cannot assume that there will be family members readily available to follow through on suggestions we make regarding client activities. The single parent, for example, may have to shoulder the entire responsibility for family financial support as well as educational, recreational, and other nurturing demands. It is not practical to request that this individual spend an inordinate amount of time assisting the child in homework assignments and enrichment activities. Sometimes, a clinician conference (by parental permission) with a non-family-member primary caregiver can be extremely helpful to the course of therapy.

Families in which both husband and wife work outside the home may find it almost impossible to devote the time and energy necessary to care for growing children or for an elderly disabled (and often disoriented) parent. Family members in situations such as these may seek the speech-language pathologist's or audiologist's advice in finding appropriate adjunct care for the client. The clinician's role in these cases may be limited to suggestions (preferably in printed form to lessen the clinician's time involved) on how to evaluate child care facilities, preschools, adult day care programs, and skilled nursing facilities, particularly in regard to provisions for language stimulation and interactions.

In these days of electronic child-tending, the clinician may help parents become aware of the value of specific television programs and provide suggestions for ways to interact with their child to take advantage of these programs. Some television programs for children are actually designed as "parent substitutes." For example, Sesame Street and Mr. Rogers' Neighborhood utilize topics that pique children's interests, multisensory approaches in introducing new concepts, and dialogue that is linguistically similar to that used by adults when speaking to young children. Mabel Rice and Patti Haight (1986) analyzed dialogue from these two television shows and found it to be well suited to young viewers. The dialogue had simplified sentence structure, a majority of present tense verbs, a high proportion of utterances about immediately visible topics or referents, a preponderance of narrative about shared immediate events, and frequent repetition of key terms. The activities and dialogue in these programs provide language stimulation for native or foreign-born young viewers. If parents take the time occasionally to watch with the youngster, these programs also provide examples that the parents can utilize in their own interactions with their children. Professionals agree that television cannot replace pleasant, stimulating, live interaction with interested humans. However, judicious television viewing can provide some enriching environmental experiences. Concerning the other end of the age spectrum, the addition of television to the environment of elderly and/or lonely homebound individuals has provided necessary stimulation and structure and has consequently enriched many lives.

Electronic media are facts of life in today's society. Television, video cassette recorders, computers, and electronic games can be the main recreational activities of family members and can occupy a large amount of time. Frequently, these activities are solitary activities and vary in quality and educational potential. It behooves family members to assess and monitor the quality of such experiences and the quantity of time absorbed. Time spent in these activities limits the time available for other pursuits, but you do not always know what activities would replace the electronic ones. In evaluating a client's environment and sometimes recommending changes, you must be aware that many things in the environment are not inherently "good" or "bad." Rather, the issue is the use made of available machines, media, and materials; the extent and quality of interpersonal contacts; and the amount of time devoted to one activity to the detriment of other potentially more enriching activities. You must be aware of the entire constellation of opportunities available to the client when making recommendations.

Speech-language and hearing specialists working to improve the communication abilities of their clients often contribute, either by design or by serendipity, to improved communication within family constellations. Effective clinicians often extend their knowledge of family systems and family communication patterns and the basic principles of family therapy so that their contacts with families will be facilitative rather than counterproductive. It is helpful for professionals to be aware of factors that family therapists consider important to effective family functioning. For example, David Luterman (1987, p. 8) stated that most family therapists in the United States agree that an ideal family would have the following characteristics:

1. *Communication among all members is clear and direct.* In an optimal family there is no hesitation or holding back, no talking around an issue. Comments are always directed to the person for whom they are intended. Talking is efficient and straightforward. Messages are congruent, containing both content and feeling. . . .

2. *Roles and responsibilities are clearly delineated, and the family allows for flexibility in role allocation.* An optimal family must have clear boundaries. There must be a clear intergenerational boundary as well as a sibling boundary. The parents must have clear authority. At the same time, the family must allow flexibility in roles to accommodate change. There must be a basis and structure for negotiation. . . .

3. *The family members accept limits for the resolution of conflict.* Conflict is ever present in families. Healthy families resolve conflict at an individual or family level. They do not avoid or deny conflict. Individual needs are always considered in attempting a resolution of any dispute, and there are face-saving mechanisms, too.

4. *Intimacy is prevalent and is a function of frequent, equal-powered transactions.* One of the basic functions of family is to provide intimacy. Human beings need environments where there is closeness

and caring. An optimal family provides intimacy while also respecting the need for space and distance. Optimal families are cohesive without being enmeshed.

5. *There is a healthy balance between change and the maintenance of stability*. Families must change to accommodate the life cycle and life's vicissitudes, such as having a deaf child, the death of parents, or sometimes social or economic catastrophe. Optimal families are able to make the necessary changes while maintaining stability; the stress of the change is accommodated and the family makes the necessary alterations.

SUMMARY

The professional's interactions with family members usually involve information getting and giving, exploration of feelings (often negative or ambivalent ones), or various aspects of problem solving, including helping to plan and carry out actions that will benefit the client. Just how directly family members will participate in habilitative and rehabilitative procedures will depend upon the personality characteristics of the family members, the nature of their relationships with the client, and the professional judgment of the speech and hearing professional.

In an ideal clinician–family relationship, there is open communication, mutual respect, and cooperation in activities and decisions that will benefit the client. The clinician fosters these characteristics by clear communication of pertinent information, utilizing active listening techniques; seeking participation of crucial family members in setting communication goals and therapy objectives; and assuring family members that they are important, knowledgeable, caring, interested, and influential persons in the client's life. More is certainly gained by this assumption than by the attitude that family members are ignorant, meddlesome, uninformed, uncaring, or unworthy. Even in the worst of circumstances, the clinician can serve as a model of attributes and behaviors that promote not only the client's growth and development, but family effectiveness and happiness as well.

REFERENCES

Becker, C. (1987 November/December). Where do we find the time? *Shhh Journal*, pp. 27–28.

Behmer, M.R. (1976). Coping with our children's disabilities: Some basic principles. *The Exceptional Parent*, 6(2), 35–38.

Beyers, B. (1988, February 2). Man in motion runs down challenges facing the family. In *The Stanford Center for the Study of Families, Children and Youth*. Supplement to the *Stanford Observer*.

Budd, K.S., Madison, L.S., Itzkowitz, J.S., George, C.H., & Price, H.A. (1986). Parents and therapists as allies in behavioral treatment of children's stuttering. *Behavior Therapy, 17*, 538–553.

DeMoss, A., Foster, L., Moore, C., Sekimoto, R., & Smith, E. (1984). *Parents as partners: A guide to oral language development in the pre-school child.* San Jose, CA: Evergreen School District.

Fuqua, R.W., Hegland, S.M., & Karas, S.C. (1985). Processes influencing linkages between preschool handicap classrooms and homes. *Exceptional Children, 51*(4), 307–314.

Grannis, P.D., & Peer, G.G. (1985, Spring). Using transactional analysis with parents of handicapped children. *Teaching Exceptional Children*, pp. 170–174.

Luterman, D. (1987). *Deafness in the family.* Boston: College-Hill Press, Division of Little, Brown & Co.

National Joint Committee on Learning Disabilities. (1987). Learning disabilities and the preschool child. *Asha, 29*(5), 35–38.

O'Neill, G., & O'Neill, N. (1974). *Shifting gears: Finding security in a changing world.* New York: M. Evans and Co., Avon Books.

Rice, M.L., & Haight, P.L. (1986). Motherese of Mr. Rogers: A description of the dialogue of educational television programs. *Journal of Speech and Hearing Disorders, 51*, 282–287.

Roos, P. (1985). Parents of mentally retarded children: Misunderstood and mistreated. In H.R. Turnbull, III & A.P. Turnbull (Eds.), *Parents speak out: Then and now* (pp. 245–257). Columbus, OH: Charles E. Merrill Publishing Co.

Schrader, M. (Ed.). (1987). *Parent articles.* Tucson, AZ: Communication Skill Builders.

Schulz, J.B. (1985). The parent-professional conflict. In H.R. Turnbull, III & A.P. Turnbull (Eds.), *Parents speak out: Then and now* (pp. 3–9). Columbus, OH: Charles E. Merrill Publishing Co.

Shames, G.H., & Florance, C.L. (1980). *Stutter-free speech: A goal for therapy.* Columbus, OH: Charles E. Merrill Publishing Co.

Sitkin, L.A., & Murdoch, B.E. (1987). *Brain injury and the family: An aid to better understanding.* Concord, CA: Simmons & Hall Publishing.

Tawney, J.W. (1983). *Analyzing the instructional process: A manual for parents.* University Park, PA: Project Next Step, The Pennsylvania State University.

U.S. News & World Report. (1986, October 27). Children Under Stress, pp. 58–63.

Witt, J.C., Miller, C.D., McIntyre, R.M., & Smith, D. (1984). Effects of variables on parental perceptions of staffings. *Exceptional Children, 51*(1), 27–32.

6

Understanding and Working with Groups

Specialists in the field of communicative disorders may find themselves working in a variety of group situations. Seven types come quickly to mind.

1. groups of clients—typically with similar problems or common therapy objectives
2. groups of family members of clients with communicative disorders
3. groups composed of professionals from various disciplines, such as a cleft palate panel or other diagnostic team
4. groups composed of professionals and a client and family members meeting together to plan a client's educational program or an appropriate educational or agency placement
5. continuing education or college classes in which the professional may be either student or instructor
6. committees functioning as part of professional or other organizations of which the clinician is a member
7. other groups in which the clinician is interested and takes part; for example, as a community service or as a recreational activity

This chapter will focus on the dynamics of group process and on aspects of group membership and leadership.

IMPORTANCE OF GROUP PROCESS TRAINING TO THE PROFESSIONAL

Professional enjoyment and success depends as much on being comfortable in the group setting as it does on being comfortable in the individual approach to therapy. Some professionals much prefer individual therapy and consequently do not make an effort to form and lead groups. As one clinician said "I don't know anything about group work so I steer clear of getting involved in groups." Another stated, "I sometimes have groups of aphasic clients or laryngectomized clients, but I find that I still pretty much do one-on-one therapy even in the group setting."

Other clinicians are comfortable and effective in the group setting. They find that appropriate group activities can be time-saving for the professional; stimulating, interesting, and economical for the client; informative and supportive for family members; and, most importantly, at times can have a more positive therapeutic effect than individual therapy or counseling.

Many professionals find that therapy conducted in group settings for selected clients can speed the accomplishment of therapeutic goals. After all, communication is a social function and, for most people, communication with more than one person typifies the daily routine. The clinician/client relationship, in which the clinician is trained to respond to the most distorted speech sounds and the slightest attempts at interpersonal communication, is a relatively unnatural one compared to the give-and-take of more ordinary conversation. In working with young children with delayed language development, for example, participation in a small group for therapy can be every bit as important to the progress of the youngster as individual sessions.

As well-trained and experienced as a clinician may be, it is unlikely that he or she has experienced personally the effects of particular communicative disorders upon one's life experiences. The opportunity for a laryngectomized client, or a dysfluent client, or a brain-injured client to share experiences with other similarly affected clients and to work together with them to accomplish common goals can be an important adjunct to private therapy. Similarly, the opportunity for family members of communicatively disordered individuals to meet together to discuss common problems and possible solutions, and to acknowledge deep-seated emotions in an accepting atmosphere, can provide needed education, expression, and encouragement.

Many professionals do not incorporate group work into their therapy activities because, as mentioned above, they feel untrained or uncomfortable. Many others, though, have found it worthwhile and rewarding to make the effort. Often the effort begins with the scheduling of some simple, "one-shot" activities (sometimes referred to as "one-session groups"). For instance, the clinician may schedule a guest speaker on language development for an evening session to which the parents of selected child clients are invited. An audiologist may invite a number of clients for whom hearing aids have been recommended to a special session on "trouble shooting" for hearing aid users.

After a few successful one-session group activities, the professional may be encouraged to attempt more ambitious group projects: perhaps a series of four one-night-a-week sessions on language facilitation for parents of severely language delayed clients; or a series of eight classes on "Improving Your English Pronunciation" for bilingual clients. As in all aspects of professional development, you need to learn basic principles and then apply those principles in actual situations. Learning the basic principles of group process and group participation and leadership has the added advantage of improving not only your effectiveness in therapy but your satisfaction in all types of group settings.

BASIC PRINCIPLES OF GROUP PROCESS AND PARTICIPATION

Technically, two or more people interdependent upon one another in some fashion can be called a group. However, for purposes of this discussion, we will consider a *group* to be composed of three or more people, to differentiate it from the *dyadic* (two person) clinician/client relationship. Much of what has been said thus far regarding working with individual clients can also apply to group work. Both types of sessions can involve work to accomplish goals and objectives. In addition to activities designed to further therapy goals, both individual and group sessions can include information getting, information giving, expression and exploration of feelings, problem solving, or planning for future action. Both can serve to meet basic social needs, motivate change, and provide morale-building and support in times of difficulty and discouragement. In either setting, the personality and skill of the clinician will be vital to the successful achievement of the desired goals.

The principles you learned in Chapter 2 about basic needs, organismic variables, and dimensions of interaction all apply to members of groups as well as dyads. Groups are, after all, composed of individuals. The physical and emotional states and needs of each person in a group—his or her defense mechanisms, coping strategies, communicative styles, and so forth—will affect the behavior and thus the atmosphere of the group and the direction the group may follow.

Whether you are communicating in a one-to-one relationship or in a group setting, messages are being sent through verbal and nonverbal channels. Being alert and responsive to both types of communication can become more difficult as the number of participants to observe increases. Moreover, as the size of the group grows, each additional member increases the complexity of interactions. This multiplies the possible subunits into which the participants may combine. There are also more triggers of interpersonal reflexes, and more possibilities for splits, alignments, scapegoating, and power struggles within the group. Perhaps that is one reason why some professionals are uncomfortable in group sessions, or why some prefer co-leaders for a fairly large group.

Types of Groups

Groups can be classified in a variety of ways. One way is by the purpose they are primarily organized to serve. We pointed out seven of those types at the beginning of this chapter. Another way is by identification of a common characteristic of the group membership (for example, graduate students in speech-language pathology, or youngsters living in a particular neighborhood).

Another classification of groups is that of *formal* or *informal*. Examples of *formal* groups are boards; standing committees; task forces; project groups; management teams; and local, state, and national governing groups and legislatures. Formal groups usually have regularly scheduled meetings, a clearly defined membership, assigned leadership roles, recorded agendas and minutes, and tasks or projects to which members devote their time and energies.

Informal groups are composed of individuals who come together in an impromptu fashion to talk over problems and issues or who are temporarily drawn together because of an immediate interest or task. Often, in an informal group, it is not possible to identify a fixed or assigned leadership. The roles people play within the group may vary depending on what is being discussed and the personalities of the people who happen to comprise the group. People do not depend upon any one person to direct the proceedings or to grant permission to speak, and there is no precise system of rules to govern procedures. Informal groups meet as needed, not as prescheduled, and participants may vary in number and identity from meeting to meeting.

Ernest Stech and Sharon Ratliffe (1985) depicted the differences between formal and informal group functioning as found in Table 6-1.

Many effective groups combine some formal and some informal characteristics. The relative proportion of formal to informal characteristics will indicate the

Table 6-1 Formal and Informal Group Functioning

Formal Group	Informal Group
Persons have titles and positions; there is a designated leader.	Roles emerge and shift; there is no designated leader.
There are written rules and procedures.	There is improvised and casual conversation.
New members receive specific training or indoctrination.	What informal training there is occurs in the course of group meetings.
There are written agendas and minutes.	Members sometimes take notes; people often rely on memory.
Meetings are scheduled.	Meetings occur as needed or as people are available.
Members are specialists.	Members are generalists.
Decision making occurs by voting or referral to a higher authority.	Decision making occurs by consensus.

Source: From *Effective Group Communication* (p. 65) by E. Stech and S.A. Ratliffe, 1985, Lincolnwood, IL: National Textbook Company. Copyright 1985 by National Textbook Company. Reprinted by permission.

degree of formality of the group and its functioning. The degree of formality that will be effective for any particular group depends upon a number of factors, including group size, primary purpose, and the personal characteristics of the group's members and leaders.

Stech and Ratliffe subscribe to what they call a "contingency" or situational view of group work. They state that the way a group functions is best determined by its: (1) *mission*—the goal or purpose of the group, (2) *environment*—the community or organization in which the group functions, and (3) *members*—the needs and expectations of the group participants.

Differences in group formality and functioning will depend on variations in these contingency factors. Discomfort or frustration can result if some members of the group expect a more formal group structure and functioning than other members, or if the group's members and its leader or leaders have differing expectations. Group members may take offense at the idea of a serious task being performed in an informal, casual manner. Some clinicians will be more comfortable and effective in a formal group setting, while others will much prefer an informal group session or discussion. You probably have definite preferences in this regard, particularly in settings in which you play a leadership role.

Combs, Avila, and Purkey (1978) reported that people in helping professions often participate in four different types of groups: (1) *conversation groups*, characterized by casual interaction of members in a social manner; (2) *instruction groups*, designed to show or tell participants something; (3) *decision groups*, formed to arrive at a decision or consensus on some matter; and (4) *discovery groups*, designed to aid participants in gaining new insights into their own behavior and their relationships with others.

Michael Argyle (1978) discussed several different kinds of small social groups including families, work-teams, committees, groups of friends, and social clubs. He pointed out that people may form or join a group primarily to carry out a task, play a game or pursue some other leisure activities, or to interact with the other people whom they like. Argyle stated that all groups have two sides to them, though the balance varies: task and sociable motivations and activities. Even in groups you form in your professional therapy setting, some members may relish social interactions with other group members more than the completion of therapy objectives. In any group, there will be alternation between concern with a group task and concern with interpersonal problems. Argyle pointed out that it usually takes some time for a group to arrive at a pattern of interaction that is relatively acceptable to all participants. In fact, ongoing groups actually go through stages of development.

Stages of Group Development

It is important for professionals to understand some of the functions that groups serve and some ways in which groups differ. It is also important to understand that ongoing groups evolve or develop in stages, all of which seem to be necessary to the ultimate effective functioning of the group. Bruce Tuckman (1965) reviewed research data on group process and concluded that a group ordinarily moves through four stages in its development: (1) *forming,* (2) *storming,* (3) *norming,* and (4) *performing.*

In the *forming* stage, group members become acquainted with one another, assess the qualities and characteristics of other group members and of the group leader, recognize the problems or tasks confronting the group, and decide whether their membership in the group should continue. In the *storming* phase, there tends to be jockeying for positions of power on the part of members and conflict and disagreement over how the group should function and what the group should do. There may also be discontent or disagreement with the leadership of the group.

In the *norming* stage of development, the group begins to develop rules of operation and methods of proceeding with its appointed tasks. It is at this stage that members begin to feel allegiance to the group, and the group itself begins to be a cohesive unit. When a group reaches the *performing* stage, the attention of the members is to the tasks at hand and the achievement of the group's goals.

Some groups are temporary, short-term assemblings of participants for a specific purpose, called together by one or two persons who assume leadership of the group and direct its form and task. The "one-shot" group sessions described earlier in this chapter are examples of this type. In such instances, the group is already "formed" by invitation; little opportunity is given for "storming"; the session is "normed" by the ways in which the leader structures the session at its beginning; and the stated task of the meeting is "performed" with dispatch. In other groups less limited in time and task, the evolution of the group through the described stages will be more apparent. Tuckman indicated that if a group is pressured to "perform" right after it is formed, rather than having time to evolve through the storming and norming phases, its performance may be ineffective and unsatisfactory.

Lawrence Shulman (1979, pp. 257–258) summarized the evolution of a group as follows:

> The group must go through a developmental process just as any other growing entity. Early tasks include problems of formation and the satisfaction of individual members' needs. Problems of dealing with the worker as a symbol of authority (authority theme) must be faced, as well as the difficulties involved in peer-group relationships (the intimacy theme). Attention needs to be paid to the culture of the group so that norms which are consistent with the achievement of the group's goals are developed. Taboos which block the group must be challenged and mastered if the discussion is to be meaningful. Finally, a formal or informal structure must be developed. This structure will include

assigned roles, assigned status, communication patterns, and a decision-making process. Effective work in the group will develop a sense of cohesion which in turn will strengthen future work.

Characteristics of Group Members

As a group evolves through its developmental stages, members begin to demonstrate their individual characteristics and begin to fill some particular roles in the group. Professionals who have had considerable experience with groups agree that various types of group members can be identified. They also agree that some of the roles members play enhance a group's functioning while some hinder progress.

Over the years, investigators of group processes (for example, Benne and Sheats (1948); Bales (1950, 1970); Lewin (1958); Satir (1972, 1983); Bates, Johnson, and Blaker (1982); and Napier and Gershenfeld (1985)) have described a variety of roles that individual members of a group may play. Some of these roles are necessary to keep the group functioning and enable it to serve its purposes and accomplish its tasks. For instance, in order to accomplish group tasks, one or more group members may serve as an *initiator* who proposes new ideas, methods, or directions for use by the group. Another member may function more as an *elaborator*, who expands on others' suggestions and develops them in a meaningful fashion.

Another role played by a group member may be *coordinator*, a person who can listen to a number of suggestions or ideas from several group members, clarify them, and pull them together into a workable plan. Another role for a group member is *evaluator*, a person who serves to critically judge the feasibility and/or merit of proposals or plans. A group that has been in existence for a relatively long time usually has at least one member who fills the role of *historian*, someone who reports on what was done and what succeeded or failed in the past.

When it comes to maintaining the existence of a group, other roles also emerge that individual members tend to fill. One of these is the *gatekeeper*, the person most likely to control the entrance and/or acceptance of new people into the group. Other group maintenance roles are sometimes designated as the *encourager*, who positively reinforces group participation and discussion by acceptance and verbal and nonverbal approval; the *compromiser*, who tries to suggest an idea or action that disagreeing members can accept; the *harmonizer*, who tries to settle conflicts and disagreements between group members by reducing or relieving tense situations; and the *humorist*, who keeps the group from becoming overly serious or intense by lightening the situation periodically and providing comic relief.

In addition to these functional roles for group maintenance and task completion that any group member, including the leader, may play at one time or another, investigators have also described individual personality characteristics that are likely to characterize particular group members and appear consistently in their interactions with other members of the group. Four roles involving personal, individualistic functions were described by Benne and Sheats in 1948 and can still be observed in today's groups. Benne and Sheats (1948) pointed out that these roles tend to serve individual members' own needs rather than group needs. One of the roles is termed the *aggressor*, who consistently acts in a hostile, negative fashion by attacking and deprecating other group members and/or their contributions. The *dominator* tries to be in control of the group and its activities by asserting authority, manipulating others, and often monopolizing discussion. Two other familiar group figures are the *help-seeker*, who uses group time to gain sympathy and advice for purely personal problems, and the *recognition-seeker*, whose major efforts in the group setting are to call attention to his or her own activities and accomplishments even though they are unrelated to the group's agenda or goals.

Virginia Satir, the well-known family therapist, described (1972) four characteristic types of responses group members often exhibit to defend themselves against the threat of rejection by other members of the group. She described these response types as *placating, blaming, computing,* and *distracting.* In a family situation or other group setting in which an individual feels threatened, he or she tends to use one of these response types fairly consistently.

The *placater* talks in an ingratiating, subservient manner, anxious to please, and never disagreeing. The *blamer* acts as though "the best defense is a good offense" and seems to go out of his or her way to be as offensive as possible. The blamer acts superior to other group members, is dictatorial and "bossy," finds fault with others and their ideas, and often talks in loud, accusatory tones. The *computer* talks in a "cool, calm, and collected" fashion, without a trace of emotion, very restrained and often tight-jawed, discussing any problem or situation in a purely intellectual fashion. The group member playing the role of *distracter* makes remarks that are completely off the subject, or uses the topic of group discussion only as a starting place, going further and further afield through irrelevant comments and inappropriate behavior.

If you have worked with families as well as other groups, you can no doubt recall examples of these various types of group participants. They constitute real challenges to a group leader or facilitator who is trying to promote the use of what Virginia Satir called *leveling*, in which communication is direct, truthful, wholehearted, and congruent (that is, both verbal and nonverbal behavior send the same message), and represents the honest effort of the participant to address the situation at hand without concern for acceptance or esteem.

It must be noted that the roles and characteristics described above are encouraged or discouraged by other group members as well as by the leader or facilitator of the group. Organismic variables, including experience and conditioning, will determine habitual behavior patterns that become evident in the group setting. "Rewards" and "punishments" meted out by current group members, including the group leader, in response to an individual's behavior will affect whether particular behavior increases or decreases. However, personal needs may be so pressing that group reinforcement may not be effective.

Sampson and Marthas (1977, pp. 149–150) stressed the importance of ongoing group interactions in creating social reality, attaching meaning or significance to the behavior of a group member, enabling a group member to establish and maintain an individual identity, and enabling other participants to confirm or deny that individual identity. Long-time association in a particular group (for example, one's family) will provide ongoing interactions that will have profound effects upon the identities, realities, and philosophies that a person develops. The authors term this viewpoint the *symbolic interactionist view*. They state that

> The essential feature of the symbolic interactionist analysis of group process is its emphasis on the role that ongoing interaction plays in creating social reality: i.e., in creating meanings and identities. To use this model, it is necessary to examine the here-and-now interaction between persons and to see that interaction as providing identities to the participants. Thus, it is vital to pay attention to one's role as a participant in the process whereby identities are being formed. In a sense, there is no such thing as pure observation; people actively influence what they are observing. Our presence and reactions to others play a critical role in influencing the identity they come to have.

As a group evolves and members begin to demonstrate their individual characteristics and assume specific roles, an observer can describe group participants on several interpersonal dimensions. Several dimensions of interpersonal behavior were discussed in Chapter 2. Bales (1981) commented that most group members characterize and describe other group members along three dimensions: (1) dominance versus submissiveness, (2) friendliness versus unfriendliness, and (3) work-acceptance versus work-resistance. Imagine yourself describing some members of a group to which you currently belong. Do these dimensions enter into your characterization of a group member? Perhaps you may also find yourself describing members in terms of the role or roles they usually play in the group, now that we have discussed those roles in some detail.

People join a group for a variety of reasons:

- to learn something
- to meet new people
- to get help for a problem that is interfering with effective functioning

- to satisfy the need for support, belonging, or human fellowship
- to have increased opportunity to express opinions and beliefs
- to combine strength and resources with others in working toward a common goal or defeating a common enemy

Group membership entails possible gains—support, self-improvement, acceptance, esteem; but also possible losses (of power, certainty, approval, or self-image). Consequently, group membership can be anxiety-producing and stressful as well as satisfying and rewarding. However, since human beings are social creatures, we find ourselves drawn to group participation more often than not.

What obligations do members owe to a group in order to have it function effectively? The two most important obligations are probably *active listening* (as discussed in Chapter 4) and *honest expression of ideas and feelings* (identified as *leveling* earlier in this chapter). Martin Lakin (1972, p. 7) listed a number of requisites for persons participating in experiential or discovery groups (groups designed to foster emotional expressiveness, insight, and personal growth in their members). He stated that such groups require the member to

1. Contribute to the shaping and coherence of the group;
2. Invest in it emotionally;
3. Help move it toward a goal;
4. Help establish its norms, and obey them;
5. Take on some specific role or function;
6. Help establish a viable level of open communication;
7. Help establish a desired level of intimacy;
8. Make contributions relevant to others;
9. Make a place for each person;
10. Acknowledge the group's significance.

Having discussed group process and group membership, let us now consider the professional's role in group leadership.

CHARACTERISTICS OF AN EFFECTIVE GROUP LEADER

Probably no single definition of an effective leader will encompass all aspects of leadership and please everyone who has belonged to groups. People asked to contribute to such a definition make comments as follows:

- "Someone I can look up to."
- "A person who gets the job done."

- "Someone who inspires people to work together toward a common goal."
- "A person who can take over in an emergency and tell other people what to do."
- "Someone who can take a bunch of people and get them to agree to do what he or she wants done."
- "The person with the most power."
- "A person who is willing to take responsibility—not only for his own actions but for other people's as well."
- "A leader has to be able to get people to stop arguing and start working."

From the above statements, we may extract some characteristics of effective leadership. The effective leader has power over others, has the respect of others, is listened to by others, can persuade others to do his or her will, and can direct others in the performance of a prescribed task. In any group, there may be several people who could qualify as a leader under this definition. One of those may be the appointed or elected head of the group; others may be members of the group who happen to possess natural or acquired leadership abilities.

Marilyn Bates, Clarence Johnson, and Kenneth Blaker (1982) stated that four important roles of a group leader are as (1) *traffic director*, alerting group members to behaviors that facilitate or inhibit communication, intervening when necessary to keep the group functioning according to its established purposes and "norms"; (2) *model*, relating to other group members, communicating, and approaching problems and situations in such a way as to provide appropriate behavioral examples for others to follow; (3) *interaction catalyst*, using techniques to get the group moving at the start of a session and to get individual members participating in the group process; and (4) *communication facilitator*, using counseling techniques, in addition to those needed in the above roles, to increase the degree and depth of each member's participation and individual growth by providing feedback for group discussion and encouraging insights into individual and group behavior. These counseling techniques may include restatement of content, reflection of feeling, and other active listening skills designed to help group members check their perceptions of others and understand their behavior. The techniques might also include helping group members to reduce their fear of self-disclosure or to resolve incongruence in their verbal and nonverbal communication.

As a communicative disorders specialist, it is unlikely that you will be leading groups in which superior physical power is one of the requisites of leadership. It is probable that some of your leadership will be the result of established professional authority and skill acknowledged by other group members. In the groups for which you are responsible, respect for all group members, acceptance and encouragement of their individuality, acknowledgement and encouragement of their positive contributions to the group's functioning, and lack of defensiveness or secretiveness on your part will be important factors in the successful continuation of the group.

Your preferred leadership style depends on a number of factors. Perhaps the most important is your fundamental opinion of people and what causes them to behave as they do. If, for instance, you believe that most people prefer to be told what to do rather than take responsibility for their own actions and direction, you will tend to be more *autocratic* in leadership style. If, on the other hand, you believe that most people are capable of governing their own behavior and are capable of changing their behavior if they see that change is to their advantage, you will tend to be more *democratic* in leadership style. If you have no real interest in leadership nor in working with other people toward a particular group goal, yet you become designated as a group's leader, you may employ a *laissez-faire* style (from a French term meaning "to allow to happen," implying that the group will develop and function on its own without active leadership).

A professional's leadership style with individual clients may lead to different results in group settings and, therefore, may require modification. Some clinicians who use a low-key, collaborative approach in individual therapy may find that, if they apply this approach to a group, the group may flounder for lack of direction or be monopolized by one or two "dominators" or "recognition seekers." On the other hand, a clinician with a strong authoritarian style may inadvertently suppress responses of group members that could be helpful and meaningful.

Speech-language pathologists and audiologists, then, will find it necessary to employ varying degrees of directiveness or authoritarianism depending on the nature of the group they are leading. For example, a group of laryngectomized clients meeting together to improve their communicative abilities may need clear direction to accomplish specific therapy objectives, thus necessitating an authoritarian approach. The professional conducting a group session with head-injured clients may deliberately choose to employ a laissez-faire style, if the therapy goal is to have the clients plan a group outing and make all the necessary arrangements. A democratic style is often the leadership style of choice when working with a transdisciplinary team where all members are experts in their own fields. It is important to realize that no one leadership style is inherently better or more praiseworthy than another. It is the ability to choose and use the most effective style for a particular group and purpose that marks a skilled leader.

Rudolph Verderber (1978) defined group leadership as *exerting influence* and *getting things done*. He listed (pp. 207–208) the following principles for aspiring leaders:

1. Think carefully about group expectations.
2. As a potential leader, you must have knowledge related to the particular group tasks.

3. Closely related to point 2, be prepared to work harder than anyone else in the group.
4. A leader must be willing to be decisive at key moments in the discussion.
5. The leader must be personally committed to the group goals and needs.
6. A person who wishes to be leader must interact freely.
7. The person who wishes to be leader must develop skill at maintenance functions as well as at task functions.

Verderber also discussed the responsibilities of leaders of work-groups—those in which the members are working toward a common goal. The specifics he included can be summarized as follows:

- Establish an appropriate "climate" by attention to the physical setting and seating arrangement.
- Plan an appropriate and workable agenda.
- Introduce the topic.
- Direct the flow of discussion.
- Keep the interaction balanced.
- Brainstorm when needed.
- Summarize frequently.
- Maintain necessary control.
- Close the discussion effectively.

Every effective session, whether dyadic or group, has three essential phases: a beginning, a middle (or body), and a closing. The leader has certain responsibilities in each of these phases. Suggestions for the group leader regarding the opening minutes of a session are as follows:

- Make the group members comfortable and at ease.
- Make sure the group members know one another, if the size of the group makes that possible.
- Alert the group members to any time limitations or procedural restrictions.
- Establish a working relationship with the group members.
- Structure an atmosphere that will facilitate the type of group session desired.
- Orient the group members to the objectives for the session.

The leader's personal objectives for the main portion or body of the session are to maintain effective interaction among the participants and to work toward the achievement of the goals of the session. Suggestions for attaining these objectives include

- Listen to group members attentively as they speak, and encourage other participants to do the same.
- Check understanding of group members' comments by restating content when appropriate.
- Be alert to expressions of positive, negative, or ambivalent feelings expressed either verbally or nonverbally by group members.
- Verbally reflect feelings expressed by group members when appropriate.
- Make certain that restatements of content and reflections of feelings actually further the purpose of the session.
- Be aware of the purposes of silence and of the fact that often if the leader is silent, other members will contribute.
- Encourage participation by all group members without pressuring anyone unduly to "perform."
- Provide sufficient time for group members to participate, but keep unproductive digression to a minimum.
- Keep the session moving in the appropriate direction to achieve the desired goal.
- Remember that positive reinforcement of behaviors will encourage continuation of those behaviors.
- Be alert to dimensions of interaction and how they affect each member's participation.
- Provide a model of the "leveling" style of communication.

The closing few minutes of any session are special. All participants need a feeling of closure: a feeling that the purposes of the session have been achieved. To bring the session to a satisfying close, the leader may utilize the following guidelines:

- Allow enough time to end the session so that there is not an abrupt cut-off.
- At an appropriate point in the session, alert the group members to the time remaining, and suggest what should be accomplished in that time.
- Summarize important points or highlights of the session.
- Request evaluation of the session by the participants.

- Plan what will take place at the next session and/or in the period of time before the next session.
- Close the session on a pleasant, upbeat note, allowing a few moments for small talk among the participants as they leave.

If the leader doesn't allow time for the closing phase of a group session, participants are likely to feel a sense of frustration. They may even engage in "closing" activities after the session has officially ended. If the leader is on a tight time schedule, he or she may have a difficult time breaking away from group members who feel the need for a more satisfying closure. It is preferable, then, to include closing activities in the allotted time period.

It is often the professional's responsibility to determine the size of the group with whom he or she will work. Just as no one leadership style is appropriate for all groups, there is no one preferred group size. The purpose of the group, the nature of its activities, and the skill and experience of the group's leader or co-leaders will all play a part in determining its most effective size.

Speech-language therapists employed in the public school system often find that working with groups of three or four youngsters with similar therapy goals is the most efficient way of handling a large caseload. In other settings, clients with similar problems may participate in group sessions involving 10 to 20 clients for general orientation and instruction and then be assigned to smaller groups for application and practice of new skills. One-session parent education groups may be planned to accommodate as many parents as will turn out for an evening meeting. For a series of parent discussion group meetings, six to ten members are often ideal; there are enough participants to provide a variety of opinions and experiences for discussion, but not so many that there is a chance that someone will not be heard. If the professional is often called upon to speak to large audiences, conduct in-service sessions, or teach college classes, training and experience in public speaking can help to make him or her comfortable and effective in these larger group settings. Some suggestions for making public presentations are given in Chapter 9.

Experience has shown that some situations typically occur in working with groups. Many leaders have had the experience of a group member monopolizing the discussion. If other group members do not raise objections to this, it is important that the group leader gently but firmly acknowledge the person's contribution but indicate that other members must also be heard. ("You've made some interesting points, Tom. Now let's hear what others have to say. Jane, it looked as though you had a comment you wanted to make.") If there is no change, and the individual continues to monopolize, the group leader may need to confront the person more forcefully. ("Tom, I'm concerned that you're doing so much talking that others aren't having a chance to say anything." or "Does anyone else have a comment about this? We don't want to have one person monopolize our discussion time.'') Comments should not be disrespectful or embarrassing; they should point out the monopolizing behavior while allowing the individual to maintain his or her dignity.

In direct contrast to the problem of the group monopolizer is that of the nonparticipator. It is important to realize that people may not participate in a discussion for a variety of reasons.

- They may feel unable to contribute anything important or worthwhile on the topic being discussed.
- They may feel uncomfortable speaking out before a group.
- They may feel their comments might be ridiculed, particularly if they have speech or language problems or if the language being used is not their native language.
- They may fear that expressed ideas or feelings might cause them to be unacceptable to the group.
- They may be naturally more observing and reflective than outgoing and verbal.
- They may be accustomed to playing a passive role in other groups and not be motivated to change habitual behavior.

It is important that the group leader encourage the nonparticipant to contribute to discussions, but it is equally important that the person not feel pressured. (''We've heard a number of ideas now. Dick, do you have any reactions? We'd certainly like to hear your opinion.'' or ''Mary, when you and I were talking the other day, you mentioned your experience with your son Keith at the grocery store. I think the other parents would find that interesting. Will you share it with us?'')

Experienced professionals can cite many other problem situations that can occur in the group setting: one member may be consistently negative and/or unpleasant; antagonism may develop between two members of the group and be overtly expressed; group members may use one member as a ''scapegoat''; or a real power struggle may erupt among group members. Time does not permit us to discuss each of these problems individually, but we can share a general principle of operation that has evolved from long experience with groups: when you sense a problem, ''level'' with the group members. Acknowledge your feelings that a problem exists and what you think the problem is. At times, this leveling will occur with a particular member in private. (''Jim, I sense that you were unhappy with the way I conducted the meeting today. I'd appreciate your input and suggestions.'' or ''Jane, I notice that you find it very difficult to work with Ellen in our group. Is there anything I should know about or any way I can help?'') At other times, you will level to the entire group about your feelings. (''I feel stymied. I'm not sure what our next move should be. I need some suggestions." or "It seems to me we are talking too much about what hasn't worked in the past. I think our time could be better spent in brainstorming new ways of dealing with the problem.") An advantage to group work is that one person does not have to provide all the answers. However, if you need the group's resources, there are times when you have to expressly ask for them.

THERAPY GROUPS FOR CLIENTS WITH SPECIFIC DISORDERS

Many speech-language pathologists and audiologists are currently working effectively with groups composed of clients with particular communicative disorders. Group therapy is often used with head-injured, aphasic, dysfluent, laryngectomized, hearing-impaired, and speech- and language-delayed clients. At times, group therapy is used as an adjunct to individual therapy. For example, a client may have an individual therapy session once or twice a week and also attend a once-a-week group session. In this way, the client receives specific instructions and practice regarding his or her particular problem, and also has the opportunity to practice newly emerging behaviors in a more natural communicative setting. The support and encouragement from group members as well as the stimulation of group interactions can be important components of the therapy process.

In these days of limited funds allocated for rehabilitation, many clients find that they are financially able to pay for group sessions when they, or their insurance coverage, can no longer pay for individual therapy. Many clients thus can continue to work on therapy goals and make significant further progress via group therapy.

Experience working with a variety of therapy groups leads to the following suggestions for working with clients with specific communicative problems.

Groups for Traumatically Head-Injured Clients

An important consideration in working with clients who have sustained traumatic head injury is the relatively young age of many of them. The increased incidence of motorcycle/automobile accidents and of assault—coupled with medical advances that save lives that would otherwise be lost—make this a growing population. The needs of many clients in this population that can be addressed in group therapy are related to vocational and social communicative skills. The clinician may provide specific therapy activities designed to improve listening and observation skills, problem-solving abilities, ability to maintain discussion topics, and strategies to compensate for cognitive impairment. In many cases, group therapy sessions are structured similarly to club meetings, at which members plan social events that will then be held. In the course of making and executing plans, the clients must practice a variety of skills that are necessary in their daily lives.

Some groups plan events such as lunches or picnics, or conduct fundraisers for service projects or future social events. Other groups focus on vocational needs and training. Guest speakers representing a variety of disciplines may be invited to meet with the group, either to talk about job possibilities or to answer questions the group has prepared on a particular topic. One of the authors of this book was invited to speak on "the brain" by a group of head-injured clients. Their prepared list of questions relating to their particular problems generated considerable discussion: "Why can't I remember as well as I used to?"; "Why do I get so mad all the time?"; "My trouble is in my brain stem; what does that mean?"

In some therapy settings, group members participate in activities conducted in a computer center and learn to use computers and a variety of software programs. There is a wealth of software that can be used in cognitive rehabilitation. If a clinician is in a setting where computers can be made available, he or she should make establishing a library of appropriate software a high priority. Even though the clients will often work individually at a computer and at their own pace, the camaraderie of the center provides needed social interaction.

The characteristic that strikes one the most in working with groups of traumatically head-injured clients is the multiplicity of their problems and the complete disruption of their former lifestyles. These problems not only affect the clients but have severe impact on family members and friends. The therapy group often provides a haven where clients can relax and interact with peers on a more equal basis and in a supportive environment. It is important to keep this in mind when planning group activities. It is also important for the group leader to realize that head-injured clients will manifest a variety of emotional problems either caused or exacerbated by the trauma. The clinician must use professional judgment as to when to ignore and when to acknowledge or attempt to change emotionally related behaviors.

Groups for Aphasic Clients

In contrast to traumatically head-injured clients, individuals who suffer from aphasia due to other causes are likely to be older. Because of this age difference, the needs of clients with aphasia may be less related to vocational and educational goals. However, the basic human needs, including the need for security, love, respect, and self-actualization, still need to be met as does the need to communicate with others. The client has usually established a fairly settled lifestyle prior to the cerebrovascular accident. Because of the nature of the lifestyle and the communication problems, the client with aphasia may be more apt to retain aspects of his or her former lifestyle to a higher degree than the traumatically head-injured client. The aphasic client is not as likely to find the therapy group a "home away from home" to the extent that the traumatically head-injured client does. The group provides support and socialization, but the client is more likely to attend for the sole purpose of improving his or her language skills.

One characteristic often noted in aphasia therapy groups is that the clinician tends to work with each client on a one-to-one basis even in the group setting. Special efforts have to be made to encourage the clients to interact with one another. Cooperative and team activities can be developed to achieve therapy objectives. Since the levels of ability may differ among the clients, the more highly functioning members of the group can provide leadership and language strategy models for the more severely impaired. The clinician needs to be aware of the different levels of functioning of each group member and plan group activities that encourage and enable each person to participate.

Groups for Dysfluent Clients

Adults enrolled in therapy for dysfluency problems are usually a relatively young age. As adults, their communication problem is essentially a speech problem rather than a language problem. In contrast to therapy with traumatically head-injured or aphasic clients, cognitive rehabilitation in a narrowly defined sense is not an aspect of group therapy with stutterers.

Most clinicians favor a particular therapy approach for dysfluency. In methods focusing upon symptom modification or fluency enhancement, the clinician often works individually with clients in the early stages of therapy. As the client becomes more proficient in techniques for achieving and maintaining fluent speech, he or she may be invited to participate in group therapy sessions. The group sessions provide opportunities for the clients to practice developing skills with people other than the clinician and provide support and encouragement to the participants. In addition, group sessions provide the clinician with an opportunity to observe clients' use of designated techniques when communicating with other people. Frequently, the clinician may have to remind group members to focus on their speech production even when highly stimulating topics are being discussed. It is more difficult for the client who is just learning the techniques to participate in lengthy and emotion-laden conversations. The group therapy session should be structured to permit each member to participate at his or her own level and speed. Often, the group therapy approach used with older dysfluent children is similar to that used with adults.

Clinicians who use a psychotherapeutic approach to treatment of dysfluency will structure group therapy sessions to reflect their particular psychotherapeutic bent. These group therapy sessions often focus on interpersonal relationships and may or may not include specific attention to modifying speech production. As with any other methods, it is important that the clinician employing a psychotherapeutic approach be well-trained and experienced in its use.

Young children with dysfluency problems frequently have underlying or concomitant language disorders. The clinician then must decide whether to work directly on the stuttering symptoms or concentrate on improving language skills. Often, the clinician will opt to work primarily on language skills. The clinician may also work concurrently with family members to modify any environmental factors that may be contributing to the dysfluency.

Groups for Laryngectomized Clients

A clinician who has worked a number of years with groups of laryngectomized clients made the following comments about the benefits of group therapy with these clients:

> What do I feel is beneficial about having a group? I think with laryngectomy groups in particular—support for each other and helping them each keep perspective. Some of them are models, one for the other, both speech models and role models. It's an information learning time because they learn from each other. They can tell each other things that I could talk 'til I was blue in the face but this is a laryngectomee telling me that my phlegm will get better. It's partly a spousal support group, because spouses are invited and they attend all the sessions, and they are right in the session. It's also extremely time saving. At least in laryngectomy therapy, it's very redundant, and the same instructions fit a lot of people. It's time saving in the sense that this person can then make several tries and rest for a minute while someone else is having a try. I think it's a very efficient use of time. I think for all those reasons the group works very well.

When working with laryngectomized clients, the clinician will often be faced with treating individuals who may have further changes in their vocal tract or general bodily condition due to recurrences of malignancy. The client's physical condition may worsen and he or she may find it difficult to concentrate on improving communication when faced with a life-threatening situation. In such circumstances, support from other group members as well as the clinician can be extremely beneficial. A group of laryngectomized clients will typically be composed of individuals using a variety of communication methods or devices. This affords an opportunity for all the group members to become familiar with various alternatives for communication. If a particular method becomes unworkable for an individual, he or she is then already familiar with other possibilities.

Groups for Hearing-Impaired Clients

There is a longstanding tradition of effective group work with hearing-impaired clients. Aural rehabilitation in the group setting provides benefits that cannot be achieved in individual therapy. For example, "stage management" techniques, such as choosing appropriate seating, asking questions to fill in missed information, and making use of all visual cues can be demonstrated, practiced, and tested in the group setting. In addition to learning specific strategies to aid communication, group members often discuss their experiences and attitudes related to their hearing loss. Members become aware of ways people deal with common problems and are often motivated to make changes in their own behavior. Suggestions from group members with hearing losses often carry more weight than similar suggestions from the clinician.

Groups for Language-Delayed Clients

As mentioned earlier, speech-language pathologists in school settings frequently work with children who have been grouped together because of common problems, common therapy objectives, or inflexible time schedules. Many of the advantages of group therapy mentioned above also apply to working with children and adolescents.

Two types of groups for preschoolers are becoming increasingly useful as services are mandated for infants and toddlers (as in Public Law 99-457). One type of group is designed to serve infants who have been diagnosed as having Down syndrome or some other developmentally delaying condition. The group program is often designated as an *infant stimulation program* and involves prescription and carrying out of stimulation activities for the infant combined with parent education and support activities for the families of the infants. One example of such a program is sponsored by two agencies serving mentally retarded citizens in an Eastern community. The program serves infants between three weeks and three years of age. It provides services that include individualized child evaluations; prescriptive programming of activities to be carried out by family members or volunteers in the home; weekly sessions in a community facility where stimulation activities are provided for infants by assigned volunteers while parents engage in parent training activities such as seminars, lectures, and conferences; and monthly home visits by a therapist/teacher who works with both the parents and the child.

Infants ordinarily remain in the program for two years, with periodic reevaluations and updating of program and prescribed activities.

Another popular type of program is the therapy group designed especially for preschool language-delayed children (most commonly between two and four years of age). Etiology for the language delay may vary among the children as will the severity of the communicative handicap. Such groups often meet several times a week for periods ranging from 45 minutes to 3 hours. They may serve as the sole therapy activity for the child, as an adjunct to individual therapy, or as a supplement to the child's participation in a general education preschool program. Parent participation is an important facet of the group therapy program. Parents learn, by observation, instruction, and sometimes by working with the group, language facilitation techniques that they can then use at home.

Group programs for adolescents are also effectively used by communicative disorders specialists. Vicki Larson and Nancy McKinley (1985) have reported that, in their experience, the majority of language-delayed adolescents benefit more from group rather than individual sessions. They state (p. 76) that

> . . . few adolescents will need the amount of one-to-one language intervention that their younger counterparts require or that they, themselves, may have received in the lower grades.
>
> Group sessions help the adolescent to recognize that he or she is not the only one with certain communicative deficiencies and permit the adolescent to derive emotional support from fellow members. In addition, because the group members participate in rendering judgments on their own and their peers' performances, the evaluation of ongoing communicative behaviors is not the sole province of the clinician.
>
> . . . Within the group process it is more natural to teach adolescents to listen assertively to one another. Many adolescents with language disorders have poor listening skills; they act as if listening is a passive process in which one has very little or no control over the speaker.
>
> . . . Small-group discussions are an effective way to assist adolescents in developing their assertive and active listening skills. Such discussions also help adolescents apply more pragmatic conversational skills before they are asked to use those skills in the classroom and more informally in home and community settings.

In expanding their suggestions for working effectively with language-impaired adolescents, Larson and McKinley (1985, 1987) emphasized the importance of naturalistic therapy contexts in which improvement of pragmatic skills is the primary goal. Barbara Hoskins (1987) also stressed the importance of group conversational interactions for language-impaired adolescents.

Human beings are social creatures, and communication is the key to human contact. Providing a natural setting with interesting materials and activities and other children can be a potent motivating force for a child or adolescent to attempt or increase communication. The therapist is responsible for structuring the setting to maximize each child's communicative attempts and to provide appropriate reinforcement for attempts that may go unnoticed or unrecognized by others in the environment. He or she is also responsible for alerting family members and other appropriate members of the agency staff to these communicative attempts and appropriate responses. The therapist must fully understand each child's present level of linguistic functioning so that individual and group therapy objectives can be formulated and appropriate materials and activities can be selected. The clinician must plan group activities that will permit a range of responses and that are sufficiently challenging yet not overwhelmingly difficult for each member of the group. When participating in such interesting and challenging activities, group members serve as stimulators, models, and reinforcers for each other.

In working with all types of groups—child, adolescent, and adult—the principles discussed in this chapter will apply. Experience has taught us that the following questions need to be addressed when establishing client therapy groups:

- What will be the general objectives for the group?
- Where will the group meet?
- Who will be the participants?
- Will group members be required to be enrolled in concomitant individual therapy?
- How large will the group be?
- When and how often will the group meet?
- How long will each session be?
- What fee schedule will be established?
- Will this be an ongoing group or limited to a prescribed number of sessions?
- Will other clients be able to enroll once the sessions have begun?
- How will participants be notified?
- Will guests or observers be permitted?
- How will each session be structured?
- Will "homework assignments" be made?
- What record-keeping methods will be used?
- What procedures, if any, will be established for handling absenteeism?
- What will be dismissal criteria if the group is ongoing?

- Will parent or spousal participation be required?
- How will the program be publicized, if publicity is desired?
- If clients are involved in other therapy or therapy programs, how will coordination be achieved?
- Is the physical setting appropriate? If not, are modifications possible?
- What provisions will be made for group members to become acquainted?
- Are necessary materials prepared and easily accessible?
- Will adjunct therapists or aides be used? How will they be secured and trained?
- Will refreshments be provided, and who will be responsible for them?

STRUCTURING EFFECTIVE FAMILY GROUPS

The communicative disorders specialist may plan parent, spousal, or family groups for several reasons. He or she may feel the need for family education in areas that profoundly affect interpersonal communication. For example, the clinician may feel it would be helpful for parents to have information on child growth and development, particularly in relation to speech and language skills. Or the clinician may be aware of the need for instruction in problem-solving techniques in a number of families within the caseload. Or it may be apparent that a support group is needed for family members of some of the professional's clients—a group where members have the opportunity to share some of their feelings and frustrations and special problems, and perhaps work through some stages of grief. Again, as with client groups, the professional considers forming family groups not only because such groups can be time-saving and more economical than private counseling, but because the educational and therapeutic benefits of group interaction and process can be greater than from dyadic sessions.

For family members, group participation can be informative, educational, stimulating, supporting, insight-inducing, change-motivating, and healing. Whether a particular group will be beneficial to a member will partially depend on the clinician's skill in meeting the needs of group members and in creating an atmosphere that will mobilize the member's coping abilities rather than arouse and prolong defensive reactions that interfere with learning and change. We say "partially depend" because no matter how skilled a clinician, the group members are still individuals who differ not only in organismic characteristics but in the complexity of their problems, in their lifestyles and environments, and in their readiness for change. Effective professionals are well aware that they can never take full credit for clients' successes, and they never need to take full blame for client failures—in either individual or group settings. Whenever possible, however, they try to be growth-promoting rather than growth-inhibiting. Experience has shown that changes in perception can result in changes of behavior; and changes in perception are more likely to result when an individual is in a coping rather than a defending state.

Family educational and support groups will vary in nature depending on their major purpose, the nature of the group membership, and the leadership style of the professional leading the group. Some group leaders maintain a leader-centered didactic approach, while others aim to establish a member-centered discussion group by using various client-centered techniques espoused by Carl Rogers (1970) and his many successors. These techniques include restatement of content and reflection of feelings expressed by clients in such a way as to guide the discussion in significant directions with a minimum of interpretation by the therapist. The therapist serving as group leader strives for empathy with group participants, for an attitude of unconditional positive regard toward them, and for congruence in his or her own inner feelings and outward communication (revealed in nonverbal and verbal behavior) when leading the group.

Whether a family member comes to a first group meeting and continues to attend depends on a number of factors: the person's feelings toward the clinician or agency who is issuing the invitation; the person's relationship to the client and whether the client wishes the family member to participate in the group; the person's awareness of problems that are affecting his or her personal happiness or effective functioning; the relevance of the announced group tasks or goals to the person's perceived needs; the extent to which the attendee feels welcomed and accepted by the leader and other group members; and the accessibility of the group to the family member in regard to time and location.

Some suggestions to be considered when establishing a new parent or family group are as follows:

- If possible, talk informally with family members with whom you come in contact in the course of therapy with the client. Ask them if they feel the need for any family educational activities or for a discussion or support group. Find out what they feel would be helpful and if they would be likely to attend. If a choice of meeting times is possible, find out if there is one time that is preferred by most people to whom you talk.

- On the basis of this preliminary needs assessment, plan a specific date, time, place, and meeting topic, and send written invitations to the people for whom the group is designed. Be sure to indicate the purpose or purposes of the group and what is planned for the first meeting. Have some way in which people can indicate if they plan to attend. Make sure you provide specific instructions for the location of the meeting and availability of parking.

- A personal or telephone follow-up to a written invitation often markedly increases attendance at a meeting, particularly if the follow-up is made by the clinician. If that is not possible, follow-up phone calls can be made by the clinician's aide or secretary or by an enthusiastic member of a client's family who has been recruited to help notify potential members of the group.

- It is important to make necessary advance preparations to ensure a satisfactory meeting: the meeting room should be arranged; refreshments, if any, should be available; any materials to be distributed should be ready in sufficient quantity; and any desired technical equipment should be available and tested. If the meeting is being held in a school or agency, be sure to let staff members including secretaries and receptionists know about the meeting so that they can give appropriate information to people calling regarding the meeting. It is also helpful to have a sign posted at the meeting place to let early arrivals know they are at the correct location.

- Plan to be at the meeting place a few minutes early to greet participants as they arrive. If the group will be a relatively small one, you will want to try to acquaint participants with one another, either by personal introduction or by supplying nametags.

- As in any new encounters, first impressions can be lasting ones. For that reason, it is important that the meeting begin on time, and that the person who has called the meeting welcome attendants, reiterate the general purpose of the meeting, and get to the business at hand. For a one-session group, the business at hand may be introducing a guest speaker or panel of speakers, or making a presentation of your own to be followed by a question-and-answer or discussion period.

- If the meeting is designed to be the first of a series of family education or discussion groups, the first session should be structured to preview what you hope will be accomplished in the group series and the general form the group sessions will take. Experience has shown that a series composed of a specific number of sessions is preferable to an "open-ended" group series with no predetermined ending date. Encourage and maximize participation of group members in making decisions regarding the group, as well as in discussion and other group activities. Even though the meeting is the first of a series of sessions, it is important that there be sufficient content and useful information gained in the first session that participants will feel their attendance was worthwhile. Parents or family members do not want to go to all the trouble of attending a meeting only to have the major business of the meeting be "All right, it's decided; we'll meet again next week." The first meeting should already begin to meet the members' needs if they are to be motivated to return for future sessions.

- The responsibilities of the group leader for structuring the session, facilitating participation and pertinent discussion, encouraging appropriate and beneficial interactions among group members, and keeping the group sufficiently on-task to achieve its objectives continue throughout the group session.

- It is the responsibility of the leader to make certain the session is brought to an appropriate and timely close. Participants should feel that the group leader noted and welcomed their presence and participation in the meeting and that the leader is looking forward to the next meeting with enthusiasm.
- Continued participation by group members depends on whether some of their important needs are being met by participation in the group. It is the leader's responsibility to keep in touch with those needs and evaluate the sessions from that perspective as well as in the light of his or her own objectives for the group.

Much more could be written about group formation, leadership, and activity. In regard to parent education, several excellent programs are available if the clinician would like to use or adapt already prepared materials (for example, Thomas Gordon's Parent Effectiveness Training (1970), the Systematic Training for Effective Parenting or STEP programs (Dinkmeyer and McKay, 1976, 1983), Active Parenting by Michael Popkin (1983), and Responsive Parenting by Saf Lerman (1984)).

SUMMARY

Improvement of group participation and group leadership skills can increase a speech-language pathologist's or audiologist's opportunities for professional advancement and service, personal satisfaction, and social influence. Improvement of these skills is facilitated by understanding the nature of group process and the various ways in which group needs and goals can be served.

Groups vary in size; in degree of formality; in their purpose for functioning; in stability and duration; in the characteristics, contributions, and commitment of their members; and in the skills, experience, and personal style of their leaders.

Groups can be vital instruments for education, emotional support, problem solving, and behavioral change. Professionals in the field of communicative disorders are therefore encouraged to seek out additional reading, training, and experience in group participation and leadership.

REFERENCES

Argyle, M. (1978). *The psychology of interpersonal behavior* (3rd ed.). New York: Penguin Books.

Bales, R.F. (1950). *Interaction process analysis: A method for the study of small groups.* Cambridge, MA: Addison-Wesley.

146   SUCCESSFUL INTERACTIVE SKILLS

Bales, R.F. (1970). *Personality and interpersonal behavior*. New York: Holt, Rinehart & Winston.

Bales, R.F. (1981). Communication in small groups. In J.A. DeVito (Ed.), *Communication concepts and processes* (3rd ed., pp. 190–197). Englewood Cliffs, NJ: Prentice-Hall.

Bates, M., Johnson, C.D., & Blaker, K.E. (1982). *Group leadership: A manual for group counseling leaders*. Denver: Love Publishing Company.

Benne, K.D., & Sheats, P. (1948). Functional roles of group members. *Journal of Social Issues, 4*(2), 41–49.

Combs, A.W., Avila, D.L., & Purkey, W.W. (1978). *Helping relationships: Basic concepts for the helping professions* (2nd ed.). Boston: Allyn & Bacon.

Dinkmeyer, D., & McKay, G.D. (1976). *STEP: Systematic training for effective parenting*. Circle Pines, MN: American Guidance Service. (Also available in a Spanish-language edition.)

Dinkmeyer, D., & McKay, G.D. (1983). *STEP/Teen: Systematic training for effective parenting of teens*. Circle Pines, MN: American Guidance Service.

Gordon, T. (1970). *Parent effectiveness training*. New York: Peter H. Wyden.

Hoskins, B. (1987). *Conversations: Language intervention for adolescents*. Allen, TX: DLM-Teaching Resources.

Lakin, M. (1972). *Experiential groups: The uses of interpersonal encounter, psychotherapy groups, and sensitivity training*. Morristown, NJ: General Learning Press.

Larson, V.L., & McKinley, N.L. (1985). General intervention principles with language impaired adolescents. *Topics in Language Disorders, 5*(3), 70–77.

Larson, V.L., & McKinley, N.L. (1987). *Communication assessment and intervention strategies for adolescents*. Eau Claire, WI: Thinking Publications.

Lerman, S. (1984). *Responsive parenting*. Circle Pines, MN: American Guidance Service.

Lewin, K. (1958). Group decision and social change. In E.E. Maccoby, T.M. Newcomb, & E.L. Hartley (Eds.), *Readings in social psychology* (3rd ed., pp. 197–211). New York: Holt, Rinehart & Winston.

Napier, R.W., & Gershenfeld, M.K. (1985). *Groups: Theory and experience* (3rd ed.). Boston: Houghton Mifflin.

Popkin, M.H. (1983). *Active parenting*. Circle Pines, MN: American Guidance Service.

Public Law 99-457. (1986). Education of the handicapped amendment.

Rogers, C. (1970). *Carl Rogers on encounter groups*. New York: Harper & Row.

Sampson, E.E., & Marthas, M.S. (1977). *Group process for the health professions*. New York: John Wiley & Sons.

Satir, V. (1972). *Peoplemaking*. Palo Alto, CA: Science and Behavior Books.

Satir, V. (1983). *Conjoint family therapy* (3rd ed.). Palo Alto, CA: Science and Behavior Books.

Shulman, L. (1979). *The skills of helping individuals and groups*. Itasca, IL: F.E. Peacock Publishers, Inc.

Stech, E., & Ratliffe, S.A. (1985). *Effective group communication*. Lincolnwood, IL: National Textbook Company.

Tuckman, B.W. (1965). Developmental sequence in small groups. *Psychological bulletin, 63*, 384–399.

Verderber, R.F. (1978). *Communicate!* (2nd ed.). Belmont, CA: Wadsworth Publishing Company, Inc.

7

Helping Clients and Families Become Effective Problem Solvers

The successful communication disorders specialist is of necessity an effective problem solver. Earlier chapters discussed some problems that must be resolved in working with each client. These are summarized in the following questions:

- What is the nature and extent of the client's communication problem?
- How can the communication disorder best be remedied or reduced?
- How can I most effectively motivate this client to devote maximum time and energy to accomplish necessary behavioral change?
- How can I most effectively promote environmental changes that will assist the client in improving communicative relationships and interactions?
- How can I assist the client to meet new problems of interpersonal communication that arise outside the therapy setting?

In this chapter, we pay particular attention to using the principles of problem solving in helping clients and their families become more effective in their daily living.

PROFESSIONAL APPLICATIONS OF PROBLEM SOLVING

One of the skills essential to speech-language pathologists and audiologists is problem solving. The premise of a diagnostic evaluation is to solve a problem: what is the nature and extent of the communicative disorder and what can be done about it? Frequently, therapy sessions involve solving problems. A person's communicative disorder affects not only the person, but family members, friends, and other listeners as well, thus causing problems in relationships. In professional settings, differences of opinion can occur related to the resolution of a client's

problem, the functioning and goals of the agency, and responsibilities or obligations of staff members, to name a few. And, needless to say, problems frequently
arise in one's personal life. Being able to resolve problems effectively is an
important factor in professional and personal success and satisfaction.

Your primary aim for clients is to enable them to operate more effectively in
their environment. Basically, therapy for a communication disorder is devoted to
addressing some type of problem that needs to be solved. The assumption is that
when this problem is solved, the person's more effective functioning will
engender greater happiness, contentment, and/or self-satisfaction in himself or
herself, and perhaps in others as well. In addition to the basic communication
problem, the client may be faced with other problems related either directly or
indirectly to the underlying speech, language, or hearing problem. Sometimes,
these tangential problems surface or are brought up by the client during a therapy
session. The clinician must then decide whether to devote time to the revealed
problem, acknowledge it but decline to take therapy time to discuss it further, or
ignore it completely. At other times, a family member will request time to discuss
a particular problem that involves the client. Whether or not the clinician will
assist either the client or family members in their efforts to cope with the problem
situation should be decided on the basis of the overall goals for the client and the
clinician's own professional philosophy. The decision should not have to be
influenced by whether or not the clinician is skilled in problem-solving techniques.

Dr. Thomas Gordon, in his workshops and publications on parent effectiveness
training (1970), teacher effectiveness training (1977), and leader effectiveness
training (1977), did a great deal to promulgate and popularize the basic principles
of problem solving. He advocated their use by family members as well as by
business and professional associates in everyday relationships and situations. He
felt that careful attention to problem-solving principles was vital in what he called
the "no-lose" method of conflict resolution—one that could result in solutions
acceptable to all people involved in the problem situation.

Robert Rutherford and Eugene Edgar (1979, p. 35) described the problem-
solving process as follows: "Problem solving involves a systematic procedure for
resolving differences, reaching solutions, or discovering sources of difficulties."
They described this systematic procedure as a four-step process: (1) defining the
problem, (2) developing the solution, (3) implementing the solution, and
(4) evaluating the results.

Naomi Brill (1985, p. 137) discussed how the scientific method can be applied
in working with people as they attempt to solve problems. Notice how all the
aspects of problem solving she described are also aspects of effective therapy.

> The classical scientific method involves recognition and systematic
> formulation of a problem, collection of data through observation and
> experiment, and the formulation and testing of hypotheses (tentative

explanations of the problem). . . . The orderly framework for working with people is an adaptation of this . . .

1. Engagement: involving oneself in the situation, establishing communication, and formulating preliminary hypotheses for understanding and dealing with the problem.
2. Assessment: appraising the situation on the basis of data (facts, feelings, persons, circumstances, and systems) involved.
3. Definition of the problem: formulating the need.
4. Setting of goals: the end toward which the effort is to be directed.
5. Selection of alternative methods and an initial mode of intervention: looking at all the possible ways of tackling the problem and selecting the most propitious one.
6. Establishment of a contract: agreeing on a definition of the roles and responsibilities of the participants.
7. Action leading toward the desired goal: the work that is necessary.
8. Evaluation: weighing the outcome of action in terms of success or failure.
9. Continuation of working plan, abandonment of unsuccessful intervention and selection of a different approach, or termination. Both continuation and selection of a different interventive strategy are based on a repetition of this basic problem-solving process.

There will be times when clients or family members will come to you complaining of unhappiness or anxiety, or with a vague feeling of unfulfillment. They may be aware of ineffective or unsatisfying functioning within their environment, but they have not been able to pinpoint any precise problem or determine whether or not circumstances can be changed. Your role as a clinician might be to assist the person in clarifying the problem before helping to explore other possible solutions.

Lawrence Brammer (1988, p. 124) described the evolution from problem awareness to goal setting as follows:

Helpees seldom come with neatly stated problems. They usually are expressed in vague feelings of confusion, dissatisfaction, or distress. Often complaints are focused on another person or institution. Thus, helpers begin, as in other styles of helping, with listening for understanding. They try to communicate this understanding, and often this is enough for the helpee to feel understood and comforted. But if the helper's listening reveals that the helpee needs to *act* differently, another strategy is needed. As helpers listen, they are gaining information about the specifics in helpees' lives—how they look at themselves and others, what they want, and what their environment is like. From these data about the helpee's initial complaints and feelings, the helper and helpee together *describe* how the helpee *acts now* and would *like to act*. Thus, goals are formulated toward which the person can work with some methods suggested by the helper.

Goals must meet three criteria: (1) they are desired by and tailored to the helpee; (2) the helper is willing to help the person work toward the goals; (3) attainment of the goals is observable and assessable. General growth goals, such as "self-understanding" and "self-actualization," are accepted by almost everyone, but to be useful in an action approach they must be stated in the unique and specific language of the helpee.

For communicative disorders specialists, however, the aim of a session is more often to solve a specific problem that has already been identified and acknowledged. Let us now examine in more detail some steps of the problem-solving process.

STEPS IN PROBLEM SOLVING

For discussion purposes, the steps in problem solving will be delineated as follows:

- identifying and defining the problem
- identifying possible solutions
- evaluating possible solutions and selecting the most feasible
- planning and carrying out necessary actions to implement the solution
- planning and carrying out evaluation procedures

Let us now note some considerations for each of these stages.

Identifying and Defining the Problem

In Chapter 5, we gave several examples of interviews with family members of clients in which problems were discussed. We pointed out that people may be aware of a problem without recognizing its causes or the possible solutions. We also pointed out the necessity of clarifying who actually "owns" a problem. Another consideration related to problem solving involves not only defining the problem in specific terms, but also assigning some kind of priority rating when more than one problem exists. Sometimes, a person can be so overwhelmed by the number and complexity of the problems owned that he or she is actually paralyzed into inactivity and thus prevented from taking any positive action. In that case, the person needs to select the most pressing problem and, at least temporarily, try to ignore the rest.

Roger Kroth, in discussing conferences between teachers and parents (1975, p. 110) made the following suggestions:

> . . . problem-solving is enhanced by being able to reduce global problems into entities that are measurable and observable. When behaviors have been defined in measurable terms then it helps place the problem in perspective, it takes away some of the subjectivity that surrounds the problem, and it is easier to determine when the problem has been solved. The teacher who serves as the catalyst in the problem solving conference will (1) reduce the problem to measurable terms, (2) restate the problem to verify her perception, (3) list the problems, (4) ask that the problems be prioritized, and (5) set up a procedure for measuring the behavior.

Some of the questions to be answered in this first stage of problem solving are as follows:

- Is there a real concern with this problem?
- Who owns the problem? If it is someone other than the person doing the problem solving, define the problem from the solver's perspective. For example, if someone in a client's family is an alcoholic, the alcoholic owns the drinking problem. However, if the alcoholic is not attempting to overcome the problem, then the client's problem is how to relate to that person, how to cope with the situations that are brought on by the person's alcoholism, or how to get the alcoholic to seek help.
- Is the problem composed of a number of smaller problems? If so, which one shall serve as a starting point?
- At the conclusion of this first step in the problem-solving process, has the problem been stated clearly, concisely, and accurately? Do all participants agree with the statement of the problem? Do all participants also agree that the problem needs to be solved? Can the problem be handled even though disagreement exists?

Identifying Possible Solutions

This is the "brainstorming" phase of problem solving, the phase in which various possible solutions are generated. Appropriate questions to consider during this phase are

- What do we already know that is vital to the problem? Is the existing information factual and reliable?
- Is more information needed regarding the problem? If so, how and where can the needed information be obtained?
- What possible solutions can be imagined, invented, or recalled?
- Is participation and creative thinking by all participants encouraged?
- Are all suggested solutions acknowledged and received nonjudgmentally, no matter how ingenious or impractical? Is evaluation and criticism prohibited at this point?
- At the conclusion of this stage, have we generated a variety of possible solutions to the problem?

Evaluating Possible Solutions and Selecting the Most Feasible

In the brainstorming phase of problem solving, judgment was suspended and efforts were concentrated on generating as many alternative solutions as possible. In this next stage, the proposed solutions are reexamined with the intent of selecting one or a few that appear to be the most promising and workable. Some questions to be addressed in this stage are the following:

- What outcomes might be anticipated from the various solutions proposed?
- Is one solution clearly preferable to the others in terms of workability, feasibility, or desirability of outcome?
- Which of the proposed solutions or actions would produce undesirable effects and hence need to be eliminated?
- Which of the proposed solutions appear to be untenable in the light of information collected?
- Is care taken not to eliminate proposed solutions only on the basis of personal biases and prejudices?
- Are personal values of all participants weighed and considered in selecting the solution to be implemented?

Robert Carkhuff and William Anthony (1979) developed a procedure for choosing a course of action when there are several possible solutions to a problem. Their procedure can be particularly helpful if there is a dilemma about which solution is best. They suggested the construction of a matrix in which the various alternatives are listed, and the client assigns a numerical weight to each solution based on personal values. Once the preferred solution is identified, implementing the solution can begin. You may find it helpful to use this or a similar procedure for assigning priorities when no one solution to a problem is clearly the best.

When examining and evaluating possible solutions to a problem, it is certainly your prerogative to make only one recommendation. You may do this because you feel that the recommendation is absolutely correct. However, you must then accept the possibility that the client may reject that one recommendation. People find themselves in situations where they initially feel that only one solution is acceptable. Experts on problem solving affirm that there are usually several acceptable solutions or resolutions of a problem. Unwillingness to consider alternatives can lead to frustration and dissatisfaction or even to outright tragedy.

Planning and Carrying Out Necessary Actions

Problem-solving techniques often include planning for future action, discussed briefly in Chapter 5. In that chapter, we pointed out the desirability of setting up specific long-range and intermediate goals when planning for action. Workers in many fields have made specific suggestions regarding the establishment of objectives and methods of evaluation appropriate for those fields. In the field of education, for example, Robert Mager (1962) detailed procedures for establishing instructional objectives that are still used by professionals in many service fields.

In the planning for action stage, some questions to be considered are as follows:

- Is the agreed-upon solution or course of action clearly and concisely stated? Is it agreed upon by all concerned?
- What exactly will be done by all people concerned to implement the agreed-upon solution or action? Are work assignments clearly made and agreed to by the person or persons assigned?
- What is the timeframe for carrying out the necessary actions?
- In attempting to put the solution into effect, have participants recognized the limitations of reality?

Often, in a problem situation, you will want to encourage a change in behavior that will lead to your client's more effective functioning. You will try to help the client plan more appropriate behavior and be responsible for carrying it out. However, you may be faced with clients or family members who are docile and dependent in their behavior, asking for your help and expressing admiration and respect for your knowledge and good judgment. Your awareness of interpersonal reflexes should remind you that such behavior on the part of a client is likely to encourage an increased amount of directiveness on your part. You may be tempted to outline specific plans of action without encouraging the respondent to participate in the development of the plans. When the responsibility for future action rests primarily on the client or on family members, the action is more likely to be carried out if the person responsible has taken an active role in formulating the plan. If actual behavioral change by the client is going to take place, the client will have to agree to a specific attainable goal and act accordingly.

As a communication disorders specialist, you naturally expect your clients to practice and employ their new speech behaviors in settings other than the therapy room. You must remember that planned action is also necessary in changing other problem behaviors that interfere with communicative interactions. Several psychotherapy approaches emphasize the planning and practice of new behaviors by clients as they progress in therapy. Psychotherapists stress the importance of developing insight into problems and awareness of alternative ways of behaving. They feel, however, for this insight and awareness to be effective, it is necessary to achieve behavioral change. For example, homework assignments are routinely included in rational-emotive therapy (RET). Clients practice new behaviors that are then evaluated and discussed with the therapist. In discussing this aspect of rational-emotive therapy, Gerald Corey (1977, p. 154) stated

> The homework-assignment method is well suited to enabling clients to practice new behaviors and assisting them in the process of their reconditioning. Reality therapy, behavior therapy, and Transactional Analysis share with RET this action orientation. Clients can gain a multitude of insights and can become very aware of the nature of their problems, but I question the value of self-understanding unless specific plans that lead to behavioral changes desired by the client are implemented. RET insists on this action phase as a crucial part of the therapy process.

Nena and George O'Neill pointed out that often significant life changes can be made in a series of small achievable steps. They discussed (1974, p. 183) the importance of genuine commitment to action.

> You find yourself in crisis. You face up to the existence of the crisis, achieving awareness, which is the first step in the process of shifting gears. By focusing and centering you refine that awareness, evaluating your situation and exploring possible alternatives. You make a decision to change, to seek a specific new path to self-fulfillment. But if you stop there, you have not shifted gears nor resolved the crisis. To resolve the crisis you must now take the risk of committing yourself to action, of testing your competence in a new situation . . .

Planning and Carrying Out Evaluation Procedures

When planning evaluation procedures to determine if the proposed actions are actually solving the problem, the following questions should be considered:

- How will we know if all work assignments have been carried out?
- How will we decide if the agreed-upon actions are solving the original problem?
- Who will conduct the evaluation? When will it be conducted?
- What if new information makes it necessary to reconsider the problem and possible solutions?
- What if the situation changes to such an extent that it is necessary to reconsider the agreed-upon solution?
- What if the executed solution creates other problems that make reconsideration necessary?

It is important to be as objective as possible when evaluating the effectiveness of any actions taken to solve a problem. If the agreed-upon actions are not working, all participants should feel free to discuss the situation. They should try to uncover possible causes for the failure, brainstorm new alternatives, and select another course of action. Attempts to fix blame for failure, coupled with charges and countercharges, tend to raise defensiveness in one or more participants and interfere with productive coping behavior.

CLIENT AND FAMILY PARTICIPATION IN PROBLEM SOLVING

Application of problem-solving techniques is illustrated in the following excerpts, each of which crystallizes a problem from the perspective of either a client or family member. Each of these statements, in effect, constitutes an invitation to the clinician to introduce problem-solving techniques. We suggest that you read each statement and consider your structuring of the ensuing conversation. We have included a summary of points the clinician might consider in dealing with such problems.

The mother of a five-year-old daughter with delayed language states

"The last few weeks Sharon cries every time we get in the car to come to the clinic."

Something is bothering the mother: her daughter cries and doesn't want to come to the clinic. The problem should be further explored and more precisely defined. Does the mother have any idea why the child cries? There could be a number of reasons. If possible, pinpoint the time of the shift. Has anything changed in the child's schedule or situation? Try to get the child's input; don't rely solely on the mother's impressions. The clinician will want to ask the mother what she has already tried to do to resolve the problem. Both participants can then generate additional solutions. When a child expresses unhappiness in coming to therapy, the clinician is likely to ask inwardly: "What am I doing wrong?" Negative statements regarding therapy made by a parent can raise a clinician's defenses. More is accomplished, however, if the clinician can remain objective and introduce problem-solving strategies. It is easy for clinicians to take full responsibility for a child's unhappiness. Both clinician and parent must take some responsibility for making therapy pleasant.

The daughter of a 75-year-old retired longshoreman states

"We bought that hearing aid you recommended for Dad, and it hasn't been out of his dresser since the first week."

In this case, the question "Who owns the problem?" must be answered. What are the father's and the family's expectations of the hearing aid? Who wanted the hearing aid and for what purpose? Do all participants understand what an aid can do? Again, the clinician must guard against becoming defensive, and should employ problem-solving techniques. For example, the client may need further hearing aid orientation. Sometimes a problem can only be minimized, not eliminated. The clinician can assist the client and family to face facts realistically. Professionals should beware of promising more than can be delivered.

A seven-year-old boy with dysfluency problems makes the following statement:

"My brothers keep teasing me when I practice my contracts."

This example reminds us that even young children are capable of participating in problem solving and learning problem-solving techniques. The clinician should explore with the boy exactly how his brothers tease him while he is working on his contracts and whether or not they tease him at other times. If he learns how to deal with teasing while he is doing his contracts, he can learn to deal with other problems. Role rehearsal, in which the child actually practices strategies with the clinician for dealing with the teasing, often proves helpful. Other techniques that could be effective might involve desensitization procedures for the child or actual manipulation of the environment. The clinician might meet with the child and his brothers to discuss possible solutions to the problem. A clinician's goal in working with any client is to help the individual learn problem-solving skills that can be generalized to other situations.

The father of a two-year-old daughter with a recently diagnosed profound hearing loss states

"There's no point in my learning sign language. She's got to learn to talk!"

In this example, a previously discussed solution (having the child and her parents learn sign language in order to communicate) is not acceptable to one of the concerned participants. The father is seeking another solution that may or may not be achievable by his daughter. The clinician may feel that learning sign language is an important and achievable goal, but may need to explore the father's feelings in more detail. The father may be afraid that he cannot learn sign language. He may not be willing to accept the reality of profound hearing loss. Or he may be afraid that his child will be stigmatized by using such an unusual form of communication. Sometimes the clinician will need to verbalize possible objections that a client or parent has not identified and/or verbalized. The clinician may want to consider developing a "pro and con" list of possible solutions with the father. In this particular example, the father's feelings may be based on limited information regarding profound hearing loss and sign language. He might also benefit from a support group composed of parents of children with similar problems.

In an interview, the parent of a teenage motorcycle accident victim says

"I know he should be getting physical therapy, but we've used up all the insurance benefits."

There is certainly a need in this situation to examine all possible alternative solutions to the problem. It may be necessary for the clinician to suggest that the parent discuss the problem with the social worker or case manager to determine if other funding is available or if free services can be obtained. The clinician may also be aware of other agencies to which the client can be referred. It is important for speech-language pathologists and audiologists to remember that they cannot solve every problem a person has—they cannot be all things to all people.

The mother of a ten-year-old hearing aid user responds to the clinician's suggestion that the parent should ask her son's teacher if his behavior has improved since he has been wearing his new hearing aid.

"If I ever get a chance, I'll ask his teacher about that."

If the clinician feels that a parent contact with a teacher is crucial, it is important to have the parent agree to a specific plan of action. It is also important that a timeline be established for that action. If the parent has not realized the importance of the teacher contact, it is likely that any action will be postponed indefinitely. A clinician's response to a statement such as the above will depend on his or her professional assessment of the importance of the planned action.

A 35-year-old attorney who is enrolled in therapy at the recommendation of her otolaryngologist for problems related to vocal abuse responds to the clinician's suggestion with the following statement:

"I'm willing to try it, but I don't think it's going to work."

In this situation, the client is expressing hesitation about following a suggestion made by the clinician. If the clinician feels that the recommended action is important, he or she may spend time to explore why the client does not think it will work. It is also necessary to share with the client the rationale for the suggestion.

The professional needs to feel confident in the worthiness of suggestions and to convey that confidence to the client. A client may need to be reminded that a planned action is more likely to succeed if it is enthusiastically endorsed and positively approached. A reminder: once a planned therapeutic intervention is completed, it is necessary to evaluate it objectively. That is why tape recordings made at various intervals throughout the therapy program are crucial. This objective documentation records actual gains rather than relying on the memory of the participants.

The parent of an emotionally disturbed child states

"You're the expert. What should I do?"

This comment exemplifies a frequently encountered attitude on the part of clients and/or family members: the professional is the expert and should make decisions regarding a variety of problems, even those that are outside the clinician's domain or area of expertise. Depending upon the circumstances, the clinician may offer a suggestion or may respond to such a statement by forcing the client to accept responsibility for suggesting possible resolutions to the problem. It is important that clients and family members participate whenever possible in the problem-solving process. In some circumstances, the clinician may feel that the most appropriate approach is to refer the client and family to another professional. In this example, the clinician may feel that the behavioral problems disturbing the parent warrant referral of the family to a psychotherapist.

The examples detailed above are a sampling of the many that will occur in the speech-language pathologist's or audiologist's practice. The problems may differ, but the approach to solving them is essentially following through on the steps delineated above.

PROBLEM SOLVING IN GROUP SETTINGS

How are the principles of problem solving applied to working with groups? Two contrasting situations come to mind regarding problem solving in groups. In one circumstance, an individual member of a client or family group may bring up a personal problem. In another situation, there may be a problem that needs to be resolved by the group. In either circumstance, the steps to solving the problem are the same as already described in this chapter. The difference from the clinician's point of view is that, in the former situation, the clinician must decide if one client's personal problem merits use of the limited group time. If the clinician determines that group discussion of the problem is warranted, it is then important to clarify the usefulness of the discussion for all of the group members. Perhaps some other members have an identical or similar problem. If not, the clinician must frame the problem in such a way that it is applicable to a number of members of the group, a technique referred to as *generalizing* or *universalizing*.

A member of a laryngectomee group practicing use of artificial larynges expresses the following concern:

> "My 16-year-old daughter won't bring her friends to the house because she's embarrassed when I use my artificial larynx."

In a case such as this, the clinician might ask if other members of the group have similar difficulties. Members of the group might respond that either they do not have children or that their children do not live at home. The clinician might restate the problem in the following manner: "Do any of you sometimes feel that your family members or friends are embarrassed by your communication?" It is likely that more members of the group will have similar dilemmas and can then relate to the problem.

Once the problem for discussion is clearly identified, the group can then move to brainstorming solutions. The clinician may need to remind the group to withhold judgment on the proposed solutions during the brainstorming phase. One of the advantages of group discussion is the extensive pool of information and potential problem-solving ideas that the group members can generate. Some of the comments generated in the group of laryngectomees during the brainstorming phase might be as follows:

- "I found that a lot of people didn't understand my surgery, so I explained it to them. Once they had a better understanding, they became more interested and less embarrassed."
- "My embarrassment caused other people to be embarrassed. When I relaxed, they seemed to relax too."
- "My grandson was afraid until I let him practice with my artificial larynx."
- "Teenagers are embarrassed by their parents no matter what."
- "I wonder if it would help your daughter to come with you to the group sessions."

It is then necessary to evaluate the proposed solutions in the light of each individual's unique situation. If the group is discussing a problem generated by one particular member's concern, that individual should be encouraged to evaluate proposed solutions in light of his or her particular circumstances. For instance, after listening to all the comments, the clinician might ask: "Joe, we've heard a lot of suggestions here. Do any sound as though they would work for you?" With luck, Joe might reply: "She did talk about wanting to come to the group, but I was embarrassed to have her come. If she did come and learn more about my surgery, that might help both of us."

Once a solution is accepted as feasible by a client, it is important to obtain a commitment to specific action. For example, the clinician could say: "O.K., Joe. Why don't you bring her to our next meeting. We'll all be looking forward to meeting her. You can let us know later if it helped."

The above example illustrates the supportive nature of group therapy. Another example of a likely candidate for group support is the mother of a young child with a severe congenital defect. In a group meeting for parents of children with palatal clefts, a mother comments

"I'm worn out just thinking about all that will have to be done for him—it's overwhelming."

The mother's feeling of being overwhelmed points out the need for a "one day at a time" approach when multiple problems exist. The clinician can assist in prioritizing problems and action items. This does not mean that problems should be minimized, but they do not have to all be solved at once. A parent's self-confidence often needs bolstering. This can be one function that a parent group or network can serve. One of the advantages of parent groups is that a participant will meet other parents with similar problems. Some of these parents may have already worked through some of the problems and can give valuable suggestions and encouragement. Some of the parents may also have progressed through the various stages of grief and are more able to cope effectively.

It is important that the clinician acknowledge the feelings that parents have when their child has a physical problem, particularly one that will require long-term habilitation. Many times parents in such circumstances need to have their feelings validated in an accepting atmosphere. Parents need to realize that all of their attention need not be centered on the child and that they should plan some time for themselves. The clinician can encourage the parents to consider their own needs as well as the needs of their child.

Knowledge of problem-solving techniques is important not only when working with clients and family members, but also when interacting with colleagues and professionals in other disciplines. The following statement made by a colleague in a staff meeting provides such an example:

"I'm getting sick and tired of people not doing their fair share of the work!"

It is not clear from this excerpt whether the statement pertains to the main reason for the meeting. If it is incidental to the main purpose of the meeting, the decision needs to be made whether to ignore the complaint or pursue it. Time restraints may be a factor in the decision. Also, the group leader must decide whether this problem must be addressed before the actual purpose of the meeting can be accomplished. Often, acknowledgment of the expressed feeling with a minimum of discussion is sufficient. The speaker may have expressed such feelings as a form of release and not have expected the issue to be addressed by the group.

PROBLEM-SOLVING STYLES

Professionals, clients, and family members all have problem-solving styles that you must take into consideration as you work with them. People differ in their methods of gathering information, in their ways of manipulating and organizing that information in order to cope with their environment, in their cognitive tempo, and in what is often referred to as their locus of control.

One customary distinction between problem-solving styles is the *systematic* style and the *intuitive* style. In the *systematic* style, a person first takes in the available information on the situation, decides what the principal problem is, decides upon an appropriate solution, and decides upon appropriate procedures to carry out the solution. The *intuitive* problem solver tends to approach a problem in what is likely to seem an unsystematic, disorganized fashion. Intuitive problem solvers try out one idea after another, quickly evaluating each and discarding an idea if it seems unworkable, following "hunches" at times, and changing their minds and methods more quickly than systematic thinkers if they encounter difficulties.

Familiarity with brain physiology reminds us that the differences between the two problem-solving approaches may represent greater involvement of either the left ("systematic") or right ("intuitive") cerebral hemisphere. As with leadership styles, no one style is inherently superior to the other; a person adept at either can solve many problems successfully. A group confronted with a problem to solve will be fortunate if both styles are represented in the group even though the different approaches may cause members some discomfort.

James McKenney and Peter Keen (1974) did extensive research on the data-gathering and problem-solving methods of nearly 200 graduate students majoring in business administration. They found that the classification of systematic versus intuitive problem solvers was borne out in their research. They also found that people tend to differ in their methods of collecting information about the problem facing them. According to McKenney and Keen, most people fall into one of two major groups when scanning the environment, taking in information, and organizing their perceptions to assist in the cognitive problem-solving process. They refer to the two types of information gatherers as *preceptive* and *receptive*.

A precept can be defined as "a command, maxim, principle, or direction given as a rule of action or conduct." *Preceptive* information gatherers tend to gather information that fits into a system or concept that they have in mind as they begin working to solve a problem. For example, a counselor trained in a particular method of psychotherapy will often gather information from a client that the counselor deems crucial on the basis of what the counselor believes are important motivating forces in human behavior. A speech pathologist who believes that certain voice disorders are a direct result of vocal strain will seek information from a client related to possible instances of vocal abuse. A clinician meeting the parent of a language-delayed child client for the first time often takes a case history, asking for information in various areas that experience has shown to be significant in speech and language development.

In contrast to preceptive information gatherers, *receptive* data processors tend to take in a wide variety of individual bits of information, focusing on individual details without necessarily trying to fit them into a preconceived conceptual framework. They are not especially concerned about discovering relationships among the facts gleaned, particularly early in their information gathering. They are willing to let the bits of information gather and to admit puzzling details that do not seem to fit any pattern, until the various data seem to permit the forming of some conclusion or hypothesis. As with the systematic versus intuitive styles of finding solutions to problems, neither the preceptive nor receptive method of data gathering is inherently superior. People just seem to fall into one category or the other as one of their organismic variables.

On the basis of their research, McKenney and Keen estimated that approximately 70 percent of the people they worked with could be clearly categorized as favoring one of four cognitive styles when problem solving: (1) systematic-preceptive, (2) systematic-receptive, (3) intuitive-preceptive, and (4) intuitive-receptive. The remaining people in their studies tended to favor one style but did not use it as exclusively as the 70 percent did. Follow-up studies conducted by the researchers and other investigators have indicated that certain occupations and careers are more likely to be followed successfully and with satisfaction by people with particular cognitive styles. For example, systematic-preceptive problem solvers tend to do well in fields such as statistics, financial analysis, logistics, and production management. Intuitive-preceptive thinkers, on the other hand, would be likely to find more satisfaction in pursuing careers in psychology, history, or marketing management.

On the basis of findings regarding cognitive styles, we can assume that workers in the field of communication disorders represent the gamut of problem-solving types. In one agency, for example, we might find a research audiologist (the systematic-receptive type); a language clinician who directs the preschool therapy group and the parent education program (an intuitive-preceptive type); a clinician who handles many of the dysfluent clients and also conducts most of the intake interviews (a systematic-preceptive thinker); and the director of the agency who is liked and respected by all the employees because of her fairness and personal concern for all and because of her ability to generate ideas for innovative agency projects and successful fundraisers (an intuitive-receptive type), even though her personal book- and record-keeping is a disaster.

Studies of variations in personal styles of inquiry, data manipulation, and approaches to problem solving continue to occupy the time and attention of researchers. Five studies that have been particularly influential in this field (in addition to those of McKenney and Keen) are those of Churchman (1971), DeBono (1972), Mitroff and Pondy (1974), Ewing (1977), and Harrison and Bramson (1982).

Harrison and Bramson, for example, have described five basic styles of thinking and have described at length the cognitive and interpersonal characteristics, strengths, and weaknesses of the people who prefer and utilize the various styles. They designate the five basic types of thinkers as follows: (1) the *synthesist*, who sees likeness in apparent unlikes, enjoys debate, and is interested in change; (2) the *idealist*, who welcomes a broad range of views and seeks ideal solutions; (3) the *pragmatist*, whose motto is "whatever works" and who seeks the shortest route to payoff; (4) the *analyst*, who is interested in scientific solutions and seeks the "one best way"; and (5) the *realist*, who relies on facts and expert opinions, and is interested in concrete results.

A group of professionals comprising an interdisciplinary cleft palate panel has just learned that its prosthodontist has accepted a position in another state. Faced with this loss, the cleft palate panel will probably utilize problem-solving procedures. There may be no disagreement about the nature of the problem: the loss of the prosthodontist will diminish the effectiveness of the cleft palate team. There may be disagreement, however, on the procedures for selecting a replacement. Some of the comments from group members during the brainstorming phase might be

- "Let's let personnel deal with this."
- "I have a niece in prosthodontia who wants to relocate."
- "Ben told me about a fellow right here in town who presented at the last conference of the American Cleft Palate Association. Ben was very impressed with his work."
- "I remember when Dr. Smith substituted on the panel last year. We had mixed feelings about him."
- "What is our procedure for replacing panel members? I'm sure this situation has occurred before."

- "Let's advertise in the county medical society bulletin."
- "Maybe we should think about reorganizing our whole operation."

In evaluating possible solutions suggested during brainstorming, the cognitive styles of the commenters can often be identified. A pragmatist, seeking the shortest route to payoff, may favor turning the problem over to the personnel department. An analyst, interested in scientific solutions and seeking the one best candidate, may argue for developing a checklist and point scale to evaluate all the candidates. A realist, who relies on facts and expert opinions and is interested in concrete results, may suggest that the expert opinion of a respected colleague confirmed by the suggested candidate's resume would be the fastest way to resolve the problem. A synthesist might state that he has heard of two different panels that operate without a prosthodontist and perhaps one is not necessary. The idealist in the group might remind the members that the panel's first responsibility is to the clients being served, and any decision must be made from that perspective.

The 1982 publication by Harrison and Bramson contains a copy of a test that can be self-administered and was developed to determine an individual's preferred style or styles of thinking. The authors point out that many people have two preferred styles of thinking that they use with nearly equal frequency and adeptness. These combinations are referred to as "two-pronged thinking styles," and ten of the most common combinations are discussed at length. Harrison and Bramson point out that, even though emotions and roles greatly influence behavior, knowledge and recognition of the various styles and combinations can help to explain affinities, compatibilities, and conflicts among people and can also help a person to influence others.

The above-mentioned studies are of interest to people in a wide variety of careers and professions because of their applications to interpersonal relationships. As a communication specialist, you often find yourself providing people with information, assisting them in problem solving, helping them to acquire new skills, and motivating them to change both behavior and attitudes. If you understand various modes of inquiry, learning styles, and approaches to problem solving, and can recognize them by identifying certain characteristics, you will be able to provide information, opportunities, and approaches for your clients that will be compatible with their cognitive skills, strategies, and preferences. Also, if you understand your own preferred styles of thinking, you can use them to their best advantage in appropriate situations. You can also endeavor to expand and improve your cognitive and problem-solving skills.

SUMMARY

This chapter has been concerned with various aspects of the problem-solving process, elucidating some basic principles the clinician and client must consider if the process is to be effective. The chapter has also considered a variety of cognitive approaches that affect individual problem solving. The discussion contrasted preceptive versus receptive data gathering, systematic versus intuitive data processing, and possible combinations thereof. Five basic types of thinkers were described: synthesist, idealist, pragmatist, analyst, and realist. We noted that some individuals use two or even three favored thinking styles, while others tend to use one style almost exclusively.

Knowledge of various approaches to data gathering, data processing, and problem solving will help the communicative disorders specialist interact with a client in a manner compatible with the client's cognitive approach and skills. Such knowledge will also permit the professional to try new ways of gathering and processing information and to utilize his or her preferred thinking style or styles more efficiently.

An appropriate goal for the communication disorders specialist is not only to serve as a model of effective problem-solving behavior, but to assist clients and family members in improving their own ability to define and work through problems that arise during the course of therapy and in other areas of life.

REFERENCES

Brammer, L.M. (1988). *The helping relationship: Process and skills* (4th ed.). Englewood Cliffs, NJ: Prentice-Hall.

Brill, N.I. (1985). *Working with people: The helping process* (3rd ed.). New York: Longman.

Carkhuff, R.R., & Anthony, W.A. (1979). *The skills of helping*. Amherst, MA: Human Resource Development Press.

Churchman, C.W. (1971). *The design of inquiring systems*. New York: Basic Books.

Corey, G. (1977). *Theory and practice of counseling and psychotherapy*. Monterey, CA: Brooks/Cole.

DeBono, E. (1972). *Lateral Thinking*. New York: Harper & Row.

Ewing, D.W. (1977, December). Discovering your problem-solving style. *Psychology Today*, pp. 69–73, 138.

Gordon, T. (1970). *Parent effectiveness training*. New York: Peter H. Wyden.

Gordon, T. (1977). *Teacher effectiveness training*. New York: D. McKay Company.

Gordon, T. (1977). *Leader effectiveness training*. New York: Bantam Books.

Harrison, A.F., & Bramson, R.M. (1982). *The art of thinking*. New York: Berkley Books.

Kroth, R.L. (1975). *Communicating with parents of exceptional children*. Denver: Love Publishing Co.

Mager, R.F. (1962). *Preparing instructional objectives*. Palo Alto, CA: Fearon Publishers.

McKenney, J.L., & Keen, P.G.W. (1974). How managers' minds work. *Harvard Business Review*, 62(3), 79–90.

Mitroff, I.I., & Pondy, L.R. (1974, September/October). On the organization of inquiry: A comparison of some radically different approaches to policy analysis. *Public Administration Review*, pp. 471–479.

O'Neill, N., & O'Neill, G. (1974). *Shifting gears: Finding security in a changing world.* New York: M. Evans and Co., Avon Books.

Rutherford, R.B., Jr., & Edgar, E. (1979). *Teachers and parents: A guide to interaction and cooperation* (abridged ed.). Boston: Allyn & Bacon.

8

When Therapy Ends

Modern psychologists stress the importance of completed patterns, or Gestalts, in human life and activities. People often feel stress or tension when activities are interrupted or conversations terminated before they have reached an intended goal. Conversely, people often experience a sense of satisfaction and relief when a job or project is completed. At that point, they can move on to a new and different activity without some of their energy and concern still being vested in the unfinished Gestalt.

In previous chapters, we have discussed the need of humans for structures that facilitate this desirable feeling of closure. Public speakers and professional writers think in terms of introduction, main body, and conclusion as they plan presentations. Clinicians find that sessions with individual clients are more satisfying if each session is structured with a beginning, main portion, and conclusion. In group work, a session will seem rushed or disorganized if time is not available for some introductory minutes in which participants can focus on goals for the session and settle into the business at hand. In addition to these opening moments, there must be time for concluding the session, a denouement of the main action, or participants may leave feeling frustrated or unsatisfied.

Your work with each client in your caseload is also subject to this general structure: you meet a client for the first time; you decide on certain goals for the relationship and work together over a period of time; and then the working relationship ends. Sometimes the relationship ends prematurely or abruptly. Sometimes it continues longer than is necessary or desirable. Ideally, the relationship ends because the original purpose for the alliance has been served. In this chapter, we will discuss some of the factors involved in the important closing stage of a professional relationship.

FACTORS INVOLVED IN ENDING THERAPY

Therapy Ended by External Circumstances

Therapy can end for a variety of reasons, some beyond the control of the client or clinician. A client may be transferred by an employer to another city. The family of a child client may move away from the community. Services may be cut back in a school system or public agency. Third party payment may be terminated because the maximum number of reimbursable sessions has been reached, and the client cannot afford to pay for any further sessions. Or the work schedule of a client may be so drastically changed that there is no possible meeting time.

Some therapy or rehabilitation programs are designed to include a specific number of sessions. For example, a military hospital may have a therapy program for military personnel with dysfluency problems. The personnel are transferred from their duty base to the hospital for eight weeks of intensive therapy and then return to their home base. Or an audiologist may be contracted by a community senior center to conduct an aural rehabilitation program for elders consisting of 10 2-hour weekly sessions. Members of these groups make varying degrees of progress during the allotted sessions. Some might benefit from further therapy and, if possible, are provided with information regarding sources where additional therapy might be obtained.

In situations such as these, termination of therapy may not be desired by either participant, but both must face the reality of the situation. Often, the closing session or sessions will be concerned with problem solving: how can the client continue to progress toward desired communication goals even though the therapy relationship is ended? The solution may involve preparation of a home program or referral to a private or public agency in the client's new location. In any case, the clinician will want to make the end of therapy as fruitful as possible.

Therapy Ended by the Client

At times, therapy may be terminated by the client or the client's family before the clinician feels termination is appropriate. From the client's or family's perspective, the progress being made is not worth the time, energy, or expense involved. Or other personal problems may be so pressing that therapy is no longer a priority concern. Sometimes, these feelings are shared with the clinician so that discussion can take place.

Occasionally, the decision is made without discussion, and the end of therapy is so abrupt that the clinician is left stunned. Whenever possible, it is wise for the clinician to contact the client or the client's family in order to determine in an objective and nondefensive way the probable cause of termination. The contact will be a learning experience for the clinician and will at least permit closing of the Gestalt through expression of concern and courteous leavetaking.

Therapy Ended by the Clinician

One-sided termination of therapy is not only the client's prerogative. Sometimes the clinician may discontinue therapy because certain behaviors on the part of the client are sabotaging the client's progress or making the clinician's life miserable. Possible causes for dismissal from therapy include the client's coming to therapy repeatedly under the influence of alcohol or other drugs; chronic, unexplained absenteeism; persistent refusal to carry out activities and assignments; and outbursts of violent, irrational, or abusive behavior. There is no reason for a clinician to work with a client against the clinician's considered judgment. However, detailed documentation of incidents leading to dismissal is of primary importance.

It is important also that the clinician share with the client (or the person responsible for the client) the reasons for terminating therapy. The agreed-upon goals for therapy should be reviewed, and the effects of the client's behavior on the progress of therapy should be discussed. The clinician will again emphasize the autonomy and responsibility of the client in the therapy process and the role of the clinician as guide and facilitator. Any discussion of the termination of therapy should be in a problem-solving mode: the problem is that certain characteristics or behaviors of the client are interfering with progress in therapy to such a degree that the clinician feels the current arrangement is not feasible or desirable. The clinician is well aware that the client in such instances needs help, but may decide that some other help is necessary before any real progress can be made in a communication therapy program. Alternative suggestions are usually considered in such problem-solving sessions and may result in referral to another agency if the clinician and client agree to such action.

There are times in practice when a clinician decides that he or she is not the professional the client needs most. Perhaps the nature and/or severity of the client's problem warrants referral to a speech-language pathologist or audiologist with more training and experience in working with that particular problem. In other circumstances, the clinician may have begun working with a client but may realize over a period of time that a different type of professional service to the client is a higher priority. A preexistent or newly developed health problem may require medical attention before therapy should continue. Or the mental or emotional condition of the client may be cause for serious professional concern. We have already discussed (in Chapter 4) the effects of high levels of unmanaged stress and of clinical depression upon clients' behavior and attitudes.

The clinician may feel that therapy by a psychiatrist or in a mental health clinic should take precedence over speech or language therapy. For example, the communicative disorders specialist often begins work with a severely language-delayed or mute youngster on a diagnostic therapy basis. As the relationship progresses and the child's responses to a variety of language facilitatory techniques are noted, the need for psychiatric intervention occasionally becomes apparent. The parents may be content with the help being received and even encouraged by some small progress that is being made, but if the clinician's professional judgment dictates that psychiatric help may be more beneficial to the child, the clinician should certainly recommend it. Terminating speech-language therapy until such help is obtained is an indication of the clinician's opinion regarding the importance of the recommended service.

In no way do we wish to imply that children or adults with speech, language, or hearing problems are more susceptible to psychiatric problems than the general population. However, communication skills and behaviors are important aspects of personality, and personality disorders sometimes first reveal themselves in disturbed interpersonal communication. People who need psychiatric help sometimes come into the caseload of communicative disorders specialists. We are encouraging you to become familiar with the symptoms of psychiatric disturbance and psychiatric emergencies so that you will be aware when a client needs a different kind of help than you are prepared or trained to give. These symptoms include suicide attempts or threats; outbursts of unprovoked and uncontrolled assaultive and aggressive behavior; exhibitionism or voyeurism; frequent anguished crying (not the whiney, manipulative kind); hallucinations, delusions, compulsions, or other bizarre behavior; delinquent behavior; and extreme depression and/or withdrawal.

Families of clients exhibiting psychiatric symptoms are often anxious and concerned but feel helpless in their ability to control the situation or make needed changes. The fact that you may be in a position to direct families to available help can be a significant service, particularly early in a child client's life. Some guidelines to assist you in making referrals to other agencies will be discussed later in this chapter.

Therapy Ended by Mutual Consent

The preferred reason for ending therapy is that the client has achieved agreed-upon goals and no longer needs the services of the clinician. The identified problem has been corrected and the client (or client's parent) perceives his or her communication abilities as satisfactory. The end of therapy does not necessarily mean that the client's speech and language is perfect; rather, it may signify that an appropriate level of proficiency has been attained. In the clinician's judgment, or in the dismissal criteria of the agency, any additional increment of gain achieved through further therapy would not warrant the professional's time and effort, or the expense involved. For example, Diedrich and Bangert (1980) pointed out in their longitudinal study of articulation therapy that they consider achievement of 75 to 80 percent accuracy during conversation to be a cost-effective dismissal criterion. They claimed that it is uneconomical to aim for an additional 10 to 20 percent accuracy in articulation since that may take 6 to 15 more treatment weeks.

In some settings, such as university clinics and school programs, clients may be retained in therapy until a higher criterion level is achieved. For example, Eger, Chabon, Mient, and Cushman (1986) reported that 99.8 percent of 443 children with articulation problems were dismissed from therapy by their public school speech and language clinicians when they had achieved 90 to 100 percent proficiency in conversational speech. The authors (p. 25) acknowledged that

> Although it was confirmed that most clinicians establish goals of near-perfect speech for their articulation-impaired children, these objectives may not be realistic or necessary. . . . It may be time for speech and language clinicians to reconsider the dismissal criteria used and base future decisions on empirically based standards of quality rather than a priori notions of acceptability.

The findings of Carol Frattali (1987), in a study evaluating treatment of articulation disordered children in a university speech and hearing clinic, closely paralleled those of Eger and her colleagues and Diedrich and Bangert.

Professionals in the field point out that dismissal from therapy is a highly individual decision. Factors to consider must include the nature and severity of the disorder, and the client's age, physical condition, motivation, family support, economic circumstances, and progress in therapy. The overriding consideration is the client's ability to communicate effectively in everyday life situations.

PREPARING A CLIENT FOR LEAVING THERAPY

The client-clinician relationship is an important and personal one. For that reason, it is crucial that the client and clinician discuss the approaching dismissal from therapy. You want your clients to feel pleased that they have made progress and feel confident that they can make continued progress independently. At the same time, you do not want the client to feel cut off or deserted. Of course, clients differ in their need to continue the relationship and maintain contact. The clinician should try to sense the client's needs in this regard and act accordingly.

Discussion regarding dismissal should focus on the client's achievement of the previously agreed-upon therapy goals. Preferably, the discussion will be initiated two or three sessions prior to dismissal. This will allow opportunity to devote the final sessions to activities deemed especially important by either the client or clinician. For instance, further testing (standardized, criterion-referenced, or informal evaluation of targeted behaviors) will be conducted if needed to document the client's progress in therapy. These test results will be discussed with the client and the client's family and compared with previous test scores. Pre- and post-therapy audio and/or videotapes can be powerful proof of the progress that has been achieved. Playing ''before and after'' tapes can stimulate discussion of accomplishments and the goals by which they were achieved. It can also stimulate discussion of feelings regarding the therapy process and the client's present communicative skills.

In these closing sessions, the clinician will also spend time discussing activities to facilitate continued improvement that can be carried out by the client following dismissal. It is important that these suggestions be summarized in writing as a tangible reminder to the client of personal responsibility for communication skills. The clinician will often encourage family members to participate in these discussions because of their vital roles in assisting the client.

The clinician may encourage the client to contact him or her if any questions or problems develop. Frequently, the clinician and client will plan for a follow-up evaluative session at some future date to note whether progress has been maintained. Such follow-up sessions are always desirable. They may be crucial if the clinician is conducting research on the efficacy of treatment and the maintenance of attained therapy goals.

In the following interview excerpt, a young elementary school teacher who had been referred by an otolaryngologist for correction of vocal abuse comments during a therapy session:

Interview Excerpt 8-1

R: I saw Dr. Cohen last week and he said my vocal folds were clear—there was no evidence of vocal nodules. He even said that my voice sounded much better and I seemed more relaxed.

C: That's great news. As we mentioned last session, you have made good progress and have really changed your speech habits. The fact that you no longer are hoarse at the end of the day is evidence of the changes. It's time to talk about concluding therapy.

R: I've been thinking about that too. When you played that tape last week of my first session here and then I heard the playback of my new voice, I couldn't believe the difference. I really notice when I strain my voice now and I know what to do about it.

C: That was our goal. Shall we make next week our last session? We can review activities that you can continue to do on your own. We will make a tape of those for you to use at home. And we'll plan for a follow-up session in three months.

If the clinician's relationship with the client has been fairly long and especially challenging, poignant, or satisfying, there may be a real sadness or reluctance to end the association. Lawrence Shulman (1979, p. 92) acknowledged this in regard to ending the relationship of a counselor and client.

> In many ways the ending sessions are the most difficult ones for both worker and client. The source of the strain stems from our general problem of dealing with the ending of important relationships. The worker–client association is a specific example of this larger problem. It can be painful to terminate a close relationship; when you have invested yourself meaningfully in a relationship, have shared some of your most important feelings, and have given and taken help from another human being, the bond that develops is strong. This is true with friends, family, working colleagues—in fact with all relationships. Our society has done little to train us how to handle a separation; in fact, the general norm is to deny feelings associated with it.

Feelings of warmth and mutual regard are evident in the following excerpt from a closing therapy session with the mother of a preschool son originally diagnosed as language delayed:

Interview Excerpt 8-2

R: These past months have meant so much to me. When we first started, I felt like crying every day. I couldn't understand why Nick wasn't speaking. My in-laws kept telling me there was something wrong with him. Now when they see him and talk to him they are just amazed.

C: Nick has certainly made good progress. He's a bright youngster; he just needed more stimulation and incentive to talk. You and your husband have done a fine job following through on the activities we've worked on in therapy and on other suggestions I've made.

R: At first, I didn't think that what you suggested would help. But it made all the difference in the world. We can never thank you enough. If Nick ever has any more problems, can we call on you?

C: Of course, but I think he's well on his way. It has been a real treat for me to work with both of you. I would really like to hear from you occasionally to find out how everyone is doing.

Peterson and Nisenholz (1987, pp. 96–97) make the following comments regarding terminating counseling that also apply to terminating speech, language, or hearing therapy:

> It is important that the counselor and client bring to closure any relationship issues through the discussion of feelings toward one another and toward the relationship. The goal is to bring about an appropriate ending in which everything that needs expression is expressed. . . . The preparation for and implementation of termination of the relationship involves a variety of the skills used in earlier stages, with the major new skill being knowing how to comfortably say goodbye to a person with whom one has developed a close relationship.

Many clinicians find that in the last sessions of therapy, feelings of closure can be achieved by summarizing, evaluating, and planning. A helpful way to look at this is attention to the past, present, and future: summarizing what has happened during the course of therapy; evaluating the current feelings of both client and clinician regarding the client's current communication skills and termination of therapy; and planning what the client may do in the future to maintain and increase communicative effectiveness.

Termination of therapy can also involve more mundane matters than leavetaking and associated expression of feelings. In some work settings, particularly private clinics or individual private practice, clinicians can be faced with the uncomfortable dilemma of collecting past due payments prior to dismissal from therapy. Richard Flower (1986, p. 112) discusses this dilemma.

> Although issues related to delinquent accounts, bad debts, and retroactive denial of claims have few direct ethical implications, they can lead to dilemmas for private practitioners who are dedicated to the delivery of human services. On the one hand, there is nothing unethical about clinicians expecting fair recompense for their services. On the other hand, there are widespread negative attitudes about health and human services providers who pursue delinquent accounts and bad debts too vigorously. Therefore, the course to be followed may be determined by professional propriety, rather than by actual ethical concerns. Clinicians may ultimately pay a high price for breaches of propriety with respect to these financial matters. Too vigorous pursuit of delinquent accounts may be viewed as improper and ultimately impair a practitioner's status in the community. The economic consequences of losses in reputation may ultimately be much greater than the losses from bad debts. Every private practitioner should become familiar with the prevailing customs

of other professionals in the community before deciding on his or her approach to such matters.

In addition to past due accounts, therapy materials or reference books may have been borrowed and not yet returned. The clinician must judge how far to pursue these matters. One or two unpleasant experiences in this regard may result in changes in your office or practice procedures. If there have been problems in these areas with a particular client, you may wish to take this into consideration prior to making a referral to another professional or agency.

REFERRAL TO OTHER AGENCIES

We have made reference in several chapters to the possibility of the communication disorders specialist referring a client to other professionals or other agencies. Experiences in this aspect of professional practice have led to the formulation of the following guidelines regarding referral:

- The clinician must know possible appropriate referral agencies. Directories of local and national services are important additions to the professional's library. Although published information regarding local agencies and services is valuable, personal knowledge of the services provided and of the professionals at the agency is preferable.
- Reasons for referral must be clear in the mind of the clinician and should be discussed in a straightforward manner with the client and/or appropriate family members.
- A description of the recommended agency, the pertinent services offered, and the hoped-for outcome of the client's work there should be shared with the client.
- It is the client's (or legal guardian's) responsibility to make contact with the recommended agency and set up an appointment. The clinician may offer to notify the professional or agency that the client may be contacting them.
- The clinician must obtain a signed release form from the client before any records are forwarded to the referral agency.
- It is important that the client not feel "abandoned," particularly if the only professional working with the client is the communicative disorders specialist.
- The clinician should document the referral, providing a copy of the written recommendation for the client and for the client's file.

- The clinician may also suggest that the client share available audio or videotape materials of his or her therapy sessions with professionals at the new agency, if this is appropriate.
- The clinician must keep in mind that the paramount concern is the client's well-being. Referral to other agencies or professionals should not be delayed because the clinician is reluctant to admit limitations in ability to provide the most appropriate service.

IMPORTANCE OF RECORD KEEPING AND DOCUMENTATION

In interviews with practicing clinicians regarding record keeping and documentation, one common theme prevailed: keeping records is absolutely essential. The format and detail of record keeping varies with the work setting, but the clinician should make every effort to maintain an individual file for each client. The following comments made during interviews with practicing clinicians underscore the importance of documentation:

"Keep a chart on each client. Keep notes in the chart for every contact or visit. After hearing aid trials, indicate type of aid and what factors contributed to its success or failure. Be sure to keep copies of reports to referral sources."

"I maintain a log using the SOAP format: Subjective and Objective comments, Activities and results, and Progress. The entries should be neat, brief, legible, and intelligible and should always be dated and signed. In charting progress, indicate percentages and ratios as much as possible. One thing I do that hospital nurses appreciate is to not only write suggestions in a patient's file, but to also write them on an 8-1/2 by 11 paper—signed and dated—and post it above the patient's bed. This is important because I can't speak to all the people who come in contact with the patient. I can't even speak to all the nurses because of the different shifts."

"I find that keeping a tape for each client in addition to the regular file is very useful. It can be used during the therapy session, for the client to take home between sessions for practice, and to document progress."

"I don't have any special suggestions regarding record keeping—only to be quite meticulous about documenting all contacts. I note not only personal contacts, but also telephone conversations. I make sure to keep all authorizations for release of information on file. I also maintain tapes for each patient as an additional record."

Clinicians working in the schools point out the difficulty of record keeping with large caseloads. They also iterate the necessity for a procedure by which the clinician can make notes regarding each client, even in group settings.

"Record keeping in the schools is very difficult because of the caseload. I use a clipboard containing a sheet of paper with everyone in the group listed. I keep charting records and jot down notes regarding each child when he or she responds in therapy. At report-writing time, I pull this information out."

The following list of items to be included in a client's file summarizes suggestions made by experienced clinicians:

- reports of the initial diagnostic evaluation and any reevaluations or additional testing done at a later date
- reports forwarded to the clinician by other professionals regarding the client
- the recommended therapy program containing a list of therapy goals and objectives
- a record of all clinician contacts with the client, often in the form of a therapy log
- summaries of interviews with the client or family members, or other professionals
- all reports prepared by the clinician in accordance with personal or agency policy
- copies of all reports sent to others, along with permission forms signed by the client or legal guardian
- copies of any referral letters sent by the clinician

The clinician should decide upon a particular order of arrangement for material in the files and adhere to it. All reports, summaries, and accounts of therapy sessions should be signed and dated by the clinician.

It is not our intention to discuss the basic principles and details of report and letter writing, even though this is a critical aspect of professional functioning. Current textbooks on diagnosis and/or therapy in speech, language, and hearing pathology contain information regarding this important subject. For example, Nation and Aram (1984) include sample administrative forms such as release forms, referral letters, requests for information, scheduling forms, and discharge summaries. Meitus and Weinberg (1983) provide a chapter on clinical report and letter writing. Another well-known publication on report writing is that of Kenneth Knepflar (1976).

Although many notations regarding clients must of necessity be made manually by the clinician, increasing use is being made of personal computers to process diagnostic and therapy information and to maintain clinical files. Computers are also being used to assist in the business aspect of a professional practice. Mariana Newton (1986a, 1986b) discussed computer application in private practice.

A professional must be aware that clients have a legal right of access to clinical records. It is important, then, that the clinician maintain the file in a professional manner and that the file contain objective and well-documented information. It is also important that files be kept in a way that will ensure confidentiality. Irv Meitus, in his text co-edited with Bernd Weinberg (1983, p. 299), comments on this.

> Clinical data, written reports and summary letters all contain confidential information. The original copy of the reports and the copies of summary letters are typically kept in the clinical folder as part of hospital, school, or clinical records. Under normal circumstances this information cannot be released to unauthorized persons without the written consent of the patient or a responsible adult . . .

> . . . It should be noted, that once information is released to another individual or agency, speech-language clinicians have no control over how that information will be used. This fact highlights the need to ensure that any piece of clinical writing represents a well-founded, objectively prepared document that places its writer in a fully accountable position.

Twila Griffith (1987, p. 110) discusses record keeping and accountability in a community hospital speech-language-hearing program.

> The need for accountability cannot be overemphasized. Documentation must be thorough and must follow the regulations of the setting in which treatment is provided. A comprehensive rehabilitation record should include: reason for referral; summary of the clinical condition; evaluation; plan of treatment with measurable goals; and progress notes. As treatment continues, the monthly summaries can discuss the patient and/ or the family's attitude regarding treatment, results of additional assessments, justification for continued treatment and expected improvement in functional ability. Recommendations for further care must be included in the discharge summary.

Kooper and Sullivan (1986), in their discussion of professional liability, stress the importance of record keeping for both speech-language pathologists and audiologists. They state (p. 76)

> The establishment of a patient record for appointments, fees and payments, insurance transactions, hearing aids dispensed, hearing aid repairs, battery sales, and hearing aid insurance is essential. This record may be kept by hand, typewritten, or placed on the computer. Initially, most records are kept manually. Appointments records can be maintained in the general appointment book. Notes should be made in the appointment book when a patient cancels an appointment or fails to come for the appointment. This information may serve as possible evidence for malpractice defense. The patient may be found responsible for contributory negligence for failing to keep appointments or obtain follow-up care.
>
> A general ledger system maintains information for billing and signals the late payment of a fee. The late payment for services may alert the clinician that the patient is dissatisfied. Daily records that track fees, payments, and the filing of insurance forms can provide patients with accurate information and prompt service. . . . These records provide the clinician with specific information needed to monitor transactions and assist in maintaining good public relations with patients. The subject of financial transactions is one of the most sensitive topics for patients, particularly when there are limited resources. Respecting this sensitivity through the accurate keeping of records lessens the possibility for misunderstanding.
>
> Audiologists, in particular, need to maintain records about the sales of batteries, hearing aid repairs, telephone calls, and hearing aid insurance. These provide important information for testimony if lawsuits are filed involving hearing aid usage. In addition, notes need to be made if there was a trial usage period and if the patient accepted or rejected the aid at the end of that period of time. This denotes in writing a respect for the consumer's rights by the practitioner in the process of dispensing.

We have stressed the importance of maintaining client files in a systematic manner. The clinician will also need to develop an efficient procedure for handling all paperwork. The development of such a system can greatly enhance personal efficiency.

Writers in the field of business provide an excellent source of suggestions in this regard. For instance, Kaufman and Corrigan (1988) give suggestions for the business executive that can be adapted by the communication specialist. Kaufman and Corrigan underscore the importance of a personal calendar and of personal files as essential to efficient organization. They discuss the creation of specialized files such as monthly and daily "tickler" files, in which items are stored that are to be handled on particular dates. These files contain reminders regarding future meetings and other events. Other specialized files include those for "work in progress," for mail, for specific meetings, and for material to be read when time permits.

FOLLOW-UP PROCEDURES

We have alluded to follow-up procedures in the preceding discussion. Two important points to be stressed regarding follow-up concern effectiveness of therapy and research considerations. Maintaining contact with clients enables the clinician to determine whether the client has maintained the level of proficiency achieved at the time of dismissal or whether communicative effectiveness has been enhanced or reduced. The clinician is also able to ascertain whether or not recommended referrals were accomplished. Some clinicians prefer to schedule a future follow-up appointment at the time the client is dismissed from therapy. Others make a note in their "tickler" file and contact the client by phone or mail after an appropriate time has elapsed to check on how things are going. In school settings, the clinician may informally check on a client's progress by chatting with the child on the playground or in the corridor, or by talking with the child's classroom teacher. As stated above, it is important that all follow-up contacts be documented in the client's file.

In recent years, practicing clinicians have become increasingly interested in researching and documenting the efficacy of various treatment programs. If a clinician is engaged in such research, follow-up of clients becomes a necessity rather than an option. Follow-up in this case may take the form of one or more scheduled client reevaluations, a telephone interview with the client or appropriate family member, the completion of a questionnaire by the client, or any other form dictated by the research design. Two books on research design specifically written for communicative disorders specialists are those by William Shearer (1982) and Leija McReynolds and Kevin Kearns (1983).

FACING THE DEATH OF A CLIENT

In a chapter concerned with the ending of therapy, we must acknowledge the possibility of the death of a client. Communication disorders specialists work with a variety of clients, some of whom suffer from terminal illness (such as AIDS, ALS, or a metastasized malignancy). Others may have conditions that suddenly worsen (for example, heart disease or vascular conditions). Occasionally, a client may meet with sudden accidental death.

It is important for the clinician to understand the grief process (discussed in Chapter 3) in order to understand what the seriously ill client and his or her family are experiencing in confronting the inevitability of death. Concentration on previously established therapy goals becomes much less significant as the illness progresses. If a client dies, knowledge of grief and mourning may help in contacts with surviving members and friends. The clinician's actions following the death of a client will be determined by personal feelings and preferences. Many clinicians may feel that a personal note of sympathy to the family is appropriate; others may attend the funeral.

If the client was a member of a therapy group, the clinician may have to help the group members work through their grief. Group members with similar diagnoses (as in an alaryngeal speech group or a stroke group) may be particularly affected. Time may be allotted during the group therapy session to acknowledge feelings regarding the death. The group members may decide to send a sympathy card or other expression to the surviving family members. The clinician must rely on professional judgment regarding the extent to which attention is devoted to the expression and exploration of feelings. It is important for the clinician to realize that it is not always possible to maintain professional objectivity. The clinician should not be surprised, therefore, if the death of a client triggers a personal grief reaction.

SUMMARY

This chapter has been concerned with closure. The pattern—or Gestalt—of therapy must be brought to a satisfying finish. At what point therapy ends is dependent upon a number of factors. Ideally, it ends when both client and clinician agree that the goals of therapy have been met. The last therapy sessions are devoted to discussion of achievement of therapy goals, of the client's present communicative skills, of activities to facilitate continued improvement that can be carried out independently by the client, and of feelings regarding the therapy process and the ending of therapy. Arrangements may be made during the final sessions regarding follow-up contacts or appointments.

This chapter included other aspects to be considered as therapy ends. It listed guidelines for referring clients to other professionals or agencies. The chapter also stressed the importance of record keeping and documentation, not only from the standpoint of completeness and accountability but in connection with personal and professional efficiency.

A variety of emotions can be aroused in clinicians as they end their associations with clients. It is hoped that these feelings are generally positive. However, feelings of loss, frustration, or sadness may be triggered if therapy ends abruptly or prematurely.

REFERENCES

Diedrich, W., & Bangert, J. (1980). *Articulation learning*. Houston, TX: College-Hill Press.

Eger, D.L., Chabon, S.S., Mient, M.G., & Cushman, B.B. (1986). When is enough enough? *Asha, 28*(5), 23–25.

Flower, R. (1986). Ethical concerns in private practice. In K.G. Butler (Ed.), *Prospering in private practice: A handbook for speech-language pathology and audiology* (pp. 101–123). Rockville, MD: Aspen Publishers, Inc.

Frattali, C.M. (1987). *Quality of care in speech-language pathology: Treatment evaluation of articulation disordered children in a university speech and hearing clinic*. Unpublished doctoral dissertation, University of Pittsburgh.

Griffith, T.S. (1987). Administration of community hospital speech-language-hearing programs. In H.J. Oyer (Ed.), *Administration of programs in speech-language pathology and audiology* (pp. 100–128). Englewood Cliffs, NJ: Prentice-Hall.

Kaufman, P.C., & Corrigan, A. (1988). *Managing people at work-at home*. Stamford, CT: Long-meadow Press.

Knepflar, K.J. (1976). *Report writing in the field of communication disorders*. Danville, IL: Interstate Printers & Publishers.

Kooper, R., & Sullivan, C.A. (1986). Professional liability: Management and prevention. In K.G. Butler (Ed.), *Prospering in private practice: A handbook for speech-language pathology and audiology* (pp. 59–80). Rockville, MD: Aspen Publishers, Inc.

McReynolds, L.V., & Kearns, K.P. (1983). *Single-subject experimental designs in communicative disorders*. Baltimore: University Park Press.

Meitus, I.J., & Weinberg, B. (Eds.). (1983). *Diagnosis in speech-language pathology*. Baltimore: University Park Press.

Nation, J.E., & Aram, D.M. (1984). *Diagnosis of speech and language disorders* (2nd ed.). San Diego: College-Hill Press.

Newton, M. (1986a). Computer applications in private practice: Getting started. In K.G. Butler (Ed.), *Prospering in private practice: A handbook for speech-language pathology and audiology* (pp. 167–174). Rockville, MD: Aspen Publishers, Inc.

Newton, M. (1986b). Standard computer software applications in private practice. In K.G. Butler (Ed.), *Prospering in private practice: A handbook for speech-language pathology and audiology* (pp. 203–222). Rockville, MD: Aspen Publishers, Inc.

Peterson, J.V., & Nisenholz, B. (1987). *Orientation to counseling*. Boston: Allyn & Bacon.

Shearer, W.M. (1982). *Research procedures in speech, language, and hearing*. Baltimore: Williams & Wilkins.

Shulman, L. (1979). *The skills of helping individuals and groups*. Itasca, IL: F.E. Peacock Publishers, Inc.

9

Professional Effectiveness in the Work Setting

Effectiveness in professional work involves many factors. Being a *competent* professional is, of course, paramount. Also, the professional person must be able to assure others of this competence. When interviewed, well-established speech-language pathologists and audiologists stressed the importance of developing expertise and becoming known for a specialty within the field. Toward that end, continuing education is a necessity. These successful professionals also mentioned the importance of liking people and enjoying what you do. Positive personal qualities, interpersonal communication skills, good business practices, and efficient time management were other factors seen as vital to success. Much of the information discussed in previous chapters is not only applicable to working with clients and their families, but to getting along with co-workers as well. Additional aspects important in professional effectiveness will be discussed in this chapter.

GETTING ALONG AND GETTING AHEAD IN THE WORK SETTING

Working as a Team Member

An important aspect of professional life is working with others. The information regarding basic human needs, organismic variables, and purposes and dimensions of interactions (Chapter 2); working with family members of clients (Chapter 5); working with groups (Chapter 6); and problem solving (Chapter 7) is particularly applicable in relating to.co-workers.

The importance of professionals working as team members to facilitate services to handicapped infants and toddlers was underscored in the 1986 passage of Public Law 99-457—an amendment that extends the range of services originally mandated in the Education for All Handicapped Children Act (Public Law 94-142). A requirement of P.L. 99-457 is that each statewide system must include components related to multidisciplinary evaluations for the handicapped infants and toddlers, the development of individualized family service plans, and interagency cooperation and agreements. Another requirement is the appointment of a *case manager* to serve as coordinator of the services provided by the interdisciplinary team members and their agencies. All of these components call for close cooperation and effective interactions among the involved professionals and family members.

Ernest Stech and Sharon Ratliffe (1985) discuss requirements and skills for working effectively with others. They point out the necessity of combining the different skills and viewpoints of team members through processes of cooperation and coordination. Thus, team members must have expertise, be willing to communicate, and be willing to coordinate their efforts with others. Stech and Ratliffe indicate that five interpersonal skills are requisite for effective and efficient group or team membership: (1) assertiveness, (2) active listening, (3) negotiation, (4) conflict management, and (5) timing (knowing when to use the other four skills). They state (p. 160)

> Assertiveness is needed to get opinions and ideas into the discussion. Listening is needed to make sure that ideas and opinions are heard and understood. The skill of negotiation helps group members seek answers that satisfy the greatest number. Conflict management allows a group to ride through the rough seas of disagreement. A sensitive, alert group member is aware that these skills are needed at different times and in various situations. An effective group member knows how to use the super skill of timing.
>
> By using the interpersonal skills appropriate to each situation, group members will have a better chance of getting along with each other. They will be able to build and maintain their relationships. All members of the group will be involved in the work of the group. The result will be a group that holds together through difficult times as well as in moments of success.

Lou Tomes and Dixie Sanger (1986) surveyed the attitudes of interdisciplinary team members (classroom teachers, elementary school principals, school psychologists, and learning disabilities teachers) toward speech-language services in public schools. They found that, in general, these professionals had positive attitudes toward the speech-language services provided. However, clinicians received lower ratings on their ability to provide helpful in-services and to offer appropriate suggestions for classroom management. The authors state (p. 238)

> A major challenge of the public school speech-language clinician is to become an active member of the educational team, who assumes lead-

ership in improving children's communication skills while being sensitive to the concerns of fellow educators who have their own objectives for the children's overall academic program. The overall positive responses obtained in this and other studies indicate that educators respect clinician's abilities to facilitate development of children's communication skills. However, the less than clearly favorable responses to some statements indicate that clinicians need to listen more intently to the concerns, priorities, and suggestions of other professionals who have contact with the children. This suggestion is further supported by the observation that the extent to which educators perceive their ideas to be integrated into the treatment program is related to their overall attitude toward the speech-language program.

Work climates certainly differ. In some, there is a high level of cohesiveness: workers enjoy one another's company and work cooperatively on many worthwhile projects. Work is a source of satisfaction and pride. In other work settings, co-workers do not achieve cohesiveness. They go their separate ways, often jealously guarding their professional territories, and finding little need to communicate. Those in leadership roles have much to do with the emotional climate of a workplace. However, the responsibility for group cohesion also rests with the team members. Even one or two workers employing the interpersonal skills mentioned above can positively influence an entire work team.

In making suggestions for being an effective team member, professionals comment

"Be honest, forthright, and polite in dealing with others. Be sure your conduct is always ethical."

"If you promise to do something, do it."

"Be aware of the needs of your work group. Your function as a team member may change when you see what your group needs."

"If you are personal friends with some of your co-workers, make certain that other members of the group do not feel excluded."

"Congratulate colleagues on professional successes. Notes of congratulation or comments regarding published articles, presentations, or a promotion are welcome when sincerely stated."

"Be aware of colleagues' schedules and their workloads. Don't take up their time unnecessarily."

"Try to separate home and office. Keep your personal problems to yourself."

"If you are working with someone who is unpleasant, be as pleasant and courteous to them as you can. But don't reward their unpleasantness."

"Be careful about criticizing co-workers. If you do, make sure it's constructive criticism made directly to the person involved. Concentrate on the behavior you would like to see changed—and why—rather than negative comments about the person as an individual."

Even in pleasant work settings, conflict may occur. Valid differences of opinion exist and, if the situation is sufficiently important, will be expressed. In such cases, it is important to acknowledge the conflict and deal with it openly. Problem-solving techniques can then be used by the persons involved to work toward a resolution of differences. In successful conflict management, each person involved feels respected and listened to by the others even though they have agreed upon a compromise solution.

Some workers avoid conflict by not expressing differences of opinion. Such behavior continued over a long period of time results in frustration and reduced self-esteem. In addition, such behavior deprives the group of what could be an important and valid consideration. Valuable employees are assertive; that is, they are willing to state their ideas and feelings while respecting the ideas and feelings of others. When they feel it is necessary to disagree, they do so assertively.

Dorothy Jongeward and Philip Seyer (1978), as well as other authors, describe steps involved in assertive disagreement. One is to pause for a few moments when something is mentioned with which you disagree. This pause enables you to review mentally what was said and frame a response indicating your active listening. Your spoken response of restatement of content or reflection of feelings will help you clarify whether there actually is disagreement. If there is, you must then decide whether the disagreement is worth pursuing. If you do pursue it, first point out areas in which you and the speaker agree. If you find no such areas, at least indicate to the speaker in some way that you respect his or her right to have a differing opinion. In stating your point(s) of disagreement, do so courteously but firmly. It is useful to give reasons for your position and supporting data or examples. After stating your position, listen actively to the other person's response. You may be able to reach an agreement at that point. If not, and you determine that it is worthwhile to continue the discussion, a compromise solution may be sought. If that is unsuccessful and you reach an impasse, the only recourse may be either to drop the issue or to enlist the help of an impartial outsider.

Jongeward and Seyer (1978) summarize the steps of assertive disagreement in a flowchart depicted in Figure 9-1.

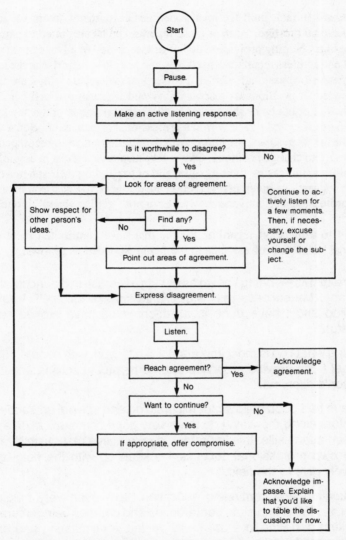

Figure 9-1 Disagreeing Assertively. *Source:* From *Choosing Success: Human Relationships on the Job* (p. 316) by D. Jongeward and P. Seyer, 1978, New York: John Wiley & Sons, Inc. Copyright 1978 by John Wiley & Sons, Inc. Reprinted by permission.

Advancing Your Career

Professionals in service fields are usually very concerned with getting *along* in their work setting. However, they frequently devote little thought or energy to also getting *ahead*. In fact, guilt feelings sometimes accompany dreams of advancement or personal prestige. Perhaps these feelings can be attributed to perceptions of the role of a "helping professional," or to association of advancement with the abhorrent and ruthless techniques used by some people in their rise to the top. And yet, competent professionals skilled in interpersonal relationships are the very people needed in positions of responsibility and leadership. Each person must decide whether or not he or she wishes to climb the corporate or agency ladder or advance in prestige and power within a professional organization. Some workers find a niche for themselves, are happy with their duties and their recompense, and have no desire to change positions. Others take an active interest in assuming new responsibilities, increasing their income, and/or expanding their spheres of influence. The suggestions given in this section are designed to assist you in maximizing your professional effectiveness, whether or not "getting ahead" is one of your goals.

In reply to a question regarding factors that have contributed most to their professional success, professionals in the field responded as follows:

"My expertise—being known as having expertise in diagnosis and therapy. My success rate with clients speaks for itself. I have studied and I have done it. My techniques have proved successful."

"Liking what I do is most important. I like to work with people. I like to feel I can provide a service and be helpful in solving another person's dilemma."

"I have had good solid academic training and special and superb mentors along the way. I do have very good communication and presentation skills. It is important to take active responsibility for your own professional success—to keep up with the field and actively *give* to the field."

"Education and continuing education have been very helpful, such as ASHA and state conferences and courses being offered. Working part-time in a university setting is stimulating and has contributed to my happiness with my career."

"Excellent training that has given me a lot of range and depth. My personal qualities: interest in people and the fun of helping them unload a burden."

"Finding an area to specialize—an area that interested me—my particular niche in the field. That keeps it exciting and opens a lot of doors. It's enabled me to publish and make presentations, which I never thought I'd be doing when I started out. You have to make it a career, not just a job. Get involved and it gets exciting."

"Being bilingual, and being in the right place at the right time. And being a good listener and sensitive to people's needs."

"Have rapport with the people you work with. Listen to your work setting and see where you'll best fit in. It's death in the public school setting to be viewed as someone above it all: often you don't have to do yard or lunchroom duty or grade papers; you have lots of exemptions. You have to show where you can put in the extras that have nothing to do with traditional speech therapy and differ with each setting."

"In this field, you have to really like people. Think of each person as a treasure box. It's like opening a treasure box and seeing each person as unique. And to do that is fun. Instead of being frustrated, you must be intrigued."

"Attend everything you can that's related to your professional interests, even if it's not in your own field. For instance, in my specialty of voice therapy I've learned a lot from psychologists and some important singers."

"You have to realize the importance of interpersonal communication skills. You also have to realize the importance of goals and of closure."

"Make the great effort to get yourself out in the community as a business person and so people take you seriously. Make a serious investment in yourself. Get other people to take you seriously. Have good business practices."

The above quotes are from professionals who work in a variety of settings, including public, private, and military hospitals; public schools; university clinics; and private practice. Yet their suggestions are applicable to speech-language pathologists and audiologists in all settings.

In their comments regarding success in their chosen field, professionals mention taking advantage of opportunities for advancement as they present themselves. Barbara Hundley (1989, p. 13), director of a university career center, noted that "being in the right place at the right time is sometimes luck, but not nearly as often as people think. On the contrary, it is often the result of careful preparation and created opportunities." Some workers may not be interested in advancement with its associated responsibilities. However, for those who are, Director Hundley (1989, p. 13) has the following suggestions:

First, size up your organization, the other players and opportunities. . . . To plan your future, take a sober look at where you are and your possibilities for the next several years. Map out several good alternatives and get started.

You can move up. You can move sideways, positioning yourself better for future moves. You can move out to find an opportunity that suits you better elsewhere. You can also not move at all; in most organizations, you can turn down a transfer or promotion and wait until a job you want is offered.

If moving up means moving out, make it clear that you are moving to a greater opportunity, not because you dislike your current job. You will need references, and it's wise to leave the door open for possible return. . . .

Sometimes, blocked avenues open when you give notice that you are leaving for a better job. Those who were unwilling to promote you or raise your pay change their minds when faced with the prospect of replacing you.

Whatever your work, you must continue to update your skills. Lawyers, accountants, scientists, doctors—even performers—know they must constantly read and retrain, or face professional disaster.

New information and technologies produce new opportunities and hazards for everyone, regardless of the field. Take advantage of every opportunity for new training . . .*

When talking with successful professionals, you may note important common characteristics. They present themselves as competent and confident individuals. They know their special skills and have found ways to express that expertise. They work well with others and yet are self-starters. They are willing to assume responsibility and follow through on commitments. They do not hesitate to assume leadership roles when opportunities arise.

Speech-language pathologists and audiologists are making more use of marketing strategies to promote public awareness of their services and enhance their professional image. The September 1988 issue of *Asha* featured a special section entitled, "Marketing Your Services." The section was described as a primer on marketing, explaining the four "Ps": practice, price, place, and promotion. Articles in the issue by Carol Ann Foxman, James P. Gelatt, Kathleen M. Griffin, Sandra C. Holley, and Cynthia B. Matthews provide valuable information. Case studies by Carolyn S. Shanoff, Marjorie B. Signer, and Sylvia A. Straub provide examples of agencies that have implemented successful marketing strategies. A

---

*Reprinted from *U of I Chicagoan*, "On the Right Track" by Barbara Hundley, with permission of the University of Illinois Alumni Association.

marketing handbook for health professionals written by Alan Bernstein, with Donna Freiermuth (1988), is another source of helpful information.

The competence and confidence of successful professionals is evident in how they express themselves both verbally and nonverbally. Much attention has turned in recent years to what is termed the "language of power." Nancy Henley (1977) devoted considerable attention to the nonverbal manifestations of power that she termed "body politics." She described how power and status, and dominance and superiority are evidenced nonverbally in interpersonal relationships. She also described how sex differences, class differences, and race differences in behavior can often be traced to differences in power.

Sometimes, people who want to get ahead in their work setting unwittingly convey messages that work to their disadvantage. For example, some behaviors that researchers have noted as signs of submissive rather than dominant behavior include the following: sitting hunched over and avoiding eye contact; smiling and nodding agreement regardless of the message; using tag questions that appear to ask for reassurance (for example, adding "isn't it?" or "wasn't it?" or "o.k.?" to statements); and using unnecessary qualifiers that give the impression of uncertainty (for example, "I think a little more time to prepare this report would help me do a somewhat better job."). Becoming aware of differences in dominant and submissive behavior can enable you to modify those behaviors that are associated with lack of status and develop those that are viewed as conveying more confidence and authority, if you are so inclined.

Communication disorders specialists interested in maximizing their effectiveness to achieve professional advancement will find a number of helpful references available. These include books written by Merna and John Galassi (1977), Thomas Gordon (1977), Carl Rogers (1977), Dorothy Jongeward and Philip Seyer (1978), Phillip Hunsaker and Anthony Alessandra (1980), Henry Lindgren (1982), Jeffrey Eisen with Pat Farley (1984), Stanlee Phelps and Nancy Austin (1987), and William Parkhurst (1988).

MAKING PROFESSIONAL PRESENTATIONS

Competence in one's profession is best demonstrated by successful work with clients and their families and by high quality reports. In effect, each time you talk with a client or family member, give or send a report, make a referral, or respond to a referral—either in person, by telephone, or in writing—you are making a professional presentation. Professional competence can also be demonstrated to a wider audience by presentations within the work setting; within the community; and at local, state, national, and international meetings and conferences. In a profession concerned with effective communication, it is crucial that its specialists are effective communicators.

Ability to convey one's thoughts effectively in a public gathering does not always come naturally. Many times, people who are effective in one-to-one or small group communication find addressing a larger audience difficult and stressful. Listed below are some guidelines regarding public speaking.

- Know what you are talking about. Clearly define the topic in your own mind and be well prepared with information regarding that topic, keeping in mind the purpose of your presentation.
- Know your audience. If possible, determine the level of professional expertise of audience members regarding the topic and what they expect to gain from your presentation.
- Keep in mind that your professional presentation begins the moment you enter the meeting room and continues until you leave the gathering. Be pleasant, courteous, and accessible not only during your presentation but before and after as well.
- Use appropriate language. Do not "talk down" to your audience, but do not assume that professionals from other disciplines or lay people know your professional jargon.
- Be sure your presentation is well organized. Select and outline two to five main points you wish to convey. Beware of trying to include more in your presentation than time allows.
- Select interesting material to support your main points. Examples, illustrations, pertinent research findings, and anecdotes—all relevant to audience experience—reinforce your message.
- Plan for an introduction, body, and conclusion. Remember: First you tell them what you are going to tell them and why it's important to them; then you tell them; and then you tell them what you've told them.
- Plan for visual aids that enhance your presentation. Slides, transparencies, or videotapes should be of high quality and easily visible to the audience. Handouts should be legible and in sufficient quantity.
- Consider your nonverbal presentation. Grooming, posture, gestures, and vocal characteristics (pitch, volume, rate, quality, intonation patterns) all convey messages that can enhance or detract from your communication. Maintenance of eye contact with members of the audience is essential.
- Be attentive to audience feedback. Audience members also communicate nonverbally. Be alert to facial expressions or other body language denoting puzzlement or confusion, boredom, agreement, or disagreement so that you can modify your presentation if necessary.
- Strive for spontaneity. Aim for a conversational rather than a stilted manner. Material that is read or repeated verbatim from a memorized script tends to

lose the attention of the audience. Judicious and unobtrusive use of note cards characterizes experienced public speakers.

- Make provision for audience participation. The form of such participation must vary depending on the size of the audience, the time allotted, the nature of the topic, and particular situational circumstances. It is the speaker's responsibility to structure the participation and to inform audience members about how they may participate.
- Listen carefully to any questions or comments from the audience, repeating the question before responding, and answer to the best of your ability, keeping in mind time and topic restraints.
- Aim for self-confidence in your presentations. Do not apologize for or belittle what you say or how you say it. Practice and experience increase self-assurance; take advantage of opportunities for growth.

It is important that communicative disorders specialists accept their professional obligation to make public presentations in order to increase people's awareness and understanding of effective communication and the prevention and alleviation of communicative disorders. In so doing, not only is the public better informed and the profession enhanced, but the individual professional reaps benefits: becoming attuned to public needs, becoming better known, making valuable contacts, and gaining experience and self-confidence. Similar advantages are incurred by presenting at professional meetings.

Invitations to give presentations and to share expertise should be accepted whenever possible. Many communities afford possibilities for speaking engagements or consultation: preschool and day-care programs, service clubs, organizations devoted to specific disabilities, parents' groups, public and private schools, and programs for the elderly, for example. The professional seeking to gain wider experience and/or professional advancement should consider submitting proposals to professional organizations for conference presentations. The submission of manuscripts to professional journals should also be considered.

Many of these opportunities for personal and professional growth do not bring immediate monetary rewards. However, other benefits need to be considered. Increased visibility may lead to more referrals to you or your agency. Added items on your vita can contribute to career advancement. Improved public speaking abilities enhance your self-esteem and leadership potential. Opportunities to interact with a variety of strangers helps you to grow in understanding and empathy. The satisfaction that comes from sharing worthwhile ideas and information with others is perhaps the greatest benefit.

EVALUATING PROFESSIONAL EFFECTIVENESS

In this age of accountability, speech-language pathologists and audiologists are more concerned than ever with evaluating the success of their professional efforts.

Some ways of measuring your professional success are obvious: Do your clients make significant progress? Are clients regular in attendance and motivated to participate in therapy? Do you receive regular referrals from several different sources? Have former clients referred others to you? Do your employers and co-workers express satisfaction and admiration regarding your capabilities? Are you happy in your work?

Rather than relying solely on their own impression of client satisfaction, some professionals make more formal efforts to secure client feedback. As mentioned in Chapter 8, final therapy sessions often include evaluation of the therapy program from the client's perspective. Some clinicians have found that sending a questionnaire to clients is an effective way of securing suggestions for improving therapy services. James Schutte (1988) provided suggestions for developing, distributing, and analyzing such a survey questionnaire. He stressed the importance of anonymity of replies; brevity of the questionnaire; inclusion of questions on the professional's manner, responsivity, and ability to explain treatment; as well as questions related to the office staff and daily operation.

Making audio and/or videotapes of sessions for later review and analysis is another method of evaluating clinical effectiveness. This method necessitates having recording equipment available and functioning. It also requires expenditure of time for reviewing and selecting procedures for analysis; however, professionals find such time and effort well spent. Some methods of analyzing clinician/client interactions have been described by Boone and Prescott (1972, 1974); Schubert, Miner, and Till (1973); Brookshire, Nicholas, Krueger, and Redmond (1978); Oratio (1979); and Molyneaux and Lane (1982).

There are several clinical evaluation forms that are designed to assist clinical supervisors in evaluating the performance of student clinicians in various settings. The forms developed by Shriberg and colleagues (1975); Baldes and colleagues (1977); Lougeay-Mottinger, Harris, Perlstein-Kaplan, and Felicetti (1984), Johnson and Shewan (1988), and those contained in Anderson (1988), for example, can be used effectively in supervising others and can also be used by the professional for self-evaluation.

Categories frequently included in evaluating professional effectiveness are listed below. You can use this list to develop your own personal rating scale (for example, by using a five-point system denoting poor, fair, average, good, and outstanding for each of the categories).

- screening skills
- diagnostic skills
- establishment of therapy goals
- therapy procedures planning
- conduct of group and individual therapy

- evaluation of client progress
- work with family members
- therapy information documenting and recording
- report writing
- selection and scheduling of caseload
- motivating and reinforcing skills
- counseling and interviewing skills
- referral skills
- consulting skills
- public relations skills
- personal communication skills
- professional appearance and grooming

Use of any evaluation device can lead to greater self-awareness and can point out areas of strength and areas that need further attention. Such knowledge can help you to capitalize on your strengths and take steps to improve weaker areas.

MANAGING AVAILABLE TIME

The response of professional colleagues to the question "What factors work against achieving maximum effectiveness in your work setting?" frequently pointed to time pressures.

"Lack of time. I like teaching, private practice, and research, but I can't do it all. I also want to spend time with my family."

"Not enough time. Being involved in activities such as professional organizations, conducting workshops, being a consultant, all take time."

"Being human and getting tired. Trying to do too much."

"The demands on my time. The size of my caseload. I can't be effective when I'm spread too thin."

"I had to learn to stay focused and be aware of my own basic needs and priorities. Often rescuers and givers become overextended."

The professionals interviewed already utilized many time management skills and still felt the need to be more efficient. We have already discussed some aspects of time management in regard to assessment (Chapter 3) and therapy sessions (Chapter 4). Following is a list of additional strategies for managing time:

- **Determine your goals.** What would you like to be doing five years from now?
- **Establish long-range and short-range objectives.** What intermediate steps are necessary to reach your goals?
- **Establish priorities.** What activities will lead to achieving your goals?
- **Analyze current activities.** How many of your current activities are related to achieving your goals?
- **Determine current activities that are unproductive.** How many of these can be eliminated? simplified? delegated?
- **Determine activities that need to be added to your schedule.** How can these be implemented?
- **Budget your time.** Are you devoting too much time to activities that do not further your goals?
- **Say "no" more often.** Have you learned to say "no" courteously but firmly to unrequired activities that do not interest you or further your goals?
- **Once you make a time commitment, honor it.** Do you use a pocket calendar to remind you of essential appointments and tasks?
- **Maintain a "to-do" list.** Do you keep a record of what needs to be done daily and weekly and check each item off as it is completed?
- **Establish a realistic schedule.** Is it possible to accomplish what you plan?
- **Allow for leisure time.** Do you include relaxing activities in your schedule?
- **Use time efficiently.** Are you taking advantage of equipment, materials, and techniques that can save you time? Do you schedule high-priority tasks for peak energy periods?
- **Evaluate perfectionistic attitudes.** Which tasks merit 100 percent perfection and which do not?
- **Handle paperwork efficiently.** Are papers being handled many times before any decision is made or any productive action taken?
- **Plan to use even small amounts of time productively.** Do you have some tasks at hand if a few minutes become available?
- **Analyze large projects.** Have you divided the work into small, manageable tasks?
- **Establish deadlines.** Have you stipulated when activities are to be completed?
- **Check priorities frequently.** Do you periodically ask yourself: "What is the best use of my time right now?"

- **Avoid procrastination.** Do you begin activities in sufficient time to meet deadlines?
- **Enjoy life.** Are you prepared to discard your schedule if an interesting opportunity presents itself? In managing your 24 hours a day, do not overlook the joys and rewards of satisfying interpersonal relationships.

There are numerous books and articles on time management. Some of these are geared to specific populations, for example, business executives, production managers, and homemakers. Barbara Travers (1983) described time management techniques for improving speech and language services. Other authors describe principles and methods of time management that can be used by any interested person. A popular book in the latter category is by the time-management consultant Alan Lakein (1973). Others that professionals find useful are those by Donna Goldfein (1977), Stephanie Winston (1978, 1983), Michael LeBoeuf (1979), Robert Moskowitz (1981), Edwin Bliss (1983), Charles Hobbs (1987), and Paul Timm (1987).

AVOIDING PROFESSIONAL BURNOUT

Many professionals who are effective in their work setting have learned how to recognize and avoid the debilitating condition known as "burnout." Herbert Freudenberger and Gail North (1985, pp. 9–10) define burnout as follows:

> Burnout is a wearing down and wearing out of energy. It is an exhaustion born of excessive demands which may be self-imposed or externally imposed by families, jobs, friends, lovers, value systems, or society, which deplete one's energy, coping mechanisms, and internal resources. It is a feeling state which is accompanied by an overload of stress, and which eventually impacts on one's motivation, attitudes, and behavior.

Symptoms of Burnout

Burnout is often the end result of continued stress. Communication disorders specialists need to be aware of symptoms of burnout, not only to be able to recognize it in themselves, but also in their clients, clients' families, and coworkers. Early recognition of the symptoms permits the individual to make changes before the condition worsens and has drastic effects on the person as well as his or her associates. There are a number of recognized symptoms of burnout that are listed below. Most people evidence at least some of these behaviors and feelings at one time or another. To be indicative of a burnout condition, several of these symptoms must be present and continue over a period of time.

- early warning symptoms: recurring headaches, digestive upsets, accelerated heartbeat, nameless anxiety
- chronic fatigue
- listlessness
- irritability
- anger
- sexual dysfunction
- feelings of futility and powerlessness
- expressions of cynicism, impatience, negativism, and alienation
- feelings of detachment from family, friends, or co-workers
- feelings of resentment towards family, friends, or co-workers
- feelings of guilt
- blurring of importance of personal values
- dulling of sense of humor
- feeling of being driven
- feeling of being depleted
- feeling of sometimes being unseen or unnoticed
- loneliness
- depression
- distortion of perceptions and judgment
- denial of personality changes and/or difficulties
- breakdowns in physical functioning
- turning to false cures: alcohol, tobacco, tranquilizers, or other drugs
- overeating or not eating at all
- feelings of paranoia or worthlessness
- anxiety over role identity
- emotional exhaustion
- depersonalization of clients and others whom one serves
- feeling of frustration and agitation for no particular reason
- defensiveness
- low self-esteem
- when overloaded, attempt to do even more

- refusal to take a break or engage in leisure activities
- inability to concentrate
- changes in sleep patterns
- increased family difficulties
- more frequent illnesses

Any professionals looking at this list may well feel that they and most of their colleagues are in the throes of burnout. As with other maladaptive behavior patterns, one or two symptoms manifested on an occasional basis should not automatically be translated into an unequivocal diagnosis. However, one of the first steps in preventing or counteracting burnout is awareness of its symptoms. As noted above, persistence, intensity, and number of symptoms must be considered in making the diagnosis. Freudenberger and North (1985), on the basis of extensive experience treating women suffering from burnout, have described the progression of burnout as consisting of twelve stages. They state that the stages are not always clearly delineated and may overlap. The stages can be summarized as follows:

Stage 1. **Compulsion to prove**—characterized by an obsessive determination to succeed

Stage 2. **Intensity**—an increased compulsion to achieve and an unwillingness to delegate work or responsibilities

Stage 3. **Subtle deprivations**—waning attention to one's self and one's personal needs

Stage 4. **Dismissal of conflict and needs**—some conscious awareness of difficulty, attributed to temporary circumstances

Stage 5. **Distortion of values**—difficulty in distinguishing between the essential (the real) and the unessential (the unreal) in daily life

Stage 6. **Heightened denial**—the unconscious defense mechanism of denial obscures personal awareness of burnout symptoms

Stage 7. **Disengagement**—the disavowing of emotions, often combined with disorientation, diminished hope, distancing from others, or ritualistic and stylized behavior

Stage 8. **Observable behavior changes**—changes in feelings and attitudes become more apparent to others

Stage 9. **Depersonalization**—a more serious form of disengagement—an increasing loss of contact with one's self, body, and priorities

Stage 10. **Emptiness**—characterized by excessive attempts to fill a perceived void

Stage 11. **Depression**—despair and self-hate, contemplation of suicide. The symptoms in this stage are similar to those of clinical depression (described in Chapter 4) but the causes are different and must be differentiated for effective treatment.

Stage 12.   **Total burnout exhaustion**—the culmination of the previous 11 stages. If a person has not yet sought help from a professional experienced in treating burnout, it is imperative at this point.

Factors Contributing to Burnout

Not only is it important to recognize the symptoms of burnout, it is crucial to be aware of factors contributing to the condition. Items listed below have been identified by a variety of researchers, including Greywolf, Reese, and Belle (1980); Weiskopf (1980); Lazarus (1981); Maslach (1982); Miller and Potter (1982); Taylor (1982); Procaccini and Kiefaber (1983); Jaffe and Scott (1984); Maddi and Kobasa (1984); Alpern and Myers (1985); Atkinson (1985); Freudenberger and North (1985); Braiker (1986, 1988); Eyre and Eyre (1987); Cherniss (1988); Pines and Aronson (1988); Raschke, Dedrick, and DeVries (1988); and Hanson (1989).

- prolonged emotional tensions
- more responsibilities and/or paperwork than can be handled
- unrealistic expectations in professional or personal life
- more daily hassles than payoffs
- threats to job security
- attempts to be strong and silent under pressure
- financial crises
- family illness
- forced relocation
- loss of loved ones
- continued threats to physical safety
- consistent denial or suppression of emotions
- unrewarded efforts
- prolonged giving of care, attention, and affection to others
- discomfort in accepting care and comfort from others
- exclusion from the "club" or "in-group"
- powerlessness in family or employment decisions
- lack of opportunities to succeed
- cultural and societal limitations

- single parent status
- lack of support with child or dependent care
- lack of a supportive confidant
- considerable time spent with people who are in emotional distress
- work primarily with or caring for people with severe disabilities

Preventive and Counteractive Measures

Fortunately for those suffering from burnout or at risk for burnout, the condition can be successfully treated and successfully prevented. Some of the professionals we interviewed had been faced with symptoms of burnout and had taken steps to reverse the condition. Some of their replies to the question "How do you avoid burnout?" are as follows:

"By getting involved in other things in the profession and by not taking any work home. Since I started not taking things home, there has been a real improvement. I go in to work early and plan; and I don't individualize as much."

"I learned from my father how to be a workaholic and yet not burn out. I go waterskiing; I work out at the gym. I talk with my husband and friends about my job."

"I do different things in the profession such as teach as well as do therapy. I like to be busy, and I am very positively reinforced. I don't think I'll ever burn out professionally."

"Variety saved me: I teach, supervise, do research, and have a private practice. My mind can shift. Variety prevents burnout; I can't do therapy full time. The key words are variety and flexibility, and being aware of available choices. These are goals not only for clinicians but for clients."

"Diversity. Doing one type of therapy in only one environment could be difficult. I really enjoy what I do: therapy, supervision, and part-time participation in a doctoral program."

"The key is variety and knowing yourself. Being very clear about what you need. I'm involved with my voice improvement groups and with a wide variety of patients. A lack of autonomy can cause burnout—a sense of helplessness, a lack of sense of control over your destiny."

"There have been times when I didn't avoid burnout. I had to change to a job with more freedom. Having competent people on my staff helps. So does the easy availability of continuing education. The other thing is to know when to take time off."

"The career that I have now is my response to your question. I have variety, and the challenges are fast and furious. Working with types of cases you don't really enjoy can contribute to burnout. There are some types of clients I don't take anymore."

The researchers mentioned in the previous section regarding factors contributing to burnout have also written extensively on ways to prevent and/or counteract burnout. Some of these ways were mentioned by the professionals in the above excerpts. Listed here are suggestions derived from experience, as well as from the referenced literature:

- Know yourself—your needs and your priorities, your strengths and limitations.
- Have the courage to be who you are.
- Break the barriers of habit. Be open to new ideas, new people, and new ways of doing things.
- Profit from the unexpected.
- Set realistic goals for yourself and your clients.
- Put some fun in your life.
- Delegate jobs and responsibilities.
- If you are in charge of an organization, build a second line of leadership so that you are not indispensable.
- Learn and use stress management techniques.
- Learn and use time management techniques.
- Learn and use problem-solving methods.
- Utilize all resources.
- Remember the importance of adequate rest, good nutrition, and regular exercise.
- Reduce overload.
- Help co-workers and employees to avoid burnout: communicate with them; recognize their individual needs as well as their contributions; use care in delegating responsibility; make sure everyone understands their duties; help maintain a pleasant, productive office climate.
- Keep your sense of humor.

- Be positive and look for the good in people and situations.
- Have patience with yourself.
- Think twice before entering a situation that is likely to produce an extreme level of ongoing stress. Make certain that the possible results and benefits outweigh the high risk of burnout.
- Cultivate and maintain a support network. Remember that isolation from friends and other professionals contributes to burnout.
- Plan for a relaxing transition or "decompression" time when you come home from work, before assuming home responsibilities.
- Be aware that burnout can be limited to one phase of your life or can be a total collapse of your personal and professional functioning. If it is limited, concentrate on effecting changes in that area.
- Learn to separate your work from the rest of your life. Develop outside interests.
- Abandon or modify unrealistic expectations.
- If your workload or work conditions are impossible, redefine the job if possible, or change jobs if necessary.
- Accept the "givens"—those things over which you have no control. You can then concentrate on changing those things that can be changed.
- Make every effort to stay mentally alert and creative.
- Avoid false "cures" for stress or tension: excessive use of alcohol, nicotine, tranquilizers, or other drugs.
- Be alert to symptoms of burnout in yourself and others. Help to make others, including clients and/or their families, if appropriate, aware of factors that contribute to burnout and of ways to prevent and alleviate the condition.

CONCLUSION

In previous chapters, we have discussed many aspects of the life of a communication disorders specialist. We talked about factors that influence not only the first meetings with clients but ongoing therapy as well. Some of these factors encompass basic human needs, organismic variables, the reasons for the relationship, the purposes contacts can serve, the dynamics of interaction, and a variety of other factors that motivate people to grow and change.

We have discussed aspects of working individually and in groups with clients, family members, and professionals from your own and other disciplines. We have tried to assist you in improving your skills in the identification of grief, stress, and depression because of the effects these conditions can have upon therapy and its outcome. We have focused attention on bringing therapy and other professional contacts to satisfying conclusions and on the importance of record keeping and referral.

In this final chapter, we have rounded out our discussion of factors contributing to professional interpersonal effectiveness by suggestions regarding public presentations, time management, and the recognition and avoidance of burnout.

Our goal for this book was to provide useful information on interpersonal skills for professionals in the fields of speech-language pathology and audiology (as well as for any other professionals who like to delve into literature outside their field to see what those fields have to offer). To make the project workable, we were forced to exclude large areas that undeniably are essential for professional expertise: namely, many specific skills of evaluation, differential diagnosis, case management, and therapy for the wide range of speech, language, and hearing disorders that present themselves to professionals in our field. We have also reluctantly foregone discussion of the realms of clinical supervision and professional consultation—realms in which many people in our profession are serving with satisfaction and distinction. However, we like to think that honing the interpersonal skills that are discussed in this book will go a long way toward making you an effective and sought-after supervisor and consultant.

In the areas that are included in this project, we have tried to share information and suggestions derived from many years of working and talking with clients, families, students, and professionals; from many years of reading and research; and from many of our own attempts to grow in professional and personal effectiveness. If you, as the reader, have adapted even a few ideas or suggestions for your personal use and if, by that means, your professional life is enriched, we will have achieved our goal.

REFERENCES

Alpern, H.L., & Myers, B. (1985, November/December). Women at work: Surviving office stress. *Rx Being Well*, pp. 54–57.

Anderson, J.L. (1988). *The supervisory process in speech-language pathology and audiology*. Boston: College-Hill Press.

Atkinson, H. (1985). *Women and fatigue*. New York: Simon & Schuster.

Baldes, R.A., Goings, R., Herbold, D.D., Jeffrey, R., Wheeler, G., & Freilinger, J.J. (1977). Supervision of student speech clinicians. *Language, Speech, and Hearing Services in Schools, 8*(2), 76–84.

Bernstein, A.L., with Freiermuth, D. (1988). *The health professional's marketing handbook*. Chicago: Year Book Medical Publishers, Inc.

Bliss, E.C. (1983). *Doing it now*. New York: Bantam Books.

Boone, D.R., & Prescott, T.E. (1972). Content and sequence analysis of speech and hearing therapy. *Asha, 14*, 58–62.

Boone, D.R., & Prescott, T.E. (1974). *Speech and hearing therapy scoring manual: A manual for learning to self-score the events of therapy*. Washington, D.C.: U.S. Department of Health,

Education and Welfare, Division of Research, Bureau of Education for the Handicapped, Office of Education.

Braiker, H.B. (1986). *The Type E woman: How to overcome the stress of being everything to everybody*. New York: New American Library.

Braiker, H.B. (1988). *A woman's guide to overcoming and preventing depression*. New York: G.P. Putnam's Sons.

Brookshire, R.H., Nicholas, L.S., Krueger, K.M., & Redmond, K.J. (1978). The clinical interaction analysis system: A system for observational recording of aphasia treatment. *Journal of Speech and Hearing Disorders, 43*, 437–447.

Cherniss, C. (1988). Observed supervisory behavior and teacher burnout in special education. *Exceptional Children, 54*(5), 449–454.

Eisen, J., with Farley, P. (1984). *Powertalk! How to speak it, think it, and use it*. New York: Simon & Schuster.

Eyre, L., & Eyre, R. (1987). *Life balance*. New York: Ballantine Books.

Foxman, C.A. (1988). Speak with sense. *Asha, 30*(9), 46–47.

Freudenberger, H.J., & North, G. (1985). *Women's burnout*. Garden City, NY: Doubleday.

Galassi, M.D., & Galassi, J.P. (1977). *Assert yourself! How to be your own person*. New York: Human Sciences Press.

Gelatt, J.P. (1988). The business of grantseeking. *Asha, 30*(9), 43–45.

Goldfein, D. (1977). *Everywoman's guide to time management*. Millbrae, CA: Les Femmes.

Gordon, T. (1977). *Leader effectiveness training*. New York: Bantam Books.

Greywolf, E.S., Reese, M.F., and Belle, D. (1980, November). Stressed mothers syndrome: How to short-circuit the stress-depression cycle. *Behavioral Medicine*, pp. 12–18.

Griffin, K.M. (1988). Quality sells. *Asha, 30*(9), 48–51.

Hanson, P.G. (1989). *Stress for success: How to make stress on the job work for you*. New York: Doubleday.

Henley, N.M. (1977). *Body politics*. Englewood Cliffs, NJ: Prentice-Hall.

Hobbs, C.R. (1987). *Time power*. New York: Harper & Row.

Holley, S.C. (1988). President's page. *Asha, 30*(9), 37–38.

Hundley, B. (1989). Moving up, moving out—or not moving at all. *U of I Chicagoan, 7*(3), 13.

Hunsaker, P.L., & Alessandra, A.J. (1980). *The art of managing people*. New York: Simon & Schuster.

Jaffe, D.T., & Scott, C.D. (1984). *From burnout to balance*. New York: McGraw-Hill.

Johnson, C.J., & Shewan, C.M. (1988). A new perspective in evaluating clinical effectiveness: The UWO clinical grading system. *Journal of Speech and Hearing Disorders, 53*(3), 328–340.

Jongeward, D., & Seyer, P.C. (1978). *Choosing success: Human relationships on the job*. New York: John Wiley & Sons.

Lakein, A. (1973). *How to get control of your time and your life*. New York: New American Library.

Lazarus, R.S. (1981, July). Little hassles can be hazardous to health. *Psychology Today*, pp. 58–62.

LeBoeuf, M. (1979). *Working smart: How to accomplish more in half the time*. New York: Warner Books.

Lindgren, H.C. (1982). *Leadership, authority, and power sharing*. Malabar, FL: Robert E. Krieger Publishing Company.

Lougeay-Mottinger, J., Harris, M., Perlstein-Kaplan, K., & Felicetti, T. (1984). UTD competency based evaluation system. *Asha, 26*(11), 39–43.

Maddi, S.R., & Kobasa, S.C. (1984). *The hardy executive: Health under stress.* Homewood, IL: Dow Jones-Irwin.

Maslach, C. (1982). *Burnout: the cost of caring.* Englewood Cliffs, NJ: Prentice-Hall.

Matthews, C.B. (1988). Strategies that work. *Asha, 30*(9), 22–25.

Miller, M.M., & Potter, R. (1982). Professional burnout among speech-language pathologists. *Asha, 24*(3), 177–181.

Molyneaux, D., & Lane, V.W. (1982). *Effective interviewing: Techniques and analysis.* Boston: Allyn & Bacon.

Moskowitz, R. (1981). *How to organize your work and your life.* New York: Doubleday.

Oratio, A.R. (1979). *"Pattern recognition": A computer program for interaction analysis of intervention and training processes in speech and hearing.* Baltimore: University Park Press.

Parkhurst, W. (1988). *The eloquent executive.* New York: Random House.

Phelps, S., & Austin, N. (1987). *The assertive woman: A new look.* San Luis Obispo, CA: Impact Publishers.

Pines, A., & Aronson, E. (1988). *Career burnout: Causes and cures.* New York: The Free Press, A Division of Macmillan, Inc.

Procaccini, J., & Kiefaber, M.W. (1983). *Parent burnout.* Garden City, NY: Doubleday.

Public Law 94-142. (1975). Education for all handicapped children act.

Public Law 99-457. (1986). Education of the handicapped amendment.

Raschke, D., Dedrick, C., & DeVries, A. (1988). Stress: The special educator's perspective. *Teaching Exceptional Children, 21*(1), 10–14.

Rogers, C.R. (1977). *Carl Rogers on personal power.* New York: Delacorte.

Schubert, G., Miner, A., & Till, J.A. (1973). *The analysis of behavior of clinicians (ABC) system.* Grand Forks, ND: University of North Dakota.

Schutte, J.E. (1988, September 19). Let patients tell you how to make your practice better. *Medical Economics,* pp. 179–186.

Shanoff, C.S. (1988). Case study 5: State association makes May a year-round event. *Asha, 30*(9), 33–34.

Shriberg, L., Filley, F., Hayes, D., Kwiatkowski, J., Schatz, J., Simmons, K., & Smith, M. (1975). The Wisconsin procedure for appraisal of clinical competence (W-PACC): Model and data. *Asha, 17,* 158–165.

Signer, M.B. (1988). Case study 2: A school system wins with team players. *Asha, 30*(9), 27–29.

Signer, M.B. (1988). Case study 3: A hospital capitalizes on opportunities. *Asha, 30*(9), 29–31.

Signer, M.B. (1988). Case study 4: A clinic profits from board members' help. *Asha, 30*(9), 31–33.

Stech, E., & Ratliffe, S.A. (1985). *Effective group communication: How to get action by working in groups.* Lincolnwood, IL: National Textbook Company.

Straub, S.A. (1988). Case study 1: A private practitioner prepares for PL 99-457. *Asha, 30*(9), 26–27.

Taylor, R.B. (1982, November). Are you heading for physician burnout? *Physician's Management,* pp. 186–196.

Timm, P.R. (1987). *Successful self-management.* Los Altos, CA: Crisp Publications, Inc.

Tomes, L., & Sanger, D.D. (1986). Attitudes of interdisciplinary team members toward speech-language services in public schools. *Language, Speech, and Hearing Services in Schools, 17*(3), 230–240.

Travers, B.W. (1983). Improving speech and language services through effective time management. *Language, Speech, and Hearing Services in Schools, 14*(2), 86–91.

Weiskopf, P.E. (1980). Burnout among teachers of exceptional children. *Exceptional Children, 47*(1), 18–36.

Winston, S. (1978). *Getting organized.* New York: Warner Books.

Winston, S. (1983). *The organized executive.* New York: Warner Books.

Index

A

Absence from therapy sessions, 72
Ackerman, N., 26, 28
Active listening, 58–59, 86
  as a group member, 128, 184–185
  in assertive disagreement, 186–187
  in combatting resistance, 73
  in stress management, 78
Adey, M., 85, 87
Adjunct care facilities, 115
Adolescent clients, 39, 42, 46, 48,
    140–141
Age of client, adapting to, 33, 34–36
Aggressor, as group member, 126
AIDS (acquired immune deficiency
    syndrome), 72, 180
Alessandra, A., 191, 205
Alexander Graham Bell Association for
    the Deaf, 113
Allen, D., 39, 54
Alper, J., 81–82, 87
Alpern, H., 200, 204
American sign language. *See* Manual
    communication
American Speech-Language-Hearing
    Association, 113
  code of ethics, 86, 87

Analyst, as type of thinker, 163–164
Anderson, J., 194, 204
Anthony, W., 152–153, 165
Aram, D., 29, 41, 44–45, 55, 177–178,
    182
Argyle, M., 26, 28, 123, 145
Aronson, E., 200, 206
Assertive disagreement, 186–187
Assertiveness, 184, 186–187
Assessment process, 29–55
  assessment goals, 4, 30–33
  assessment materials, 12, 29, 38–41,
    45
Association for Children and Adults with
    Learning Disabilities, 113
Atkinson, H., 200, 204
Audience feedback, 192–193
Audience participation, 193
Aural rehabilitation. *See* Hearing
    impaired clients
Austin, N., 191, 206
Autocratic leadership style, 130
Avila, D., 123, 146

B

Baldes, R.A., 194, 204
Bales, R.F., 125, 127, 145, 146

SUCCESSFUL INTERACTIVE SKILLS

H

Haight, P., 115, 118
Hamilton, M., 85, 87
Hanson, M., 29, 55
Hanson, P., 200, 205
Harmonizer, as group member, 125
Harris, M., 194, 206
Harrison, A., 163, 164, 165
Hate-love dimension, 26
Hayes, D., 194, 206
Haynes, W.O., 29, 36, 44, 55
Hearing aids, 14, 47, 59, 156
Hearing-impaired clients, 11, 35, 38, 43, 47, 67–68, 112–113, 139
Heersema, P.H., 85, 87
Hegland, S., 111, 118
Help–seeker, as group member, 126
Henderson, M., 26, 28
Henley, N., 191, 205
Herbold, D.D., 194, 204
Historian, as group member, 125
Hobbs, C., 197, 205
Holley, S., 190, 205
Holmes, T.H., 78, 87
Homeostasis, 18, 23, 75
Homework, by client, 64, 68, 73, 154, 169
Hoskins, B., 141, 146
Hospital settings, 2, 3, 168, 189
Humorist, as group member, 125
Hundley, B., 189–190, 205
Hunsaker, P., 191, 205
Hutchinson, B.B., 29, 55

I

Idealist, as type of thinker, 163–164
Identification, as defense mechanism, 74
IEP meetings. *See* Individual Education Plan meetings
"Imaging", 78
Individual Education Plan (IEP) meetings, 110–111, 114
Individualized Family Service Plan, 184
Infant stimulation programs, 139–140
Informal groups, 122–123
Information getting, 4, 14, 90–93, 104

Information giving, 4, 14–15, 93–95, 104–105
Initial concerns of clients, 78
Initiator, as group member, 125
Inservice training, 2, 133, 184
Intellectualization, as defense mechanism, 74
Interdisciplinary teams, 163–164, 183–187
International Association of Laryngectomees, 113
International Cleft Palate Association, 113
Interpersonal reflexes, 25, 153
Interpersonal skills of successful professionals, 23, 183–187
Interpersonal style, 25
See also S-O-R variables
Interview analysis, 13, 104–106
Interview excerpts
  excerpt 3–1, 31–32
  excerpt 3–2, 51–52
  excerpt 4–1, 60
  excerpt 4–2, 60–61
  excerpt 4–3, 61
  excerpt 4–4, 62–63
  excerpt 4–5, 63
  excerpt 4–6, 64
  excerpt 4–7, 65
  excerpt 48, 65–66
  excerpt 4–9, 66–67
  excerpt 4–10, 67–68
  excerpt 4–11, 68
  excerpt 5–1, 92–93
  excerpt 5–2, 93–94
  excerpt 5–3, 94–95
  excerpt 5–4, 96
  excerpt 5–5, 97–99
  excerpt 5–6, 99–100
  excerpt 5–7, 100
  excerpt 8–1, 172
  excerpt 8–2, 173
Interviews, 13–14
Intuitive, as problem-solving style, 161–163
Itzkowitz, J.S., 108–109, 118

About the Authors

Dorothy Molyneaux earned her Ph.D. from Stanford University in speech-language pathology and clinical psychology, and holds ASHA Certificates of Clinical Competence in both speech-language pathology and in audiology. She served as a professor, clinical supervisor, and director of the parent counseling program in the communicative disorders area at San Francisco State University from 1963 to 1987. She was a recipient of the California Speech-Language-Hearing Association's Outstanding Achievement Award in 1986, and was elected a Fellow of that association in 1987.

Dr. Molyneaux has more than 30 years of experience working as a speech and language consultant to parents, classroom teachers, preschool personnel, and special educators. She has served on boards of directors and professional advisory committees for a variety of service agencies. Her interests in consultation and effective interpersonal communication have led to extensive study of individual and group dynamics, problem-solving methods, and stress management. She has conducted workshops in those areas for professional, business, parent, and religious groups. She is co-author, with Dr. Vera W. Lane, of *Effective Interviewing: Techniques and Analysis.*

Vera W. Lane earned her Ph.D. from the University of California, Berkeley, and San Francisco State University in special education and holds the ASHA Certificate of Clinical Competence in speech-language pathology. She is a professor and clinical supervisor in the area of communicative disorders at San Francisco State University. She has served as director of the communicative disorders program, graduate coordinator for the School of Education, and as chair of the university's Academic Senate. She chaired an interdisciplinary faculty council that developed a certificate program, an undergraduate minor, and a master of arts degree in gerontology at the university.

Dr. Lane has approximately 25 years of experience in the profession—working in public school, university, and private practice settings. She works effectively with clients and their families, and with colleagues from a variety of disciplines. She was awarded the Honors of the California Speech-Language-Hearing Association in 1979.